0269778

7 Day Loan

This book is due for return on or before the last date shown below

St Ma

D1471397

KEY TOPICS IN SOCIOLINGUISTICS

Series editor: Rajend Mesthrie

This new series focuses on the main topics of study in sociolinguistics today. It consists of accessible yet challenging accounts of the most important issues to consider when examining the relationship between language and society. Some topics have been the subject of sociolinguistic study for many years, and are here re-examined in the light of new developments in the field; others are issues of growing importance that have not so far been given a sustained treatment. Written by leading experts, the books in the series are designed to be used on courses and in seminars, and include useful suggestions for further reading and a helpful glossary.

Already published in the series:

Politeness, by Richard J. Watts

Language Policy, by Bernard Spolsky

Discourse, by Jan Blommaert

Analyzing Sociolinguistic Variation, by Sali A. Tagliamonte

Forthcoming titles:

World Englishes, by Rakesh Bhatt and Rajend Mesthrie

Bilingual Talk, by Peter Auer

Language and Ethnicity

CARMEN FOUGHT

CAMBRIDGE
UNIVERSITY PRESS

CAMBRIDGE UNIVERSITY PRESS
Cambridge, New York, Melbourne, Madrid, Cape Town, Singapore, São Paulo

Cambridge University Press
The Edinburgh Building, Cambridge CB2 2RU, UK

Published in the United States of America by Cambridge University Press, New York

www.cambridge.org
Information on this title: www.cambridge.org/9780521612913

© Carmen Fought 2006

First published 2006

Printed in the United Kingdom at the University Press, Cambridge

A catalogue record for this publication is available from the British Library

Library of Congress Cataloging in Publication data
Fought, Carmen, 1966–
Language and ethnicity / Carmen Fought.
   p. cm. – (Key topics in sociolinguistics)
Includes bibliographical references and index.
ISBN-13: 978-0-521-84843-5 (hardback)
ISBN-10: 0-521-84843-1 (hardback)
ISBN-13: 978-0-521-61291-3 (pbk.)
ISBN-10: 0-521-61291-8 (pbk.)
1. Anthropological linguistics. 2. Ethnicity. I. Title. II. Series.
P35.F67 2006
306.44 – dc22

ISBN-13 978-0-521-84843-5 hardback
ISBN-10 0-521-84843-1 hardback

ISBN-13 978-0-521-61291-3 paperback
ISBN-10 0-521-61291-8 paperback

To John R. Rickford and Walt Wolfram

charismatic colleagues,
pioneering contributors to the study of language and ethnicity,
and outstanding mentors to generations of other scholars

Contents

Preface

This book is an introduction to the relationship between human language and **ethnicity**. Its purpose is to provide an overview of the main concepts, issues, and debates, as well as a guide to the key research findings in the field. It is the next volume in the Cambridge series "Key Topics in Sociolinguistics," which is appropriate because language and ethnicity is perhaps the epitome of a key topic in our field. Many of the early **sociolinguistic** studies, which launched an entire research tradition, dealt with the relationship of language to ethnicity. Since then, numerous studies of individual communities in which ethnicity plays a role in language variation have been conducted. There is no single work, however, which provides an overview of the main issues and implications of these studies. There are several volumes with the terms "language" and "ethnicity" or "**ethnic identity**" in the title (e.g. Dow 1991, Fishman 2001), but these have tended to focus on questions of nationalism, language rights, and the role of language competence in group identity, rather than variation within a particular language. In other words, books that say they are about "language and ethnicity" are, in practice, more often about "bilingualism and nationality." Because these macro-issues have been well covered in the literature, I have chosen not to address them in detail here, although where bilingualism or **code-switching** illuminates some interesting facet of identity construction, I have included it in the discussion. Mainly, though, I hope to provide a clear and accessible introduction to how ethnicity affects variation within a language or **dialect**, and particularly how that variation is significant for individuals within a group as they seek to express who they are.

Given theoretical shifts in the field of sociolinguistics such that the construction of identity is now treated as central, it is surprising that we have numerous recent works surveying the role of language in the construction of **gender**, for example (e.g. Coates 1998, Talbot 1998, Eckert and McConnell-Ginet 2003), and almost none that survey its role in the construction of ethnic identity at the individual level. There are in-depth studies of particular **ethnic groups** (e.g. Rickford 1999, Fought 2003) and more recently a few eclectic collections that unite contributions on very disparate topics (e.g. Harris and Rampton 2003), but no one comprehensive work on how the process of constructing an ethnic identity through language works, from start to finish. My goal is to offer the reader a window into the social and psychological processes that are involved in the construction of ethnic identity, and to show how language is both a mirror for reflecting these processes and a part of the process itself. By drawing on research from a wide range of different ethnic groups around the world, I hope to provide readers with a larger picture of how language and ethnicity are related. Moreover, my focus will be on both *form* (**linguistic variables**) and *function* (uses of language), tying together the **variationist** sociolinguistic approach and other, more **discourse**-oriented approaches, which are sometimes treated as secondary in sociolinguistic research but provide valuable insights that cannot be neglected.

I have divided the book into three sections. The first looks at general issues in ethnicity and language, beginning with the question of what we mean by "ethnicity," and moving on to an overview of the complexities of how ethnic identities are constructed through language. The second section looks at the process of constructing ethnic identity in specific groups. There is a chapter each on African Americans and on Latino groups in the USA, both of which have been the focus of copious research. These groups offer two very different windows into the relevant issues, particularly because in one group the variation occurs within dialects of English, while in the other language choice and code-switching both have an important role. Another chapter compares and contrasts the construction of ethnic identity in three very different multiethnic settings around the world. There is also a chapter on the construction of ethnic identity by dominant "white" groups, and one that looks at dialect contact in interethnic settings and how research in this area has informed sociolinguistic theory. The last section focuses on questions of language use. It explores the role of **pragmatics** and **discourse features** in ethnic identity, and how these can lead to miscommunication. It also looks at issues of language prejudice and the consequences of linguistic biases for society. Finally, there is a chapter exploring the relatively new topic of "**crossing**": the use of language associated with an ethnic group to which the speaker does not belong.

I don't know if I would say that language is a sensitive topic, but ethnicity most certainly is, and so I have thought hard at every turn about how to discuss these topics in a way that is both informative and ethically responsible. I have done my best to respect everyone. I have tried not to use the words "the African-American community" as if it were one big entity, or talk about what "Latinas" do, as if there were a consensus among them all. I have tried not to act as though the United States is the center of the known universe. I have tried not to claim anything that I could not possibly know without going through the day as a Black South African or an elderly Maori man, or a member of any other group to which I do not belong. I have written about these complex topics in my own voice, which I feel is the only way I could have any hope of addressing them truthfully, even if it means that I deviate at times from the level of formality we normally associate with academic styles. I have tried to tackle complicated and emotionally charged questions with honesty and open admission of the many ways in which I (in particular) or we (in general) simply may not have answers.

Acknowledgments

As I thank the people who have helped me so much in this endeavor, please remember that wherever I have failed in any regard it is my failure alone. I am grateful for the input of the two colleagues to whom I have dedicated this book, John Rickford and Walt Wolfram. When I talk to people in other fields about the mentoring I received as a young scholar in the field of sociolinguistics, they react with envy. I am thankful for all that these two brilliant and compassionate men have done for me and for so many other young scholars in the field, including many women and people of color. I am also grateful to my students. The discussions I have had with them, both in and out of the classroom, inform every aspect of my research and my thinking about language and identity. I am also thankful to Andrew Winnard for a number of helpful suggestions. Finally, I am grateful to my friends and family: my mother and brother who have seen me at my best and at my worst (and made it clear that they love me either way); my friend Martha, who sang "Another One Bites the Dust" over the phone to me when I finished a chapter; and my husband John, who, in addition to everything else he does for me, contributed by 1) agreeing to become the most overqualified research assistant in the country, and 2) making however many pots of (excellent) coffee it took for me to complete each section. Every linguist and author should be so blessed.

Part I General issues in ethnicity and language

1 What is ethnicity?

Race is not rocket science. It's harder than rocket science. (Christopher Edley, Jr., Foreword to *America Becoming: Racial Trends and Their Consequences*, vol. 1, 2001)

As a professor, I've noticed a recent trend of resistance among my students to forms that ask them to specify their ethnicity by checking a box. They see it variously as racist, irrelevant, inaccurate, or nobody's business but their own. Several students have told me that they respond to such forms by marking "other____" and writing in next to it simply "human being." I respect their choice to do this and I applaud their small protest against the way that such forms over-simplify the question of ethnicity in our diverse and complex world. However, I also know as a social scientist that most "human beings" do *not* see themselves as members of a great undifferentiated whole. Whatever our political leanings, however open and accepting of others our character might be, we nonetheless tend to cling to the distinctions among us. Most teenagers in Western societies, for instance, would die of embarrassment if somebody thought that they dressed like, acted like, or talked like their parents. They go to great lengths to avoid this possibility, including developing new **slang** terms and discarding them like used tissues, in an attempt to stay one step ahead of the game. In our heterosexually oriented modern communities, men do not usually like to be mistaken for women and vice versa. Even drag queens, a group that would seem to contradict this idea, enact an identity that relies on the audience's knowing that they are, in fact, biologically male (Barrett 1999). And in any country where multiple ethnic groups are represented, from Australia to Zimbabwe, ethnicity (however we define this term, and it won't be easy) will be a salient factor that social scientists must take into account.

The study of ethnicity (which, you'll notice, I still have not defined) is a field unto itself. Although it has formed a crucial part of the development of sociolinguistic theory, most linguists, with a few notable exceptions, have spent relatively little time on the definition of ethnic categories in the abstract. But the sand has run out. I cannot in good conscience write a book on the topic of "language and ethnicity," and bring to it expertise only in language, hoping the other half will sort itself out. So I will draw here on the substantial literature that has been produced exploring the central relevant questions: What is ethnicity? How is it related to race? What is an ethnic group? Everyone who knew that I was writing this book has said, "You have to give a definition of ethnicity." Yes, I tell them, thanks so much for the advice. But when volumes have been devoted to exploring this single question, I can hardly get by with hammering out a two-line blurb at the beginning and then just moving on. So I will try in this chapter to give a feeling for the discussion that has taken place in the history of research on race and ethnicity, among scholars much more qualified than I am to address this topic, even though it is impossible to cover the discussion comprehensively in this short space. And, despite the well-meaning advice of friends and colleagues, I leave open the possibility that I may not be able (or willing), in the end, to pin down one single definition of ethnicity for the purposes of this book.

1.1   AREAS OF AGREEMENT ABOUT ETHNICITY

Many (if not most) native speakers of English hear the term "ethnicity" and recognize it as a word they know. But actually delimiting the exact meaning of this word, as is so often true with **semantics**, turns out to be a complex endeavor. Scholars in the fields of anthropology, sociology, ethnic studies, and even linguistics, have approached this problem in a number of ways, which will be discussed further below. There are, however, a few areas of preliminary agreement about ethnicity across the approaches and disciplines, particularly among the most recent writings on this topic, and I will begin by giving an overview of those commonalities.

First, scholars across the disciplines (and I include the linguists here as well) agree that ethnicity is a *socially constructed category*, not based on any objectively measurable criteria. For a while the term "ethnicity" was used as if it were the socially defined counterpart to the biologically defined "**race**." The problem, of course, is that years of scientific research have failed to yield any reliable biological rubric for grouping human beings into racial categories. As Zelinsky reports:

> After decades of effort during which many classificatory schemes were proposed, then rejected, physical anthropologists have finally admitted defeat. It has proved impossible to arrive at a set of quantifiable morphological and physiological features whereby we can unequivocally compartmentalize all human beings into a small array of discrete races. (2001:8)

Omi and Winant use the term "racial formation" for the social construction of race, more specifically for "the sociohistorical process by which racial categories are created, inhabited, transformed, and destroyed" (1994:55). I will return to the relationship of ethnicity and race in a moment, but the main point here is that both of these categories must be treated as socially constructed, and this reality must be incorporated into any definition we might use.

On the other hand, the fact that "ethnicity" and "race" may be socially constructed *does not mean they are purely hypothetical concepts that have no basis in reality*. A number of studies acknowledge the presence of a line of thinking of this type in the earlier research, and Bobo, for example, notes that even up to the present some scholars have "argued vigorously for discontinuing the use of the term 'race'" (2001:267). However, a majority of recent works insists that these concepts are both real and crucial, and it is perilous to dismiss them as mere constructs. Zelinsky notes, "In terms of practical consequences, race as something collectively perceived, as a social construct, far outweighs its dubious validity as a biological hypothesis" (2001:9). In a similar vein, Smelser et al. say:

> The concepts of race and ethnicity are social realities because they are deeply rooted in the consciousness of individuals and groups, and because they are firmly fixed in our society's institutional life. (2001:3)

Regardless of the social relativity of their definitions, or of whether we believe that race and ethnicity should or should not have the prominent role in society that they have, we cannot dismiss them as having no basis in reality. The ideologies associated with them create their own social reality.

Another point of general agreement is that *ethnicity cannot be studied or understood outside the context of other social variables*, such as gender or social class. Urciuoli (1996:25ff.), for example, discusses in detail the conflation of class and race, and how, in the dominant ideologies, this can lead to an automatic association of certain ethnic groups with "the underclass." As will be discussed in Chapter 2, the speakers in the Puerto-Rican American community that Urciuoli studied often equated becoming more middle class with becoming more white. With respect to gender, Bucholtz notes that "any performance of ethnicity is always simultaneously a performance of gender" (1995:364); Omi and Winant express a very similar idea, saying, "In many respects, race is gendered and gender is racialized" (1994:68). As noted earlier, the construction of identity by individuals is a complex and multifaceted process in which ethnicity may be only one note, possibly not even the dominant note, at a particular moment. I have touched on these ideas only briefly here, but I will return to and develop them repeatedly throughout the discussion.

In addition, most works on race and ethnicity acknowledge the important roles of *both self-identification and the perceptions and attitudes of others* in the construction of ethnic identity. As Smelser et al. note, the categories of race and ethnicity are to some degree imposed by others and to some degree self-selected (2001:3). In modern societies that value self-determination and respect the right of each individual to define himself or herself, it is easy to fall back on the utopian idea that a person's race or ethnicity is whatever he or she says it is. But while this can be true on one level, on another level one cannot be completely free of the views and attitudes of others in the society. There are numerous references in the literature to the explicit need of community members to be able to categorize others ethnically (and in other ways). Omi and Winant see this as particularly true of race:

> One of the first things we notice about people when we meet them (along with their sex) is their race . . . This fact is made painfully obvious when we encounter someone whom we cannot conveniently racially categorize – someone who is, for example, racially "mixed." (1994:59)

A Puerto-Rican American woman in Urciuoli's study commented, "[T]he people at work try to categorize me, keep trying to get out of me what I am *really*. Really Spanish? Really black? Really East Indian?" (1996:144). **Phenotype** may play a particularly crucial role in the community's categorizations. Anulkah Thomas (personal communication) reports the experience of a Panamanian girl of African descent who was told by a teacher to check "black" on the census form because "that's what people see when they look at you." The need of others to categorize an individual's race and ethnicity forms a part of the context in which that individual constructs his or her identity.

I myself have been the subject of **ascription** to an ethnicity I would not normally claim. My father was a generic white American with no association to a particular European ancestry. My mother is from Madrid, Spain. On census forms, I would normally check "white" as my race. Still, the legal definition of Hispanic by the US Office of Management and Budget is: "All persons of Mexican, Puerto Rican, Cuban, Central or South American, or other Spanish culture or origin, regardless of race" (Smelser et al. 2001:xxviii). By this definition, I qualify as at least half-Hispanic. Phenotypically, some people have told me that I look to them like I could be "a Latina," a perception which is probably enhanced by my being a native speaker of Spanish and my being named "Carmen." My students usually know that I am fluent in Spanish, and that I have conducted research on Chicano English. As a result of these factors, I believe, an undergraduate who thanked me and another professor (who was from Mexico) in her senior thesis referred to us as "two strong Latinas." Among other things, I think this points to the important role of language in ethnic identity ascription. The fact that I felt a small thrill of pleasure at this involuntary moment of "**passing**" also says something about what it means to be a member of the dominant ethnic group, a topic to which I will return in Chapter 6.

A good **ethnographic study** of the role of the community in defining ethnic membership is Wieder and Pratt's (1990) research on the Osage tribe. All communities (and **communities of practice**) will have norms for evaluating who is and is not a member, sanctions for behaviors the group considers unacceptable, and so forth. Probably because of the historical implications of membership in certain tribes, there is much overt discussion in some Native-American communities of who is or is not "a real Indian."[1] The answer to this question about ethnic identity can have repercussions in many practical areas, such as determining who is registered as a member of a particular tribe, who is entitled to government services or health care, or who can vote in tribal elections. Side by side with these is a completely different set of concerns, related to the historical oppression of Native Americans, including issues about who has "sold out" versus maintaining pride in their culture.

Wieder and Pratt (1990) found that a number of factors outsiders (particularly European Americans) might consider to be important in defining group membership are quite useless and may even disqualify the individual in question from true status as a "real Indian." Instead, they treat being a "real Indian" as a process, rather than a static category. What is of most interest here is the constant reference to others (and the recognition of others) in how Wieder and Pratt set up the framework for the construction of ethnicity in this community. Osage community members "discuss the obvious Indianness, or lack of it, of a candidate Indian. 'Is he [or she] really an Indian?' is a question that they ask, and they know it can be asked about them" (1990:47). In addition, many if not most of the "actions" they identify as relevant for this particular community involve language, language use, or **speech events** in some way.

A similar situation is described for African Americans in some communities by Fordham and Ogbu (1986). They note that "being of African descent does not automatically make one a black person" and that one can be denied membership in the larger African-American group (which they term a "fictive kinship system") because of actions that signal a lack of loyalty or some other lack of adherence to the norms considered appropriate to group membership (1986:184). Although the relative roles of "other" versus "self" in defining one's identity, particularly one's ethnic identity, may vary a great deal from one community to another, the groups discussed here illustrate the strength and multiplexity that the "other" component can have.

1.2 POSSIBLE DEFINITIONS OF ETHNICITY

Almost all the large-scale works on the topics of race and ethnicity begin by trying to define one or both of these elusive terms, and many also start by taking apart the definitions posited by earlier generations of researchers. Scholars from the various relevant disciplines, including sociolinguistics, seem to have taken three basic approaches to this problem: 1) trying to define *ethnicity* in isolation; 2) trying to define *ethnic group* instead, then defining *ethnicity* as a corollary term; and 3) trying to define *ethnicity* in relation to *race*. Each of these has advantages and disadvantages. Below is a small sampling of the types of definitions of *ethnicity* or *ethnic groups* that can be found in the literature:

> Ethnicity, then, is a set of descent-based cultural identifiers used to assign persons to groupings that expand and contract in inverse relation to the scale of inclusiveness and exclusiveness of the membership. (Cohen 1978:387)

> [Ethnic groups are] human groups that entertain a subject belief in their common descent because of similarities of physical type or of customs or both, or because of memories of colonization and

migration . . . it does not matter whether or not an objective blood relationship exists. (Weber, cited in Smelser et al. 2001:3)

[An ethnic group:]

1. is largely biologically self-perpetuating
2. shares fundamental cultural values . . .
3. makes up a field of communication and interaction
4. has a membership which identifies itself, and is identified by others, as constituting a category distinguishable from other categories of the same order. (Barth 1969)

The ethnic group is a modern social construct, one undergoing constant change, an imagined community too large for intimate contact among its members, persons who are perceived by themselves and/or others to share a unique set of cultural and historical commonalities . . . It comes into being by reasons of its relationships with other social entities, usually by experiencing some degree of friction with other groups that adjoin it in physical or social space. (Zelinsky 2001:44; italics removed)

We see among these definitions certain similarities, which I will return to in a moment, and also some contradictions. Barth, for example, views the ethnic group as "interacting," while Zelinsky seems to suggest that if the members of the community actually have a lot of intimate contact, they are disqualified from being an ethnic group. Although Zelinsky's definition (along with the accompanying discussion) nicely sums up the main features found in many of the others, this particular element of it seems questionable to me (what about groups that are dying out, for example?). The summary of the definitional problem that I most admire is found in Omi and Winant (1994), the second edition of a well-respected, much-cited work on the sociology of race. The authors give a detailed and insightful analysis of how these concepts function, but, rather than attempting to define them they say, simply, "The definition of the terms 'ethnic group' and 'ethnicity' is muddy" (1994:14).

1.3 POSSIBLE DEFINITIONS OF RACE

The definition of race is complicated in many of the same ways as that of ethnicity. As noted above, we must acknowledge race itself as a constructed category, but that still leaves us with the problem of defining it. In some cases scholars make no explicit attempt to separate race from ethnicity, as in this definition from W. E. B. DuBois:

> What, then, is race? It is a vast family of human beings, generally of
> common blood and language, always of common history, traditions
> and impulses, who are both voluntarily and involuntarily striving
> together for the accomplishment of certain more or less vividly
> conceived ideals of life. ([1897] 2000:110)

Omi and Winant (1994), as noted above, give no explicit definition
of ethnicity, although they clearly have the understanding that it is
different from race, as shown by the fact that they discuss these concepts in separate sections. Their definition of race is "a concept which
signifies and symbolizes social conflicts and interests by referring to
different types of human bodies" (1994:55).

In other cases, race and ethnicity are deliberately separated by some
criterion, the most frequent one being elements related to physical
appearance:

> "[R]ace" is a social category based on the identification of (1) a physical
> marker transmitted through reproduction and (2) individual, group and
> cultural attributes associated with that marker. Defined as such, race is,
> then, a form of ethnicity, but distinguished from other forms of
> ethnicity by the identification of distinguishing physical
> characteristics, which, among other things, make it more difficult for
> members of the group to change their identity. (Smelser et al. 2001:3;
> italics in original)

Interestingly, Smelser et al. do not actually provide a separate definition of ethnicity that can be referenced as part of the explanation
above. Here is another definition linking these two terms:

> Common usage tends to associate "race" with biologically based
> differences between human groups, differences typically observable
> in skin color, hair texture, eye shape, and other physical attributes.
> "Ethnicity" tends to be associated with culture, pertaining to such
> factors as language, religion, and nationality. (Bobo 2001:267)

Bobo adds that, "[a]lthough perceived racial distinctions often result in
sharper and more persistent barriers than ethnic distinctions, this is
not invariably the case, and both share elements of presumed common
descent or ascriptive inheritance" (2001:267).

There are a large number of scholarly works that focus on how race
is constructed (including, among many others, Davis 1991, Anthias
and Yuval-Davis 1992, Omi and Winant 1994, Gandy 1998). In particular, it is enlightening to look at how different sociopolitical contexts
affect this process in different countries around the world. A number
of scholars have argued convincingly that the dominant ideology of
race in the United States, for instance, centers around a black–white

dichotomy, in which other groups (like Asian Americans) and variations within groups are pushed to the side. People of mixed black–
white ancestry are classified as black under the "one-drop rule" (see
Davis [1991] for a full discussion). Even as late as 1986, the US Supreme
Court refused to overturn a ruling against a woman who sought to
have her race reclassified as white, legally; the woman, Susie Phipps,
had one African-American ancestor six generations back (Davis 1991:
9–11). In this view, skin-tone differences between African Americans
or European Americans are downplayed in racializing discourses (even
though these may have practical repercussions of their own). This ideology can lead to some paradoxical situations, such as the idea suggested by Ignatiev that in the USA "a white woman can give birth to a
black child, but a black woman can never give birth to a white child"
(1995:1).

On the other hand, in South Africa, historically a similar range
of phenotypes has been broken up differently. There, Europeans and
Africans are treated as different racial groups, but there is also a
third relevant group (leaving aside South Asians for now), people
who were classified by the Apartheid government's oppressive system as "Coloured," corresponding to people whose racial ancestry was
believed to be mixed.[2] This means that the same three individuals –
one of unmixed African (Bantu) descent, one of unmixed European
descent, and one of mixed African and European descent – are grouped
differently by the ideologies of the two countries. In the US hegemonic
dichotomy, the European-descent individual would be seen as different and the other two would be grouped. In South Africa, they represent three different racial groups. In fact, McCormick suggests that,
in post-Apartheid South Africa, allegiances are developing between
mixed-race and European descent groups focused against the black
majority (2002a:4). There are also locations and times in the history of
the United States when the ethnic groupings would have been more
like those of South Africa, such as antebellum Louisiana (which will
be discussed in detail in Chapter 5).

The distinctions that national and community ideologies make
between ethnicity and race are also crucial to explore in terms
of understanding how these concepts are constructed (and indexed
through language). Urciuoli gives one perspective on such ideologies
in the USA:

> When people are talked about as an ethnic group . . . the ideological
> emphasis is on national and/or cultural origins. This emphasis gives
> them a rightful place in the United States and their claim to

language is seen as a point of pride. When people are talked about as a race (and every group now seen as ethnic was once or is still seen as a race as well . . .), the emphasis is on natural attributes that hierarchize them and, if they are not white, make their place in the nation provisional at best. (1996:15)

As Omi and Winant note, the meanings of the terms *ethnicity* and *ethnic group* in the USA developed in the context of a theory that focused on white immigrants of European descent, and was not concerned with the experience of those who were identified as racial minorities (1994:16). They also argue that one effect of the US civil rights movement was to shift elements of experience that had been previously interpreted as being about "ethnicity" into the arena of "race" (1994:95–6).

Certain ideologies clearly exist on a national level and form part of a large-scale consciousness of race and ethnicity; what Omi and Winant (1994) might call national "racial projects." But smaller communities may have their own local perspectives on race and ethnicity, and in some cases these may contradict the dominant national ideologies. For example, the Rhode Island community that Bailey (2000b) studied does not apply the "one-drop rule" mentioned earlier as characteristic of the USA in general. Among the young people he talked to, individuals whose parents represented more than one ethnic group were always referred to clearly as "half-X and half-Y," and if a person with a single African-American parent described their ethnicity as "black," it was sometimes challenged.

In sum, then, the definitions of ethnicity and race have been approached from a number of perspectives. While some common themes emerge in the discussion, each scholar tends to give these terms a slightly different focus. Since my primary training is in linguistics, I do not feel qualified to solve the problem by wrangling a perfect definition out of the multifaceted perspectives represented here. I must, though, make some decisions about what will count as an ethnic group, or as "ethnicity," for the purposes of this book. In this spirit, I will delineate what I see as the main issues to keep in mind when exploring connections of ethnicity and language.

Many of the definitions cited above acknowledge the significance of contact between groups in defining and highlighting ethnicity, for instance the fourth element in Barth's definition, which is the one he identifies as "critical" to defining ethnicity (Barth 1969:13). Zelinsky goes so far as to suggest that there must be not only contact, but also "friction," and Cohen states simply, "Ethnicity has no existence apart from interethnic relations" (1978:389). This definition of the ethnic "self" in contrast with an ethnic "other" fits well with what we know about other identities and how they are constructed: to be masculine, for example, means not to show feminine characteristics, at least in the dominant ideology. Someone living in an isolated mountain village who has never been in contact with any people who look or act differently from the family and community around them, then, might be said not to have an ethnicity, in accord with Cohen's statement above (although they would, of course, have a culture!). Without investing too much in that particular point, I will begin here from the premise that ethnicity is something that is highlighted most clearly where ingroup/outgroup boundaries are part of the context, and I will situate the discussion of language and ethnicity within a particular community's ideologies about such boundaries.

Some scholars have raised the issue of whether qualitatively different *types* of boundaries exist between groups. Often this discussion centers on race, as in Bobo's comment above that race results in more persistent barriers. The observation that race is undeniably different from other criteria that might contribute to the definition of a particular ethnic group seems compelling to me. As Zelinsky warns:

> [W]e dare not overlook a crucial distinction between race and any of the several cultural elements that can contribute to defining the ethnic group. Specifically, none of those attributes is subject to anything so virulent and ineradicable as racism. (2001:10)

Whichever other factors – religion, language, customs – might be involved, race, Zelinsky argues, is in a category of its own. It is worth repeating that what "race" means here is the perception of racial difference on the part of the groups involved, not any biologically definable quality. However, the entity involved when we use the term "race" is not *solely* a social construct, in the sense that societies use phenotype differences to classify people (unscientifically), and these elements of physical appearance affect the ascription to ethnic groupings by others in the community (and, as Smelser et al. [2001] noted above, make it difficult for members of the group to change their identity).

One perspective that appears to underlie some of this discussion, although the sources I have consulted do not make it explicit, is the idea of a continuum of differences among ethnic groups. This continuum might be conceptualized as comprising perceptions of interethnic difference, combined with the saliency of the physical and cultural markers involved, with race being a particularly crucial piece of the puzzle. So, for example, toward the low end of the difference scale we might have group differences that are viewed as ethnic, not racial, and are associated with few outward signs in terms of phenotype, culture, etc. At least in some parts of the USA the distinction between Irish-Americans and Italian-Americans (which historically was much more salient than it is now) might fit this category. It is also possible that the distinction between these groups would fall at a different place on the continuum for these two groups in an older area of settlement like New York City versus, for example, Seattle, Washington on the West Coast. The case of French Canadians and Anglo-Canadians would fall higher on the continuum than either of these, due to the sociopolitical context and the saliency of language use as an outward sign of difference.

Other significant outward signs might include dress (as with the Amish of Eastern Pennsylvania), religious customs, food, and music, all of which come up repeatedly in the literature on ethnicity. Among these categories there might be internal distinctions in terms of their effect on perceptions of difference. For instance, language (either a different native tongue from the mainstream or a different native dialect from the standard) may not be a factor at all, but where it comes up it may be less mutable than the other factors. Dress, though highly mutable, is the type of factor that is clearly perceptible in any interethnic contact situation, whereas food preferences may not be immediately evident to outsiders. My sense from having lived in Pennsylvania is that the clothing norms of the Amish contribute strongly to the sense of them as a very distinct ethnic group. Still, any of the groups discussed so far could "pass" physically for a member of the dominant (white) group.

Further along on the continuum we might have groups where there is a perception of both ethnic and racial difference, and any groups of which this is true would, in my view, represent a qualitatively different type of division. In a particular setting, there also might be internal variations such that some groups are perceived as more racially different than others, as in the case of the three South African groups discussed earlier, where the dominant European group treated the "Coloured" group as less racially different from them than the "Black" group, though both were clearly distinguished on the basis of race. In addition, the variations in phenotype that are used for characterization, as well as the interpretations of a particular set of characteristics, can differ significantly. Bailey (2000b) notes, for instance, that Dominicans are often classified as "black" by others when they immigrate to the USA, but in the Dominican Republic those same speakers count as "white," and only individuals of Haitian descent are classified as "black." He cites this as an illustration of the idea that one "can 'change one's race' with a plane ride between countries" (2000b:556).

A related issue, which can be very controversial, is the imposition of hierarchical rankings on ethnic groups by the dominant ideology. Usually the dominant group is positioned as superior in the ideology. A Puerto-Rican American woman in Urciuoli's study, for example, articulated this explicitly, saying, "[W]e tend to be more like the white race, because we see them as superior to what we are" (1996:149). Within particular communities, however, there can be local countercurrents to this ideology running in the other direction. When I was conducting fieldwork in Los Angeles, for example, a Mexican-American boy I interviewed revealed to me with great ceremony that his father was white, but asked me not to tell anyone else. He had kept this information secret from his peers, presumably indicating that, in his particular peer group, having European-American descent, or at least claiming this descent, was disfavored or shameful.

There are also hierarchies among non-dominant ethnic groups. In Bucholtz's (1995) study of multiracial women, one individual of Latin-American and Japanese descent noted that she sometimes pretended not to know Spanish, to avoid being classified as Latina. She expressed negative judgments of her own behavior in this regard, but justified it in terms of USA ideologies where "it [is] kind of bad to be Latino because you know just this big stereotype of Latino and Chicano people being so, like, dirty or bad or lazy" and, in contrast, "the Japanese part . . . that's, like, the better side" (1995:363). Within groups that the dominant ideology treats as a single entity, such as Asian-Americans, there may nonetheless be crucial hierarchical distinctions made by those within these overgeneralized categories. Among the Korean-Americans studied by Lo (1999), Korean and Chinese ethnicities were ranked highest, followed by Japanese, and then all the Southeast Asian ethnicities were seen as strikingly less desirable, in contexts such as the appropriateness of people from these backgrounds as potential marriage partners.

Another type of ideological hierarchy exists in relation to skin tone in many groups. As noted above, phenotype often plays a key role in the understanding and construction of race and ethnicity. The role of skin tone in ethnic ascription is often overtly discussed in minority ethnic communities. A young mother in Zentella's study of Puerto-Rican Americans in New York City, for instance, commented on phenotype differences in her two sons: "This one is dark and that one is light, didn't you notice? Dark and light, white and black" (1997:224). Zentella notes that she herself could not perceive any clear difference, which is not surprising, since (as we have seen), concepts of race, like concepts of ethnicity, are socially constructed. A detailed discussion of skin-tone issues in an African-American community is portrayed in the movie

Jungle Fever (1991), where a darker-skinned woman asserts that more options (especially in terms of partners) are open to lighter-skinned black women (see also Spears [2001] for a discussion of "colorism" in an African-American community). The effects of such hierarchies on language ideologies will be discussed in Chapter 2.

Finally, the discussion so far has mostly proceeded as if people have a single ethnic identity, but of course this view is too simplified, particularly (but not solely) when we consider **mixed-race individuals**. Davis (1991) provides an excellent overview of the many different ways that **multiracial** populations are integrated into the social hierarchy in countries around the world. In some societies, for example, the mixed group has been seen historically as lower in status than either parent group, while in others this group may have an intermediate status, or occasionally even a higher status than either parent group. The population of "mixed-race" individuals is increasing dramatically in a number of countries, including the USA (Zelinsky 2001:22–3), which by itself may end up having a dramatic effect on definitions of ethnicity. Currently in the USA, individuals with parents from two different ethnic groups might choose to identify themselves as belonging to both of these ethnicities, to one of them only, or to neither (Bucholtz 1995, Azoulay 1997), and these choices may shift over time. In fact, Bucholtz (1995) notes that ethnic self-definition may shift for a multiracial individual even within the span of a single conversation. Le Page and Tabouret-Keller found a very high number of individuals in Belize who would describe themselves as "Mixed," so much so that claiming a mixed background seems to be in itself a feature of Belizean ethnic identity (1985:244).

The assigning of a single ethnic identity is problematic in other ways as well. For example, immigrants of African descent who come to the USA from Spanish-speaking countries such as Panama may see themselves as having a "combined" ethnicity, e.g., "Black Latina" (Thomas 2000). As seen in Bucholtz's research (1995), an individual's ethnic choices in terms of identity may shift over a time period that may be quite brief, and an individual may choose to "pass" as a member of some other group than those in their biographical history (see Chapter 10). A group's perceptions of and labeling for their own ethnicity can also shift over different generations, for instance going from Mexican to Mexican-American (Fought 2003), Chinese to Singaporean (Escure 1997), or Indian to Belizean (Le Page and Tabouret-Keller 1985). In sum, then, we cannot expect ethnicity to be essential, static, or uncomplicated. We can only study ethnicity as a complex process of constructing and reproducing identities within a particular community, a process intertwined with social, historical, ideological, and biographical factors.

In moving on to explore the relationship of ethnicity to language, then, I will be focused on the role of language in the construction of identity by the speaker, as well as in the ascription of ethnic identity by others. I will start from the assumption that ethnicity is linked to boundaries between groups and, more importantly, ideologies about those boundaries. Language may be used as a way to preserve those boundaries, cross them, or subvert them altogether. I will attempt to address questions related to the perceived closeness or distance of particular groups. For example, in the community studied by Urciuoli in New York City, there is no fixed boundary between Puerto Ricans and African-Americans, who see themselves as members of different ethnic groups, but also as a coherent group in contrast with European-Americans. Does this perception of reduced ethnic distance have correlates in the area of language? In this respect, situations of interethnic contact among more than two ethnic groups are particularly interesting, since they provide for a more complex comparison. Because of the unique role of perceived racial distinctions in maintaining group boundaries, I have chosen to privilege somewhat in the discussion those settings where perception of ethnic and racial difference reinforce each other, exploring the role that language and dialect differences play in these types of communities. Nonetheless, in Chapter 5, I look at a specific case where both a minority group perceived as *ethnically* different and a minority group perceived as *racially* different are present. Also, although the literature on people of mixed race is still sparse, I have tried to include some examples of the specific roles that language might play in the construction of multiracial identities.

DISCUSSION QUESTIONS

1. What do you think of the criteria used to define ethnicity here? Are there any you think should be added?
2. Do you think it is important to make a distinction between "ethnicity" and "race"? Why or why not?
3. How do you characterize yourself in terms of race and/or ethnicity? Have you ever been categorized by someone else in a way that surprised you? Explain the circumstances, the event, and how you felt about the misunderstanding.
4. Suppose the parents of a mixed-race child were to say to her, "Don't let anyone tell you what race you are. You're not any

specific race. You're just a human being." What advantages and/or disadvantages do you see to such an approach?

SUGGESTIONS FOR FURTHER READING

Barth, Fredrik, ed. 1969. *Ethnic Groups and Boundaries: The Social Organization of Culture Difference*. Boston: Little, Brown.

This is a classic study, often cited when the concept of ethnic groups is discussed in sociology and other fields.

Davis, F. J. 1991. *Who is Black? One Nation's Definition*. University Park, PA: Pennsylvania State University Press.

Despite the focus of its title, this study is actually very broad. It discusses topics such as laws about race, effects of skin tone, construction of race in other countries (Brazil, Korea, Haiti, etc.), and transracial adoptions.

Le Page, Robert and Andrée Tabouret-Keller. 1985. *Acts of Identity: Creole-Based Approaches to Language and Ethnicity*. Cambridge: Cambridge University Press.

A classic study of race and ethnicity from a sociolinguistic point of view. The concept of "acts of identity" has since become a staple of the sociolinguistic literature.

Omi, M. and H. Winant. 1994. *Racial Formation in the United States: From the 1960s to the 1990s*. New York and London: Routledge.

A respected and much-cited modern study of the political history of "race," as well as class-based and other theoretical approaches to race and ethnicity.

Smelser, Neil J., William Julius Wilson, and Faith Mitchell, eds. 2001. *America Becoming: Racial Trends and Their Consequences*, vol. I. Washington, DC: National Academy Press.

The first of two substantial and thorough volumes commissioned by the National Research Council, focusing on the most current research in the area of ethnicity. It is a collection of chapters from a number of behavioral and social scientists looking at different demographic and social trends in race and race relations in the US.

Zelinsky, Wilbur. 2001. *The Enigma of Ethnicity: Another American Dilemma*. Iowa City: University of Iowa Press.

In this work, Zelinsky traces a number of modern trends in the study of race and ethnicity in the USA, including the definition of ethnicity and ethnic groups, and the ways in which these concepts play a role in the construction of identity in general.

2 Language and the construction of ethnic identity

When people ask me [about ethnicity] I say Mexican but, but then they say, "No you're not. You don't speak Spanish." They, they just tease me to get me mad . . . I guess a lot of people think if you don't speak Spanish you're not like full Mexican or whatever, but, but I am! I think so. (Veronica, a 17-year-old Latina from Los Angeles, from Fought 2003)

A few years ago, I watched a television documentary called *Urban Invaders*, a somewhat lighthearted treatment of the topic of rats in New York City. The residents who were interviewed about their experiences with rats included an African-American woman, a Puerto Rican American woman, and a European-American man. Each of these people clearly sounded like a New Yorker, and yet none of them spoke exactly like the others. All of them exhibited some features characteristic of New York City in their **phonology**, such as **raised** [ɔ°] (found in, e.g., *more* or *floor*), which occurred across all three speakers; however, each of these individuals also used **variants** linked to his or her ethnicity. The African-American woman used phonological features of **African American Vernacular English** (**AAVE**), such as [f] for [θ] in *teeth* and **monophthongization** of [aj] as [a] in *climbing*. For the Puerto-Rican American woman, the vowels [i] and [u] were realized with no **glide** and slightly higher than in other dialects. Presumably, the European-American man who was interviewed also indexed his ethnic identity in some way. But how? By non-use of the other features I've mentioned? By a more intense use of the variants associated with New York City speech? Given that the features of the "New York City dialect" have traditionally been defined with reference to the majority group of European-American speakers, to say that he uses more of these seems redundant. I will leave this question open for the moment, returning to the exploration of "white" ethnicities in Chapter 6. Even in the simplest of examples, though, we see that the role of language in constructing ethnicity quickly becomes complicated.

We know from decades of social science research that the identities of human beings in modern societies are complex. We live our lives constantly balancing different roles and expectations, even when we have no awareness of doing so. On a particular Wednesday, I may spend most of my time highlighting my role as a professor at a liberal arts college. The following Saturday, I may spend all day playing the role of loving daughter for my mother's birthday celebration, an occasion at which the fact that I am a professor may be more or less irrelevant. Language is a key element in this balancing act, the means by which we both point to and reproduce our nuanced identities. As Barrett (1999) puts it:

> Speakers may heighten or diminish linguistic displays that index various aspects of their identities according to the context of an utterance and the specific goals they are trying to achieve . . . This practice implies that speakers do not have a single "identity" but rather something closer to what Paul Kroskrity . . . has called a "repertoire of identity," in which any of a multiplicity of identities may be fronted at a particular moment. In addition, . . . speakers may index a polyphonous, multilayered identity by using linguistic variables with indexical associations to more than one social category. (1999:318)

With respect to ethnicity specifically, we know that individuals construct complex identities in which ethnicity is only one component, which may be highlighted more or less in a given situation. (It has even been shown experimentally that this is true, as will be discussed below.)

A person who happens to be African-American, for example, is very likely to index his or her ethnicity through language in some way, whether by using a particular dialect (or range of dialects), following certain norms for discourse, or participating in oral traditions such as call and response. However, there are many things that this person may want to express simultaneously, such as "I am a woman, and I identify with other women" or "I grew up in the middle class, and I'm proud of my education, but at the same time I don't want to sound white." As discussed in Chapter 1, ethnicity does not occur in isolation from other elements of identity such as class and gender. Language must provide ways of reflecting and constructing the many facets of our identities, and of course it does. This complexity is what Le Page and Tabouret-Keller (1985) sought to address with their model of linguistic behavior as *acts of identity*. In this framework, individuals' use of language is seen as "reveal[ing] both their personal identity and their search for social roles" (1985:14). For any particular ethnicity that we might study, then, there will not be one single way of speaking that marks that ethnicity. Rather, there will be a range of ways of speaking that are appropriate to the complexities of identity construction by individuals, a pool of resources from which members of a **speech community** draw the linguistic tools they need.

2.1 WHAT LINGUISTIC RESOURCES DO INDIVIDUALS HAVE IN CONSTRUCTING IDENTITY?

There are a number of types of linguistic resources available in multi-ethnic communities for speakers to use in indexing ethnic identity. In some of the Latino groups that will be discussed in Chapter 4, for instance, there may be as many as ten different **codes** that community members may draw on: **Standard English**, regional varieties of Spanish, code-switching, and so forth. In research on the connections between language and ethnicity, the following resources often emerge as important to the construction of ethnic identity:

- *A heritage language.* There is a multitude of studies focusing on the important role that a separate language tied to ethnic identity can play in defining an ethnic group, and in a sense of ethnic pride. Speakers in Bailey's study of Dominican-Americans, for example, articulate this concept explicitly, saying that "they SPEAK Spanish, so they ARE Spanish" (2000b:556). In the local **language ideology**, speaking a language makes them members of a particular ethnic group. In cases where a heritage language is dying out through **language shift**, revitalization efforts may be undertaken to prevent this loss, as has happened among the Maori in New Zealand, with numerous Native-American groups in the USA, and in many other places. At the individual level, **language acquisition**, as well as the maintenance or loss of a language, can be a complex process. Schecter and Bayley (2002), in their study of Mexican-Americans, found that commitment to maintaining an ethnic language is not a one-time event, but rather a series of choices individuals make over the course of their lifetimes. Just as identity can be fluid and changing throughout an individual's life, so can a person's relationship to the minority and dominant languages.
- *Code-switching.* There are a number of excellent works detailing the forms and functions of code-switching (too many to list, but Poplack 1980, Myers-Scotton 1993, Zentella 1997, and Auer 1998

are good places to start). The use of code-switching as a way of indexing ethnic identity specifically, though, is less thoroughly documented, and it is this latter role that is of interest here, and I will return to it particularly in Chapter 4. One benefit of code-switching in constructing ethnic identity is its inherent voicing of multiple identities – for example, the ability to index an affiliation with the local community as well as with one's ethnic heritage, a process which will be discussed further below.

• *Specific linguistic features.* Linguistic features within a variety are a key element in the indexing and reproduction of ethnic identity, just as they are for other aspects of identity, such as gender or social class. Many variationist studies of the use of particular features will be discussed throughout the book. One interesting issue that arises in looking at ethnicity and language is that different types of variables (**phonetic, syntactic,** or **lexical items**) may play completely different roles in the construction of identity at the individual and community levels. For example, in Hewitt's (1986) study, use of Creole phonology by white speakers in South London was more likely to trigger a negative reaction from Afro-Caribbean peers than use of Creole **grammar** and lexicon, suggesting that phonology is seen in more proprietary terms as an index of ethnic identity. Some features are so closely tied to ethnic identity that a single use of that feature can serve to identify a speaker as belonging to a particular group; for example, a listener in Urciuoli's study identifies a speaker on a tape as black, because he used **habitual** *be* (1996:116).

• *Suprasegmental features.* For many ethnic varieties, **suprasegmental features** are part of the signaling of ethnic identity, either in conjunction with linguistic features or independently. Fought and Fought (2002), for example, show that **syllable timing** is an important factor in the English used by Mexican-American speakers in Los Angeles. Green (2002:124) discusses evidence for the claim that some African-Americans who speak a completely **standard dialect** nonetheless use **intonational** patterns that reveal and index their ethnicity.

• *Discourse features.* In addition to the structural elements of language, ways of using language may be crucial to the performance and recognition of ethnic identity. This topic will be covered more fully in Chapter 8.

• *Using a borrowed variety.* By "**borrowed**" variety, here, I mean a code that originates outside the ethnic group, but is appropriated by individuals or entire communities for use in constructing their own ethnic identity. At the individual level, this might include crossing, as when a Korean-American speaker uses AAVE to construct his masculinity (Chun 2001). It can also occur at a broader level, e.g., when Puerto-Rican American speakers as a group, or at least some speakers, incorporate features of AAVE into their **vernacular** (Wolfram 1974, Zentella 1997). This phenomenon will be discussed more in Chapter 7.

In discussing the resources available to speakers in multiethnic communities, we must remember that not all uses of language represent choices involving the indexing of ethnic identity. A particular code may be selected for its communicative value in a specific situation, for example, without conveying anything deeply symbolic. The reverse may also be true. A language may have a highly important symbolic value for an ethnic group, despite the fact that few people have access to learning it and so cannot choose to use this particular resource. In addition, as sociolinguistic research expands into new areas, we may find communities using resources not on this list.

2.2 INDEXING MULTIPLE IDENTITIES

In looking at the complexities of how individuals index ethnic identity through language, we might begin by considering what additional factors are likely to play an important role in an individual's identity. The factors besides ethnicity that have been the focus of the most intense sociolinguistic study include *age*, *gender*, and *social class*, and all of these are crucially important to understanding the construction of ethnic identity. Rickford (1999), for example, suggests that younger African-Americans may express a more secure attitude about the use of African American Vernacular English than older African-Americans in the same community. Hewitt found that boys in some areas of South London were much more likely to know Creole than girls, a factor which sometimes caused the girls embarrassment, because of the "equation of black cultural identity with creole speech" (1986:106). I've mentioned only a few studies as examples here, but interactions of language and ethnicity with factors like age, gender, and social class will recur throughout the discussion. The full range of elements that shape identity, however, goes well beyond this brief list. Many other factors have been observed to affect patterns of language and ethnicity across a number of communities. These include, for example, *sexual orientation*, as in Barrett's (1999) study of African-American drag queens or Liang's (1997) study of Asian-American and European-American coming-out narratives, and *religion*, as in Chun's (2001) analysis of Christian Korean-Americans or Ngom's (2004) study of linguistic markers of religious identity among different ethnic groups in Senegal.

In addition, a factor that is less often discussed, but that seems to play a particularly crucial sociolinguistic role, is **local** or **extralocal orientation**. Researchers have used different terms for this factor, but it basically refers to whether a speaker mainly has strong ties to the local community, or instead is oriented toward contacts and future opportunities outside the community. One of the earliest studies to look at this factor in relation to ethnicity is Labov's classic (1972b) Martha's Vineyard study. Labov found that, among the younger generation of speakers on the island, the **centralized** variants of [ay] and [aw], associated with local island identity, were used less by residents of English descent than by residents of Native-American or of Portuguese descent. Labov attributes this correlation with ethnicity to the desire of the speakers in the two minority ethnic groups to assert their ties to local island identity, ties which have been contested historically due to ethnic prejudice against these groups. Similarly, Hazen (2000) found that this factor (for which he uses the terms *expanded identity* and *local identity*) correlated strongly with the use of local variants across three different ethnic groups in North Carolina. This correlation occurred both for locally significant variants used by all the groups and also for those that specifically indexed ethnic identity.

A related but slightly different factor is that of *strength of ethnic ties*. One example of research that focuses on this factor is the work of Lesley Milroy and Li Wei (Milroy and Wei 1995, Wei et al. 1992) on a Chinese community in Britain (Tyneside). The researchers constructed an "ethnic index" of the strength of ties that a particular individual had to others of the same ethnic group in Tyneside. They found that this ethnic index helped to explain patterns of language choice that could not be predicted by a model based on age and generation, and that ethnic network also influenced the use of certain code-switching strategies. Strength of ethnic ties may also be relevant in Gordon's (2000) study of the Northern Cities Shift. He found that most of the Mexican-descent speakers in his study did not use features of this shift, which are more prevalent in European-Americans, but one participant from this ethnic group had substantial use of such features. The individual in question lived in a mainly European-American neighborhood, and reported that her close friends were all white except for her. In addition, this speaker showed less enthusiasm about her Mexican heritage than other participants, and stated explicitly that ethnicity did not have a central place in defining her identity.

Finally, there are relevant social factors that may be very specific to particular communities. As an example, Hewitt (1986) found that a more extensive use of Creole than usual, for speakers who were not black, was found in the speech of a boy who was the only white member of a "sound" crew, a group of boys who brought sound equipment to perform music at parties. Fought (2003) describes a category among young Mexican-American speakers of people who "know gangsters," meaning that they are not themselves in a gang, but are connected with gang members in some form. This variable turned out to be crucial in understanding sociolinguistic patterns of the young adult group in the study. Sociolinguists conducting research on ethnicity and language must be vigilant for these types of factors, which can easily pass unnoticed because they do not have obvious parallels in previous studies.

It is too simplistic, however, to view the construction of ethnic identity as just being influenced by or correlating with other factors, as though the effects were separable but cumulative. Speakers often index "polyphonous identities" (Barrett 1999) through their use of language, so that utterances reflect the nuances of identity in multilayered ways that cannot be broken down into smaller components. For example, the African-American drag queens studied by Barrett (1999) used language to present themselves simultaneously as African-Americans, gay men, and drag queens. In Chun (2001), a Korean-American speaker uses AAVE to draw on stereotypes of African-American identity that reinforce his masculinity, but also to voice a distinctly Korean-American identity in opposition to ideologies about how Asian-Americans should behave. Hewitt (1986) found that young white speakers in South London would often use Creole **grammatical** forms, but with a standard phonology, deliberately indexing both their affiliation with their black friends and their own ethnic identity as members of an outside group. These examples illustrate the framework that Bakhtin (1981) labels "double-voiced discourse," where a speaker's utterances contain within themselves a "dialogue" about identity.

Almost by definition, code-switching can be seen as another form of indexing multiple identities. Myers-Scotton discusses how in many parts of Africa ethnic identity is signaled by use of the mother tongue, while use of the official language of the area is associated with membership in a "multi-ethnic elite" (2000:146). Code-switching allows speakers to index these two types of membership simultaneously. One teenage Mexican-American speaker cited in Fought (2003) articulated

the important role of code-switching in ethnic identity particularly
clearly:

> *Es que así nos- se hablan los Chicanos, los Mexicanos. Los que viven aquí.*
> *Como los de México no hablan- no saben na' de eso, pero los que viven*
> *aquí sí hablan Chicano- "Chicano language."*
>
> [It's like, that's how we- how the Chicanos speak, the Mexicans. The
> ones that live here. Like, the people from Mexico don't speak- don't
> know nothing about that, but people that live here do speak
> Chicano- "Chicano language."] (Fought 2003:209)

The tensions that exist in the Los Angeles community between
Mexican-Americans born in the USA and immigrants from Mexico
can lead to serious conflicts, as will be discussed in Chapter 4. This
speaker identifies code-switching as part of the construction of *Mexican-
American* or *Chicano* ethnicity, in contrast with immigrant Mexican ethnicity, which might look superficially similar to outsiders. By code-
switching, speakers born in the USA are able to index simultaneously
their Mexican heritage and their claim to a specifically US identity.

A slightly different pattern involves the linguistic signaling of different identities where the components can be separated out from each
other to an extent, but follow each other in rapid succession within
a particular speech event. In these cases, the multiple voices that are
performed may not overlap completely or at all, but are linked together
sequentially by the speaker into a complex chain. Bailey (2000b) gives
an example of this type of performance by a Dominican-American
teenager. Over a very brief period of time, this speaker used Spanish
to give a compliment to a Dominican girl, AAVE to boast about his abilities, and switched between Spanish and English to negotiate an activity with a friend, invoking a number of different facets of his identity.
The African-American drag queens studied by Barrett (1999), who often
voiced multiple identities simultaneously, also engaged in this type of
sequential switching of codes. In this case, some of the identities they
performed even seemed to contradict each other. For example, the drag
queens would use stereotyped **"Women's Language"** features (e.g., **tag
questions**, or "empty" adjectives like *cute*) to perform a hyper-feminine
identity. But they might switch suddenly to a low-pitched voice and
the use of **taboo words** to highlight masculinity and signal their biological identity as males. This ability to draw on contrasting gender
norms formed a crucial element of the drag performance. In highly
multilingual environments, speakers may use different languages altogether for this function. Myers-Scotton, for instance, gives an example

of this type from Kenya, where in a single conversation a speaker uses Kikuyu to signal her ethnic pride, Swahili to index her urban identity, and English to index her education (1993:104–5).

2.3 ETHNIC PRIDE OR ASSIMILATION?

One important issue that arises in the construction of ethnicity by minority ethnic groups in a region is that of **assimilation** versus "ethnic pride." Cultural ideologies often pit these two concepts against each other, promoting the idea, more or less, that you are either "one of us" or you are "one of them," and language is often seen as a key indicator of an individual's positioning with respect to this dichotomy (see, e.g., Fordham and Ogbu 1986). Often, though not always, class distinctions play a role in this process. A person may get a higher-paying job, for example, or go to college, and be expected to speak in a different way there, usually involving use of the dominant variety of the area. Upon return to the community, the person may be perceived as speaking like an outsider, forgetting where he or she came from, or thinking that he or she is "better" than other people.

The theme of **linguistic assimilation** came up repeatedly in Urciuoli's (1996) study of Puerto-Rican Americans in New York. One woman, for example, responded to a general question about what it meant to be "middle class" by saying:

> [W]hen somebody goes from one stage to another, they've changed, . . . they start talking differently. They don't talk slang or street stuff anymore. They talk like businesspeople . . . And usually when a black or Spanish person goes from being a poor person to a middle-class person, then everybody says – then it's like they can't come back to the old friends that they had because it's like "Oh! You act like you white! . . . What's this 'how are you doing, and how are you feeling?' When the fuck you learn to talk like that?"[1] (1996:142)

This accusation of acting "white" comes up frequently in discussions in many minority ethnic communities, and will be discussed further in Chapter 6. The same sorts of issues arise for many middle-class African-Americans, who find themselves in a position where standard varieties of English are a key part of the work and often home lives, but speakers may be criticized in the wider African-American community for sounding too standard (Fordham and Ogbu 1986, Rickford 1999). On the other hand, AAVE is viewed negatively outside the community, and by some members within it, but is also necessary for complete participation in many aspects of community life. (Options for resolving this tension will be discussed in detail in Chapter 3.) Mesthrie (2002b) reports a similar situation among Indian South Africans, who use varieties of English that parallel the **acrolect–mesolect–basilect** continuum found in **creole-language**-speaking communities. Indian South African speakers must balance conflicting pressures: use of the more basilectal forms may be seen as unsophisticated, but use of the more acrolectal forms, according to Mesthrie, may be viewed as "putting on airs" or "being cold" (2002b:345).

Similarly, not knowing (or using) the code that is most closely tied to the ethnic identity in the community can be a source of shame, embarrassment, or criticism. African-American college students who are native speakers of standard varieties of English, for example, will sometimes attempt to use AAVE, even if they make mistakes ("hypocorrection") (Baugh 1999: Chapter 11, Rahman 2002). One of the speakers in Rahman's (2002) study commented, "I tried talking Black English but felt awkward and fake. I wish I was raised speaking Black English as well as Standard English." Similarly, Hewitt (1986) discusses the use of Creole among young speakers of Afro-Caribbean descent in South London. Because the variety is stigmatized, and in fact many parents discourage their children from using it, a large number of young people do not speak Creole, but, as Hewitt comments, "because of the equation of black cultural identity with creole speech, many are loth to admit when their command of the language is poor" (1986:106). Often they will report that they speak Creole, even if they don't.

Where bilingualism is seen as an important component in the language norms of the community, monolingualism can sometimes be seen correspondingly as unfortunate, or even as weakening ethnic membership in some way. Monolingual English-speaking Mexican-Americans in Los Angeles, for instance, reported being criticized for not knowing Spanish (Fought 2003). The citation from the monolingual Latina that opens this chapter is a particularly striking example of this phenomenon, where the speaker feels the need to defend her "full" Mexican ethnicity because she doesn't speak Spanish.[2] A young middle-class woman from the same study, who was bilingual, commented, "A lot of people don't know how to speak the language [= Spanish]! Which shocks me, to see somebody with a last name like Lopez or Bracamontes or, that doesn't speak [Spanish]!" (2003:201). The use of the phrase "the language" is quite interesting in its own right, reinforcing the symbolic association of Spanish with Mexican-American ethnic identity.

If the *inability* to use a code associated with ethnicity is stigmatized, the *refusal* to use that code is even more negatively sanctioned. Rickford (1999:275) gives several examples of this type with respect to the use of AAVE. Similarly, Ogbu (1999) describes conflicts between parents and children, when the children came home from school using a standard variety, and would even try to correct their parents' use of AAVE. McCormick (2002b) found that among mixed-race speakers in the community of South Africa where she conducted her research, a "mixed" linguistic code, a combination of English and Afrikaans, was seen as the ingroup variety. If community members used an unmixed variety in an ingroup setting, it was seen as inappropriate, leaving the speaker open to accusations of acting "high and mighty" (2002b: 224).

Negative sanctions on the refusal to use a code are particularly prominent in bilingual communities. One young Mexican-American woman in Los Angeles, who was bilingual, commented, "Some people are like that. I hate people like that, that are Mexican, and they try to act like if they don't know Mexican [= Spanish]" (Fought 2003:202). Another bilingual Latina talked about her cousin, a recent immigrant to the USA:

> She changed. She started acting like she didn't know Spanish. And she came from Mexico, barely like, three years ago . . . and all of a sudden she changed, like, she started acting like she didn't know Spanish. And she tried to act too American. And I told, you know, I told her, "What happened to you?" you know. (2003:202)

What makes this example even more dramatic is that the issue eventually escalated to a physical fight between the teenage girl and her cousin. Simply not knowing the language well is not always seen as a reasonable excuse for refusal to speak it. A speaker from Zentella's study said, "Even if you don't wanna talk Spanish at least talk it all mixed up" (1997:206). The pressure to use the heritage language can be particularly strong where the language tied to an ethnic identity is perceived as threatened. Myers-Scotton gives an example from Nairobi, where English is often seen as threatening local languages and cultures; a student at the university reported that two boys were scolded by an older man for speaking English at a party: "Who are those speaking English? Are they back-biting us?" (1993:31). In sum, then, speakers must often strike a balance between the desire to use outgroup codes, for practical or symbolic reasons, and the pressure to use ingroup codes for signaling ethnic solidarity and being accepted within the community.

2.4 *HOW IS AN INDIVIDUAL'S ETHNICITY CO-CONSTRUCTED BY THE COMMUNITY?*

As noted in the exploration of ethnicity in Chapter 1, ethnic identity is negotiated in a social context where ascription by others in the community can be a critical factor. But how do community members make these decisions about individuals, particularly with respect to the role of language in ethnic identity? To begin with, phenotype, as has been discussed, is crucial and often deeply intertwined with expectations about both ethnicity and language. In Bailey's Rhode Island study, a young Dominican-American man says:

> a lot of people confuse me for an African American most of the time. They ask me, "Are you Black?" I'm like, "No, I'm Hispanic." . . . They'll be thinking that I'm just African American. Because sometimes the way I talk, my hair, my skin color, it's just that my hair is nappy. I use a lot of slang. You can confuse a lot of Dominicans as African American by their color. (2000b:565)

One interesting aspect of this account is the way in which phenotype and language are presented as so completely interconnected, as though "nappy" hair and slang form a natural grouping. Bailey notes that Dominican-Americans resist categorization as African-Americans due to their African-descent phenotype by invoking the Spanish language as the crucial factor in ethnicity, which will be discussed more below.

The hierarchies of skin tone, discussed in Chapter 1, can have direct effects on ideologies about language and ethnicity. For example, a mixed-race-descent South African woman in McCormick's study commented that she had decided that if her children were light-skinned, she would raise them as English speakers, since both lighter skin and command of English are seen as associated with upward mobility (2002a:103). Urciuoli (1996) conducted an experiment in which she played speech samples of people of different ethnic backgrounds for Puerto-Rican American listeners, who were asked to identify the speaker's ethnicity. In one case, listeners in the experiment were surprised to find out that a particular speaker on the tape was Dominican-American, as she lacked the linguistic characteristics they associated with this background. One of the listeners concluded, "she's probably a light-skinned Dominican" (1996:112). It is fascinating to me that speakers would think they could identify skin tone from a tape, and this example reveals how ideologies about race and language are inextricably linked to each other.

In addition to phenotype, each community has a repertoire of language ideologies that come into play in the ascription of ethnicity. In Urciuoli's (1996) experiment, discussed above, the linguistic features used by her listeners in making decisions about the ethnicity of speakers are very revealing, in terms of ideologies of language and ethnicity. Among other things, **non-standard dialect** features were strongly associated with either Puerto-Rican or African-American ethnicity (and never with European-Americans). So, for instance, one man commented about a speaker, "I'd say he's black, he's definitely black, and he has that sort of like street-talk English, the way we use it with very poor grammar" (1996:119).[3] Their comments suggest that in a number of communities, particularly in the USA, speakers expect minority ethnic group members to use non-standard forms, and members of the dominant ethnic group to use a standard dialect. Ogbu (1999) found both of these assumptions in the California community he studied. A number of African-Americans in the community expected European-Americans to "naturally" speak proper English, as something they are "born with," while African-Americans were expected to "talk slang dialect" (1999:162). Similarly, Baugh (1999:135ff.) found that individuals whose speech was perceived as standard were identified as "white," even though several of the speakers were actually African-American. I will return to these assumptions in Chapter 6.

As discussed above, fluency in a heritage language can also be used as a way of organizing expectations about ethnicity within the community. Individuals who do not speak the language may find their ethnicity called into question, and speaking the language, as in the Dominican-American example above, may be a way of explicitly asserting ethnic identity. Although I have focused here on the attitudes of community members within an ethnic group, many of these ideologies may be shared by members of other groups in the same area. In Bailey's (2000b) study, two Dominican-American boys try, as a joke, to convince a Southeast-Asian classmate that one of them is African-American. The very first thing that the skeptical classmate asks in response is: "Can he speak Spanish?" (to the other boy). Throughout the interaction, Bailey notes that the participants "treat Spanish language as the key to determining social identity, both for ratification as Spanish and for disqualification from the category 'Black'" (2000b:572).[4] In cases where the heritage language is being lost, however, the strong tie between language and ethnicity may be lost also, as was found by Zentella (1997) in the Puerto-Rican American community she studied. In the case of the Lumbee, a Native-American group of North Carolina, there are have been no speakers of any heritage language for many generations. As a result, their status as a separate group has been questioned by outsiders, including the government, which gives them only partial recognition. These situations highlight another crucial point: language ideologies are constantly in flux. As the context of a particular community changes historically, views about the value and use of particular codes may also change.

Not only the code used but also the norms for interaction can be crucial in the community's ascription of ethnicity. This process is illustrated in Wieder and Pratt's (1990) study of the Osage tribe, which was discussed in Chapter 1. The researchers put together a list of criteria for being a "real Indian" according to their ethnographic work in the community. Although they presumably were collecting *any* types of behaviors related to ethnicity that were the topic of discussion in the community, it's interesting to see how many items on their list relate in some way to language and interaction. The following behaviors are the ones they list that particularly focus on language:

- reticence in interacting with strangers
- razzing: ritualized teasing of others
- harmony in face-to-face relations, maintaining an appearance of agreement
- modesty, not bragging about personal achievements or putting forth personal expertise in an area
- appropriate use of silence, in the many situations where this is culturally appropriate
- public speaking, participating appropriately in certain types of (spontaneous or somewhat planned) public speeches

Many of these ideas about how real Indians behave seem to have grown out of **interethnic** contact with European-Americans. In other words, it seems doubtful that the Osage tribal members thought there was anything culturally important about their way of interacting with strangers until they discovered that European-Americans treat this speech event in a different way. A **speech act** such as razzing, on the other hand, that carries a particular label of its own, probably existed as a cultural factor before interethnic contact increased. Again, this example highlights the role of interethnic boundaries in the defining of ethnicity.

One final factor relevant to how the community co-constructs identity with the individual is the amazing power of language to transform, in this case specifically to transform ethnicity. As Bucholtz puts it, "the ideological link between language and ethnicity is so potent that the use of linguistic practices associated with a given ethnic group may be sufficient for an individual to pass as a group member" (1995:355).

It was discussed earlier, for example, that Dominican-Americans treat the Spanish language as a key factor that can in and of itself include or exclude a person from certain ethnic categorizations (Bailey 2000b). In Hewitt's study, the failure to use Creole is seen as having the power to classify someone as "not black" (1986:107). An even more striking case of this transformative power of language occurs in Sweetland (2002). Sweetland looked at the case of a young European-American woman, "Delilah," who grew up in a predominantly African-American area of Cincinnati, Ohio, and who speaks AAVE as her primary linguistic code. Sweetland spoke with one of the African-American men in this woman's peer group, asking him if the way Delilah spoke bothered him at all. He responded that it did not, and added, "Well, she basically black" (2002:525). The young man knew the woman's biographical identity as a European-American, but he felt that her cultural and linguistic attributes disqualified her from being white. In this case, we see the power of language to contribute to an individual's being, as Sweetland puts it, **"re-raced"** by community members.

2.5 LANGUAGE AND THE CONSTRUCTION OF ETHNIC IDENTITY: THREE INDIVIDUAL CASES

In many of the discussions of language and ethnicity presented here, the focus will be on patterns typical of communities or groups of speakers rather than individuals. It is through the behaviors of individuals, however, that such group patterns become established in the first place. The field of sociolinguistics as a whole has been working toward a more in-depth understanding of how individuals construct their social identities, and ethnographic studies of individuals can reveal nuances of language and behavior that researchers looking only at larger group patterns may miss. In this section are brief descriptions of three individuals in the United States, exploring how they reflect and reproduce their ethnic identity through language.[5] Each of their life histories illuminates different elements of the complex ways in which ethnicity and language are connected.

Muzel Bryant

> Interviewer: *Do you think you have a brogue?*
> Muzel: *Me? I don't know, I may have.*
> (Wolfram et al. 1999:168)

Muzel Bryant (Wolfram, Hazen and Tamburro 1997, Wolfram et al. 1999) was born in 1904 and grew up as part of the single African-American family on Ocracoke Island, North Carolina. Ocracoke is one of a set of islands, called the "Outer Banks," that are almost completely populated by European-Americans. Her family had been on the island for 130 years at the time she was interviewed, and she herself had lived there her entire life. She had worked as a domestic worker on the island, and had daily interactions with the other islanders, who, in her later years, have provided some support for her with meals, rides to the doctor, and so forth. Nonetheless, Wolfram et al. (1999) report that Muzel was never integrated into the social life of the community. Additionally, in her relatively isolated island life, she had no significant interactions with African-Americans on the mainland, only with her immediate family.

Muzel's situation is very interesting because there is a clear ethnic boundary between her and the European-American islanders, yet there is no separate minority ethnic community to which she belongs, and which we might expect to influence her speech patterns. So, in this long time on the island, has she simply assimilated to the patterns of the European-American Ocracokers? Or is the ethnic line strong enough for her dialect to maintain its own, separate norms, even without interaction with a larger African-American community?

Based on the interviews conducted with Muzel by the researchers, there is stronger support for the latter hypothesis, although the picture is quite complex. The researchers compared Muzel's speech with that of two elderly European-American women who are also lifetime residents of Ocracoke. Muzel shows relatively few phonological features of the local island dialect. In particular, she does not use [ɔj] for [aj] (as in the pronunciation of *high* as [hɔj]), which is probably the most salient marker of Ocracoke speech, often the subject of explicit commentary. Muzel's phonological system has features typical of AAVE (see Chapter 3) instead, such as **postvocalic /r/-lessness** and extremely high rates of **consonant cluster reduction**, which the European Americans do not show. Muzel did have some assimilation to the local dialect in her use of [a:] for [aj], though.

In terms of grammatical structures, Muzel uses both AAVE features (e.g., **copula deletion**, third singular –s absence, plural –s absence) and features of the local Outer Banks variety of English (e.g., marking of third plural noun phrases with –s, as in *The dogs goes*). Her use of AAVE features often differs slightly from the patterns found among mainland African-Americans, though, either in terms of frequency, or in terms of how the **linguistic constraints** affect the variation. There are also core AAVE features that Muzel does not seem to use, such as habitual *be*, or **remote-past *been***, and she has a very low frequency of use of **negative concord**, as compared with the mainland African-American community.

One final area of interest is lexicon. There are a number of local terms strongly associated with Ocracoke identity. While Muzel was familiar with the oldest of these **lexical items**, she did not recognize more recent ones, such as *dingbatter* for "outsider." She also seemed to be unfamiliar with the term *O'cocker*, a very significant local term referring to members of established island families. Wolfram et al. (1999) suggest that the phonology and lexicon are the components of the Ocracoke brogue that are most often identified as unique, and thus it makes sense that the social distance experienced by Muzel's family would be reflected more in these components, rather than in the **morphology** or syntax.

When Muzel Bryant speaks, then, she does not simply sound like any other O'cocker. Her construction of identity through language reflects the social distance between her family and the rest of the island community: she has a few features of the Ocracoke dialect, but in general she lacks those that are most closely tied to local identity. At the same time, it is not simply an absence of certain key local features that marks her speech. Despite the lack of regular contact with an African-American community, Muzel preserves a number of clear features of AAVE in her dialect. She sounds African-American. Muzel's speech highlights the importance of the individual's specific life history in the expression of ethnicity through language, regardless of external (interethnic) contact patterns. Her way of speaking reinforces the idea that ethnicity can be a very strong boundary indeed, even in small, isolated communities where a more complete integration than among large urban populations might be expected.

Foxy Boston

> Foxy: When I get home, I use slang and everything; when I'm at school I talk different. (Rickford and McNair Knox 1994:153, n. 42)

Foxy Boston (Rickford and McNair Knox 1994, Rickford 1999) lives about as far away from Muzel Bryant as one can get and still be within the boundaries of the United States. She grew up in a working-class family in East Palo Alto, California, and was interviewed by sociolinguistic researchers from Stanford over the course of several years when she was a teenager. While she shares with Muzel the fact that she is an African-American woman, the two of them live extraordinarily different lives, and their individual cases show the inadequacy of picking out categories like "African-American" or "woman" and expecting them to explain adequately the identity construction of real people, with respect to language or anything else.

East Palo Alto is a multiethnic suburban community near Stanford University. At the time Foxy was interviewed, it consisted primarily of families with a relatively low socioeconomic status, and over 60 percent of the residents were African-American. Up until age 15, Foxy attended predominantly African-American schools, but then she began attending a mostly European-American high school outside the local area. She is a very outgoing individual, and by age 18 she had become the president of the Black Student Union at her school. In terms of the interviews themselves, Foxy's style with the interviewers was highly animated, and she initiated or built on a number of controversial topics, such as teen pregnancy or race relations. In contrast, Wolfram et al. (1999) describe Muzel Bryant as quite reticent in the interview, not initiating conversational topics, and so forth.

If Muzel represents someone at the borders of AAVE, using some AAVE features but not others as part of her construction of ethnicity, Foxy represents what might be called the AAVE core. Among other things, she is a teenager, and the critical role of adolescents in sociolinguistic research and language change has been well established for all types of communities (cf. Eckert 2000). She also lives in a relatively urban, working-class setting, with a high density of local contacts. So, as expected, Foxy exhibits high frequencies of all the AAVE features that were studied in the project (Rickford 1999): habitual *be*, copula deletion, **possessive** –*s* absence, third singular –*s* absence, plural –*s* absence, unmarked past tense. Since adults in the same area use these features relatively less, Rickford concludes that Foxy's speech may be indicative of a change in progress, such that AAVE is becoming relatively more distinct from European-American varieties, at least with respect to certain features.

Perhaps more interesting than Foxy's high use of AAVE features in general is the way in which she varies her usage depending on context. The Stanford researchers set up the interviews with her in a way that was designed to reveal differences in the use of ethnically marked variables across different situations. In particular, one interview consisted of Foxy (age 18) speaking with a 41-year-old African-American woman and her 16-year-old daughter, both community residents, while a second interview was conducted eight months later by a 25-year-old European-American graduate student who was an outsider to the community. As might be expected, Foxy used certain AAVE variables (e.g., copula deletion, habitual *be*) significantly more in the former, ingroup interview than in the latter one. Topic shifts also influenced her use of certain variables to some degree. Although it is difficult to know how much the various factors of age, insider status, and ethnicity contribute individually, it seems likely that ethnicity, shared with the women conducting the first interview but not the woman in the second, was a large factor in Foxy's shifts in the use of AAVE. This serves as a good reminder that the construction of ethnicity does not take place in a vacuum or simply inside the individual's head. It is emphatically a social process as well, involving interactions with others, ingroup or outgroup members, who may influence the linguistic processes involved.

The researchers also uncovered another effect on Foxy's speech at an even broader level of context. There were two earlier interviews with Foxy, at ages 13 and 15, that were conducted by the same African-American women from the community. In the earliest interview, Foxy's use of AAVE features was "at a peak" according to the researchers (Rickford and McNair-Knox 1994), even higher than in the later interviews. But in the interview conducted when she was 15, Foxy uses AAVE variants much less, at a rate that approximates her low levels of use in the interview with the European-American interviewer. Rickford and McNair-Knox see a possible explanation for this phenomenon in Foxy's life history. As mentioned earlier, at age 15 she had just begun attending a predominantly European-American school, and she had also taken part in a number of tutorial and college motivational programs the previous summer. Foxy herself commented in this interview that African-American friends had said that she sounded "white." In addition, Foxy encountered a number of instances of prejudice against African-Americans at her school at first, a situation which in later years seemed to improve, or which at least she was able to handle more easily. All these factors in her personal history could account for the use of fewer AAVE features in her construction of ethnicity at age 15 than at ages 13 or 18. While it is often acknowledged that ethnic identity may be constructed differently in different contexts, there is much less discussion of how an individual's ethnic identity might vary at different times across the lifespan. Foxy's speech patterns highlight the fact that the teenage years, such a key focus of sociolinguistic research, are not necessarily an uninterrupted stream, but can also comprise a number of distinct stages.

In his discussion of whether Foxy's speech represents ongoing changes in AAVE, Rickford makes some comments that seem highly relevant to the consideration of how language and attitudes about ethnicity interact in the identity construction of individuals. He says:

> One external factor that strikes me as very relevant to divergence . . . is the differences in attitudes towards black identity and culture, including vernacular language use, between successive black generations. Black teenagers are less assimilationist than their parents and especially their grandparents, and more assertive about their rights to talk and act in their "natural way." By contrast, black adults, affected by the demands of the work-place, seem to be impelled away from distinctively black patterns of language and behavior. (1999:274)

Rickford backs this up with attitudinal evidence and comments from a number of speakers in the East Palo Alto community. So we see here a third type of context: the changing attitudes of the community towards ethnicity and the norms for its expression.

Looking at the cases of Muzel and Foxy, then, and thinking about matters of ethnicity and language, we cannot say that any two African-American women will construct their identities in the same linguistic way. We cannot even say that *one* African-American woman will construct her ethnic identity in the same linguistic way all the time. The same, of course, applies to members of ethnic groups all over the world. Though these facts are hardly controversial in current sociolinguistic theory, they still bear repeating as a caution against the overgeneralizations to which most of us fall prey at least occasionally. In addition, we must be aware of different types of contexts for the construction of ethnicity through language, including at the very least: a) the situational context which can vary from one conversation to the next or even within a single conversation, b) the broader context of an individual's life history, and c) the social context of how the community, or a segment of the community, views ethnicity at a particular point in time.

Mike

> Mike: Yo, tell me that shit is not phat!
> (Cutler 1999:432)

Reading the quote from Mike above, someone who is unfamiliar with him might conclude that he is the third working-class African-American individual to be discussed. But he is not. Mike is an upper-middle-class, European-American teenager, living on Park Avenue in one of the wealthiest sections of New York City (Cutler 1999). At the time he was interviewed, he attended an exclusive private high school and, perhaps surprisingly, given his speech, his peer group consisted mostly of European-American friends.

At age 13, Mike developed a strong interest in and identification with hip-hop culture.[6] He began wearing the clothing associated with this style and listening to rap music. In addition, he displayed outward signs of allegiance with African-American culture, including criticizing groups he felt were anti-African-American and accusing his mother of being racist. He adopted behaviors that he associated with a certain stereotype of inner city youth, such as writing graffiti on nearby buildings, playing pool and using drugs. Many of his ideas about "the gangster life" seem to have come from films on African-American inner-city life (such as *Boyz N the Hood*), which he had watched repeatedly, as well as from the lyrics of rap songs. Mike also joined a gang, leading to his having several encounters with the police. When he was 14, he was involved in a violent incident where rival (mainly white) gang members broke his arms with baseball bats.

The development of Mike's tough/urban identity was accompanied by a shift in speech style: Mike began crossing into AAVE. "Crossing" (Rampton 1995) will be explained further in Chapter 10. Like the acquisition of any new speech style, the use of AAVE by someone who is not a native speaker has an accompanying learning curve. This process is illustrated in an excerpt from Mike's speech, reported by Cutler, that amuses me every time I read it. Mike, in speaking to a friend on the telephone says, "I gotta ask, I mean aks [æks] my mom" (1999: 429). This utterance catches our attention, because we are used to hearing speakers self-correct in the direction of standard or **prescriptive** norms. Mike corrects himself not *towards* the standard, but *away* from it, in his quest to master AAVE patterns.

Mike used many phonetic features of AAVE (e.g., **stopping** of fricatives – "then" pronounced [dɛn]), and a number of **prosodic** features associated with AAVE as well. In addition to the changes in his phonology, he exhibited a very high use of lexical items associated with hip-hop culture (such as *yo* and *phat*, in the utterance quoted at the start of this section). Mike did not, on the other hand, use the core features of AAVE grammar which were used so consistently by Foxy in her speech. A number of linguistic studies (e.g., Ash and Myhill 1986) suggest that the grammatical elements of a variety may be harder to acquire than lexical items or the phonology. It makes sense, then, that individuals with limited access to these varieties might fail to acquire the grammatical component, although alternative explanations will be explored in Chapter 10.

By the conclusion of Cutler's study, Mike was 19 and in his second year at a private college. He had abandoned the tough "gangster" persona, changed his style of clothing, and, according to Cutler, tended to modify his speech more toward the standard, although he retained elements of AAVE phonology, as well as continuing to use many of the same hip-hop terms. Like Foxy, then, Mike's teen years did not constitute one undifferentiated period, either developmentally or linguistically.

From looking at just three individual cases it is clear how complex the interactions of language with ethnicity can be. Even where two speakers might identify as members of the same ethnic group (as Foxy and Muzel presumably would), their life histories may lead them to construct ethnicity in strikingly different ways, so that their use of language in reflecting and reproducing elements of their identities varies accordingly. In the following chapters, I will expand the discussion to a group level, looking at how larger communities of speakers draw on linguistic resources in defining the boundaries of their ethnic group. However, I will continue to incorporate the experiences of individuals within these groups to illuminate at a more personal level what can otherwise seem like very abstract processes.

DISCUSSION QUESTIONS

1. Think about all the factors that might play a role in the construction of ethnic identity (e.g., religious practices or ways of dressing) and imagine you are going to rank them in order of their importance. Where do you think language would fall? Is it one of the most important factors in constructing ethnicity, or one of the least important? Explain.

2. Can you list some features of your language or language usage that you think might signal your ethnic identity? When you consider this question, do other factors such as gender or age come up as well?

3. There has been relatively little study of mixed-race groups in sociolinguistics. When more studies of this type are conducted, what questions should researchers address? What might speakers whose ethnic identity includes multiple groups contribute to our understanding of language and ethnicity?

4. Do you think the mass media in the USA (or any other country you are familiar with) play a role in people's ideas about the language of other ethnic groups? In what way?

SUGGESTIONS FOR FURTHER READING

Bailey, Benjamin. 2000b. Language and negotiation of ethnic/racial identity among Dominican Americans. *Language in Society* 29:555–82.

An article in the modern sociolinguistic tradition of focusing on the construction of identity by individuals, looking at the case of a Dominican-American teenager in Rhode Island.

Cutler, Cecilia. 1999. Yorkville crossing: white teens, hip hop, and African American English. *Journal of Sociolinguistics* 3:428–42.

One of the first studies of crossing in the USA, also focusing on the study of a single individual, in this case a white middle-class boy in New York who uses AAVE.

Rickford, John and Faye McNair-Knox. 1994. Addressee- and topic-influenced style shift: a quantitative sociolinguistic study. Reprinted in J. Rickford, *African American Vernacular English: Features, Evolution, Educational Implications*. Malden, MA: Blackwell. 112–54.

A key article in the study of style and sociolinguistic variation. It presents a rigorous variationist analysis of a teenage girl in a series of different conversations, varying a number of factors including the ethnicity of the conversational partner.

Urciuoli, Bonnie. 1996. *Exposing Prejudice: Puerto Rican Experiences of Language, Race, and Class*. Boulder, CO: Westview Press.

This book focuses on the experiences, beliefs, and attitudes of Puerto-Rican Americans in New York City. It gives an excellent view of how larger social and political structures shape discourses of race and ethnicity at the community level.

Wieder, D. Lawrence and S. Pratt 1990. On being a recognizable Indian among Indians. In D. Carbaugh, ed., *Cultural Communication and Intercultural Contact*. New Jersey: Lawrence Erlbaum. 45–64.

An article focused on the construction of Native-American ethnicity that has applicability to a general understanding of how ethnicity is constructed in both ingroup and outgroup interactions.

Wolfram, Walt, Kirk Hazen, and Natalie Schilling-Estes. 1999. *Dialect Change and Maintenance on the Outer Banks*. Tuscaloosa: University of Alabama Press, for the American Dialect Society.

A long-term study of North Carolina's Outer Banks area, focusing on how various ethnic groups construct their identities in the midst of social and linguistic changes.

Part II   Linguistic features and ethnicity in specific groups

3 African-American groups

Suburban America or upward America is not my audience. My audience is mostly grassroots people. And I sound mostly like they uncle, so . . . See like, I said, "I sound mostly like they uncle." And I was cool with that. That sound good to me. (Steve Harvey, African-American talk show host from PBS documentary *Do You Speak American?*, 2005)

African American Vernacular English. AAVE. Black English. **Ebonics**. African-American English. African-American Language. Spoken Soul. Whatever name we give to this variety, it stands at the center of so much that is crucial in sociolinguistics, and in the study of language and ethnicity specifically. It is one of the most studied dialects in the world. It is at the heart of a long-standing and often heated controversy in the field, over where it came from originally. It is a political hot potato in the public arena, a topic capable of flinging otherwise peaceful and private linguists into the center of a national spotlight during the debate over the Oakland Resolution. And it is the context for one of the best chances American linguists have to give something back to the society in which they live, both by providing tools for the teaching of standard dialects to AAVE speakers and by raising the level of awareness of the beauty and complexity of AAVE so that its speakers won't continue to be maligned by teachers and employers. Or so that AAVE speakers at least will recognize the ignorance and inaccuracy of such prejudiced behavior when it happens.

It is impossible to cover here all that we know about AAVE, or all that studies of AAVE have contributed to the field as a whole. Besides, a number of others have already produced works with this kind of broad coverage in mind (e.g., Labov 1972a, Smitherman 1986, Mufwene et al. 1998, Rickford 1999, Smitherman 2000b, Rickford and Rickford 2000, Green 2002, Morgan 2002). It is also beyond the scope of this book to cover in detail the controversy over AAVE's origins, particularly whether or not it developed from a creole. Several of the works mentioned above address this question, as do some quite recent studies

(Poplack and Tagliamonte 2001, Wolfram and Thomas 2002). What I will do here is highlight the aspects of research on AAVE that most directly illuminate the construction of ethnic identity.

In particular, this chapter will look at how the forms and structures of AAVE are used by a wide range of African-American speakers of different backgrounds to construct ethnicity, in a country where race and ethnicity are such salient factors. I will begin by giving a brief overview of the structure of AAVE. Like most dialects, this one encompasses a great deal of variation, and in fact this variation itself is crucial to understanding language and ethnicity among African-Americans, so the sketch provided here is not intended to be definitive or immutable. I will focus on grammar and phonology, because, although lexicon can be significant too, there is a good deal more variation, and less research, in this area.[1] Then, I will look at the role of these linguistic variables in the construction of African-American identity, and the attitudes associated with AAVE, by ingroup and outgroup members. Among other things, I hope to explore some relatively neglected issues in the field, including the importance of regional dialect differences within AAVE, the use of prosodic features as ethnic markers, and the way middle-class African-Americans index their ethnicity through language.

3.1   WHAT IS AAVE?

This question has both a short answer and a long answer. For the short answer, we might simply say that AAVE is *a variety spoken by many African-Americans in the USA which shares a set of grammatical and other linguistic features that distinguish it from various other American dialects.* This definition, though, does not address some issues that have come up in studying AAVE. First of all, there is the question of labeling. This variety has had a number of labels historically. Here, I follow Rickford (1999:xxi) in using AAVE to refer to a system that contains distinct (non-standard) grammatical elements, reserving the broader "African-American English" for all varieties used by African-Americans, even if they are completely standard ones. But different researchers in sociolinguistics and other fields have made different decisions about terminology.[2] Both of these terms, additionally, encompass the word "English," suggesting that, whatever its origins, current-day AAVE is a variety of English.

From this discussion of labels, a related point emerges, which is that the totality of varieties used by African-Americans encompasses a tremendous amount of diversity. In early research, primary attention was given to the most vernacular varieties, especially the speech of working-class communities and teenagers (especially male teenagers), so that the current label, whatever it might be, would be applied to these varieties and no others. More recently, though, scholars have moved to the position that the full spectrum of varieties used by African-Americans is of sociolinguistic interest. Which ones, then, will we call AAVE? If a middle-class speaker uses a dialect that contains no non-standard grammatical features, but does have elements of phonology that identify the speaker as African-American, is that AAVE? What if there are no phonological differences, and the distinguishing features used are interactional patterns such as "**signifying**"? If one of these varieties is being used by a middle-class European-American teenager, does that count as AAVE? There is no single scientific answer to any of these questions; the answers are as much social and political as they are linguistic. Issues related to the standard end of the spectrum, though, will be discussed more in the section on the middle class, below.

3.2 AAVE GRAMMAR

When undergraduate linguistics students first encounter the grammatical and morphological complexities of AAVE, the experience quickly sweeps away any ideas they may have picked up about AAVE being just slang and sloppy grammar. I get great personal satisfaction out of the panicked questions during the class session before the midterm in my class on "language and ethnicity," where students who are not native AAVE speakers try to nail down nuances of form and meaning that still elude them. Maybe it's cruel to enjoy their panic, but it is also a great illustration of how difficult the rules of AAVE can be for someone who is not familiar with them. Even the undergraduates who do speak AAVE, like native speakers of all languages, may have difficulty articulating their tacit knowledge. My students may not remember all the rules of AAVE after the test, but they probably won't forget the experience of having to struggle to learn them.

Different studies of AAVE have reported different lists of core features. I have included in my list most of the features given by Rickford and Rickford (2000:109ff.), which reflect the areas of greatest overlap among studies. It should be noted that some of these features are shared by other dialects as well, especially Southern USA varieties of English, and are not necessarily tied to African-American ethnicity;

rather it is the combination of these features in AAVE that defines the grammar. Also, a majority of these features are variable, so that the same speaker may use the AAVE variant on one occasion, and a more general or standard variant on another occasion. Morphological and syntactic features of AAVE include:

> **Existential** it: AAVE speakers often use *it* as the empty subject where speakers of other dialects would use *there*, as in *It's some coffee in the kitchen*. Often it's pronounced as *i's*.
>
> *Absence of plural* –s *marking*: For example, *four girl*. Not a very common feature overall. Based on a survey of existing studies, Rickford and Rickford report that –s absence occurs from 1 to 10 percent of the time.
>
> *Absence of possessive* –s *marking*: For example, *at my mama house*. Rickford and Rickford note that this feature is more frequent than plural –s absence, and report it occurring at a rate of over 50 percent in a number of studies.
>
> *Absence of third person singular* –s *marking*: For example, *It seem like . . .* or *She have three kids*. Rickford and Rickford report that this feature is very frequent, occurring at percentages that range from around 50 percent to up to 96 percent or 97 percent.
>
> **Zero copula** (either *is* or *are*): For example, *She φ in the same grade*. The first person singular copula (*I am*) cannot be deleted. Rickford and Rickford note that deletion is also very unusual in the forms *it's*, *that's*, and *what's*, which tend to have a phonological process that deletes the [t] instead.
>
> *Invariant (or habitual)* be: As in *Your phone bill be high*, meaning "Your phone bill is usually or often high." Most frequent with –*ing* forms as in *He be getting on my nerves*.
>
> *Unstressed* been: Similar to *have been* or *has been* in other dialects, as in *I been playing cards since I was four*.
>
> *Stressed (remote-past or emphatic)* BEEN: Indicates an action that has been true for a long time or is emphatically true. For example, *She BEEN tell me that*, meaning "She told me that a long time ago."
>
> **Completive** done: an **aspect** marker signaling completion, as in *I done already finished that*. Rickford and Rickford note that it may differ slightly from perfective forms in other dialects, in that speakers report that *done* has a higher degree of intensity.
>
> *Future perfect* be done: For example: *I be done did your hair before you know it*, meaning "I will have finished doing your hair before you know it."

Use of ain't *for negation*: For example, *I ain't lyin'*. This form is of course extremely common in dialects other than AAVE, as a variant for forms of *isn't* or *hasn't*. The usage that is more unique to AAVE is its alternation with *didn't*, as in *He ain't go no further than third or fourth grade*.

Negative concord: For example, *I don't want nothing nobody can't enjoy*. Again, this feature (which may also be referred to as "multiple negation") is common to other dialects as well. **Negative inversion**, though, seems to be more specifically characteristic of AAVE, as in *Can't nobody beat them*.[3]

Preterite **had**: Use of *had* + past tense verb to refer to a simple past event, as in *I had slipped and fell* to mean "I slipped and fell." (Rickford and Rickford suggest that preterite *had* may be age-graded, so that speakers stop using it as they get older.)

Steady: Used to emphasize the intense or persistent nature of an action, as in *Them students be steady trying to make a buck*.

Come: Used to express indignation, as in *Don't come acting like you don't know what happened*.

Finna: Used to mark an action that is about to take place, as in *I'm finna get up out of here*, meaning "I'm about to leave." Related to *fixing to*, used throughout the South.

Other syntactic features can be found in studies of AAVE, depending slightly on the focus and sample involved in a particular study, but these are the items that recur in the literature as being central to AAVE grammar.[4]

3.3 AAVE PHONOLOGY

Bailey and Thomas (1998:85) call phonology "the neglected stepchild" of research on AAVE, and there is some good evidence for their view. Given the complexity of the syntactic and aspectual patterns discussed in the previous section, it is not surprising that linguists have flocked to the task of identifying the situations in which remote-past *been*, for example, is or is not appropriate. On the other hand, the differences between the phonology of AAVE and other varieties are not notably greater than the phonological differences among regional varieties, for example. Perhaps for this reason, it has drawn less study than the more saliently different aspectual system. However, in terms of language and the construction of ethnicity, we will see that phonology has a number of crucial roles to play. The features listed here are selected from Bailey and Thomas (1998), and, following their example, I have grouped them by the degree to which they are shared with other dialects.

Features characteristic of AAVE and Southern European-American dialects:

- **metathesis**: *ask* pronounced as *aks*[5]
- **vocalization** or loss of postvocalic /r/: *four* pronounced [fou] or [foə] (like *fo'*); can also occur with **intervocalic** /r/ in words like *hurry*
- **glide reduction** of /ai/: *tide* pronounced [ta:d] (like *tahd*)
- **glide reduction** of /ɔi/: *oil* pronounced [ɔɑɫ] (similar to *all*)
- **merger** of [ɪ] and [ɛ] before **nasals** (the "pin/pen merger"): so that words like *pin* and *pen* sound the same
- merger of **tense** and **lax vowels** before /l/: so, for example, *bale* and *bell* or *feel* and *fill* sound the same
- fricative stopping before nasals: so that *isn't* sounds like *idn't*

Features that seem to be unique to AAVE (or at least most frequent in AAVE):

- reduction of final nasal to **vowel nasalization**: *man* pronounced [mæ̃]
- final stop devoicing: so that *bad* sounds like *bat*; there may also be a **glottal stop** coarticulated with the final segment
- substitution of /k/ for /t/ in *str* clusters: so *street* sounds like *skreet*

Features shared by other non-standard dialects:

- loss of single final consonants:[6] *five* pronounced [fa:], like *fi'*
- loss of /r/ after consonants: *throw* pronounced [θou] (like *th'ow*), *professor* pronounced [pəfɛsɚ] (like *p'ofessor*)
- substitution of **labiodentals** for **interdental** fricatives: *bath* pronounced [bæf] (like *baf*), *bother* pronounced [bavə] (like *bava*)
- stopping of interdental fricatives: *those* pronounced [douz] (like *doze*); *with* pronounced [wɪt] (like *wit*)

Features shared by many other English dialects, possibly more frequent in AAVE:

- final consonant cluster reduction: *cold* becomes [koul] (like *cole*). (Wolfram [2000] notes that reduction before a following vowel in particular may be more characteristic of AAVE than of other dialects)
- vocalization of postvocalic /l/: *bell* pronounced [bɛʊ] (with the [l] absent)

There are also some processes related to syllable structure that characterize AAVE. For example, unstressed syllables may be deleted so that *about* becomes *'bout* and *government* becomes *gov'ment*. Also the syllable stress may be moved to the front, so that a word like *police* is pronounced with the stress on the first syllable (also found in other Southern dialects).

Interestingly, one of the most salient features of AAVE phonology is also one of the least studied: its prosody. Some studies have suggested that the ethnicity of AAVE speakers can be determined from intonation alone (see Green 2002). Rahman (2002) found that AAVE prosody contributed to the perception of speech samples as less standard, at least when evaluated by middle-class African-Americans. Probably the most detailed analysis of AAVE prosody so far is in Green (2002:124–32). Green begins by noting that a wider pitch range than in other dialects has often been reported for AAVE by researchers. She also provides data that show the use (variably) of a final level tone in yes-no questions in AAVE (as compared with the final rise that is most common in many other dialects). These intonational patterns, combined with the syllable structure patterns mentioned earlier, presumably contribute strongly to the sense that AAVE has a rhythm of its own.[7] There also seems to be an association of AAVE with low voice **pitch**, particularly in men, although it is not clear to what extent this view corresponds to actual usage by AAVE speakers, as opposed to a general stereotype.

One area that has not been discussed so far is pragmatics. Speakers of AAVE, like speakers of all dialects, have particular discourse strategies, ways of doing things with words. Rather than presenting these here, they will be discussed separately in Chapter 8 (and to some extent in Chapter 9 as well).

3.4 VARIATION IN THE USE OF NON-STANDARD FEATURES IN AAVE

As mentioned above, not every AAVE speaker will use all of the features from the lists above. Also, a majority of the features (particularly the grammatical ones) are variable, meaning that the same speaker may use the AAVE variant (*She my friend*) on some occasions and the more general variant (*She's my friend*) on others. A large body of sociolinguistic research has demonstrated that this variation is far from random. So many independent variables, linguistic and social, can affect the frequency with which one variant or the other is produced that articles exploring this variation can read like a chapter from an introductory statistics text. In this, as in other areas, AAVE provides a good case study for an important issue that was raised earlier: *intraethnic* **variation** is in some ways just as crucial as *interethnic* **variation** in understanding the construction of ethnic identity. I cannot cover the full body of work on variation in AAVE here, but I have selected a few key studies that give different relevant perspectives (see Fought [2002] for a more complete discussion).

One of the most salient factors affecting the use of AAVE features is socioeconomic status, a variable that correlates with non-standard grammatical and linguistic elements in most communities. One of the earliest studies of social class variation in AAVE is Wolfram's (1969) Detroit study. Wolfram found strong correlations of social class with all the phonological and grammatical variables that he analyzed. The grammatical variables included copula deletion, habitual *be*, *-s* absence (for plural, possessive, and third singular forms), and negative concord. Many of these features were categorically avoided by a majority of the middle-class speakers. On the other hand, a mostly quantitative difference was found for the phonological variables (including consonant cluster reduction, realization of /θ/ as /f/ or /t/, **glottalization** or deletion of final stops, and postvocalic /r/ absence). Middle-class speakers used these features less than working-class speakers, but even upper-middle-class speakers showed at least some use of each of the phonological variables. Grammatical features are generally more salient, which may account for their sharper differentiation by class. These data provide an excellent illustration of the claim made in Chapter 2 that different linguistic components may have different significance for the construction of identity through language.

Gender is also a crucial factor in determining the use of various AAVE features. Many of the variables in Wolfram's study showed effects of gender as well as social class. More recently, the work of Edwards (e.g., 1990, 1996, 1997), also in Detroit, provides a detailed analysis of gender as it affects the use of various phonological features of AAVE. Interestingly, one of the earlier studies, Edwards (1990), found a strong correlation between use of AAVE phonology and the interaction of gender and social class. However, a later study, Edwards (1997), found no gender differences in the use of four linguistic variables within a single working-class African-American neighborhood. Edwards attributes this finding to the very similar social roles filled by men and women in this community. Again, this confirms an idea that has come up before: gender, like ethnicity, is not constructed in the same way everywhere. A majority of the studies that have been done on AAVE features (and on the use of non-standard variants generally) find that women use them less. But we cannot expect this pattern to hold universally, and must look at the specifics of both ethnicity and gender in a particular community to understand their role in identity construction, especially as it involves language.

In addition, the focus in the discussion so far has been on phonological and grammatical variables, and in fact a large body of the sociolinguistic research on AAVE has concentrated on these two areas. Research suggests, though, that the interaction of social factors such as gender with variation in other areas such as **lexicon** or rhetorical style might be different. For example, there is a growing body of research on African-American women, specifically, and the unique discourse features and styles that mark their particular construction of identity in terms of both ethnicity and gender. Troutman (2001) presents an analysis of a number of phenomena that characterize African-American women's language, from collaborative discourse modes to the use of "culturally toned" **diminutives** such as "girl." Morgan (2002:84ff.) looks at uses of indirection by women, as well as some characteristics of their narrative style. Although discourse features of AAVE will be discussed in Chapter 8, it is worth mentioning these studies here as a reminder that gender can be a powerful factor in intraethnic variation.[8] Of course, as the individual speakers in Chapter 2 illustrate, specific African-American women, for example, can construct their identities in very different ways.

3.5 ATTITUDES TOWARDS AAVE

Attitudes towards AAVE can be described as both very simple and very complex. They are simple in the sense that they follow the all-too-familiar pattern in which a non-standard variety is the target of negative prejudices: it's "bad" or "lazy" or a "broken" version of the standard variety; it holds you back; it sounds terrible, etc. (what Wolfram and Schilling-Estes call the **"linguistic inferiority principle"** [1998:6]). In a pattern widely characteristic of speakers of undervalued language varieties in contact with more highly valued ones (e.g., French and English in Canada until quite recently), many of these negative views will be assimilated by speakers of the vernacular themselves (although see Hoover [1978] for a discussion of how complex **language attitudes** can be). The instantiation of all this with respect to AAVE particularly can be seen clearly in the controversy over the Oakland Resolution, which will be discussed in Chapter 9. At the edges of this simple model, though, a complexity in attitudes towards AAVE emerges. To begin with, and this is also true in other settings with a non-standard variety, although AAVE may draw criticism from speakers within the community, among them it will also evoke more positive associations: solidarity, community, "keeping it real." There are also other, more subtle differences between the attitudes of ingroup and outgroup members. Nuances of context may affect the perspectives of both groups. This section will cover some of the basics of what we know about attitudes toward AAVE; further information on negative attitudes from outside groups, including the results of experiments on dialect perception, will be presented in Chapter 9.

We have already seen how different components of the linguistic system may play different symbolic roles in the indexing of ethnicity through language. Lippi-Green (1997) notes the importance of this phenomenon in differentiating attitudes toward AAVE exhibited by African-Americans versus other groups. She proposes that "whites seem to be most comfortable voicing overt criticism about phonological matters and sometimes about grammar, but black concerns focus almost exclusively on grammatical issues" (1997:179). One piece of evidence she considers is the extremely prejudicial view that outgroup individuals often have of the pronunciation of *ask* as "aks" [æks]. Lippi-Green gives a heartbreaking example from a former mayor of New York City who was attending an event at which African-American high-school students read formal essays. He comments that the content of one student's essay was "excellent" but that because she pronounced *ask* as "aks" at one point, "regrettably, the substance of her essay was [thus made] less important" (1997:180). As Williams notes, "[e]ven solidly middle class blacks with . . . perfect command of standard grammatical structure can face discrimination if their accents are deemed in any way identifiably 'black'" (1997:8).

In contrast, while African-Americans may exhibit negative attitudes about AAVE as well, these do not generally involve phonetic features. The focus is mostly on grammar, and in particular on the need to use standard grammar in order to "get ahead." Lippi-Green gives the example of USA talk show host Oprah Winfrey, who hosted a show devoted to the topic of "Black English" in 1987; Winfrey says at one point in the show, "To me standard English is having your verbs agree with your subject" (1997:193). She seems to take the view that a variety which featured standard syntax but AAVE phonological features would not count as AAVE. Rahman's (2002) study of African-American students and staff at a major university similarly found that they generally defined "Standard English" in terms of grammar rather than phonology. With respect to the lexical component, some African-Americans clearly share the widespread misperception of AAVE as "slang." An African-American woman in one of my classes, for example, on the first day that I discussed AAVE with the class, raised her hand and said, "But that's not a language, that's just me talking slang with my friends!" Rickford notes that a number of public comments about the Oakland Resolution came from older African-Americans who misidentified AAVE with the slang vocabulary of hip-hop (2004:206).

Of course, attitudes are not uniform in either European-American or African-American communities. As noted earlier, class differences play a key role in the use of AAVE features. Rickford and Rickford note that most of the commentary heard on the subject of AAVE from African-Americans comes from the middle class; they argue that a class component is inextricably involved in negative attitudes about AAVE within the African-American community (2000:8). Age can also be a factor. Particularly with respect to the lexical component, older African-Americans, as noted above, may draw a distinction between their own AAVE usage and that of younger speakers in the community, criticizing the latter in much the same way that older generations have always criticized the supposedly "degenerating" speech of youth. Rickford notes that "the distance between the younger hip-hop generation and older African-American generations – marked by the politics of dress, music, and slang – has in some ways . . . grown more stark in the 1990's," and it is the older group's views that are most often aired in public debates (2004:206).

As with other communities that include a non-standard variety, we can also find many positive associations with AAVE among African-Americans. Here are just a few celebratory remarks on AAVE, from African-American writers and linguists:

> [It] possesses a pronounced lyrical quality which is frequently incompatible to any music other than that ceaselessly and relentlessly driving rhythm that flows from poignantly spent lives. (Claude Brown, cited in Rickford 2004:198–9)

> [T]he beauty and power of the idiom lies in its succinctness . . . Black English . . . is a language mixture, adapted to the conditions of slavery and discrimination, a combination of language and style interwoven with and inextricable from Afro-American culture. (Smitherman 1977:3)

> [It is] a language that permits the nation its only glimpse of reality. (Baldwin 1997:6)

> AAE [African-American English] is much more than the dialect and language of a culture; it is the evidence of what happened to the people who speak it proudly. (Morgan 2002:151)

> [It is used] to survive in the streets, to relax at home and recreate in playgrounds, to render our deepest emotions and embody our vital core. (Rickford 2004:206)

These are individuals whose education and status in our society, along with their personal articulateness, has helped get their views into print. The positive feelings expressed, however, are certainly shared by a large number of individuals in African-American communities whose voices we have not heard, and will not ever hear.

A final issue that seems important to discuss is the attitudes surrounding the possibility of being **bidialectal**; in other words, speaking both AAVE and some other, more standard variety. To me, it seems obvious that one need not give up one language or dialect in order to acquire another. As Rickford so eloquently puts it, "[i]t is certainly not *necessary* to abandon Spoken Soul to master Standard English, any more than it is necessary to abandon English to learn French or to abandon jazz to appreciate classical music" (2004:207; italics in original). Still, a surprising number of writers, scholars, and leaders seem to believe exactly this. Rachel Jones ([1982] 1998), for example, seems to be taking this point of view throughout. She says that it "hurts" her to hear children speaking AAVE because she knows they will be at a disadvantage in the educational system, but how can she know a priori whether or not they use another variety in school? Similarly, comedian Bill Cosby, in a number of very public and negative comments he has made recently, talks about AAVE as if it holds individuals back from the fruits of success *all by itself*, even before Standard English enters the picture. On the other hand, Morgan points out that "mono-dialectal" speakers (of either variety) in African-American communities may experience linguistic insecurity because "they cannot shift their variety according to the appropriate social context or topic" (2002:68). All of this discussion is not intended to suggest either that becoming bidialectal is simple and straightforward, or that there is no possibility of negative sanctions for this choice, within and outside the community. The latter point, in particular, will be crucial to the discussion of middle-class African-American culture, below.

3.6   REGIONAL VARIATION IN AAVE: IS AAVE CONVERGING TOWARD A SUPRAREGIONAL NORM?

Some scholars in the field of sociolinguists acknowledge clear regional differences in AAVE. Green, for instance, on the very first page of her comprehensive study of AAVE, notes:

[T]here are regional differences that will distinguish varieties of AAE [African American English] spoken in the United States. For example, although speakers of AAE in Louisiana and Texas use very similar syntactic patterns their vowel sounds may differ. Speakers of AAE in areas in Pennsylvania also share similar syntactic patterns with speakers in Louisiana and Texas; however speakers in areas in Pennsylvania are not likely to share some of the patterns that the Louisiana and Texas speakers share with other speakers of southern regions. Also, speakers from the three different states have different vowel sounds. (2002:1)

The issue of regional variation in AAVE, however, generally has not been directly addressed by sociolinguistic research. Fought (2002) lists a number of questions that arise in connection with AAVE in different geographic locations, including: 1) Is AAVE strikingly more homogeneous across the USA than European-American vernacular varieties? and 2) Is the degree of cross-regional similarity different for different components of the grammar (e.g., syntax vs. phonology)? Because there have been so few cross-regional studies of AAVE, we do not yet have the data available to address these types of questions thoroughly.

Nonetheless, sociolinguists have often attempted to extrapolate a sense of how much AAVE varies geographically by piecing together the results of research on AAVE done in different locations. A passage from Wolfram and Schilling-Estes (1998) sums up the prevailing viewpoint on the issue of regional variation in AAVE within the field of sociolinguistics:

Certainly, some of the Northern metropolitan versions of AAVE are distinguishable from some of the Southern rural versions, and South Atlantic coastal varieties are different from those found in the Gulf region. While admitting some of these regional variations, we hasten to point out that one of the most noteworthy aspects of AAVE is the common core of features shared across different regions. Features such as habitual *be*, copula absence, inflectional *-s* absence, among a number of other grammatical and phonological structures, are found in locations as distant as Los Angeles, California; New Haven, Connecticut; Meadville, Mississippi; Austin, Texas; and Wilmington, North Carolina, as well as in both urban and rural settings. Thus we recognize regional variation in AAVE while concluding, at the same time, that the regional differences do not come close to the magnitude of regional differences that exist across Anglo varieties. (1998:174–5)

One concern with this approach is whether or not the techniques employed by different researchers are truly comparable. Bailey and

Tillery (2004), for example, make a strong case for the many ways in which the field methods used can affect sociolinguistic data, sometimes significantly.

A further question which has been the subject of some recent research is whether the dialects of AAVE across the country are converging toward a **supraregional norm**. In general, research on this issue has been a secondary corollary to research on the issue of **convergence** or **divergence** with respect to European-American dialects. The convergence/divergence issue will be presented in the discussion of dialect contact in Chapter 7. However, the question of a supraregional norm for AAVE is worth discussing here, particularly because of its implications about the construction of ethnic identity among African-Americans. It is important to remember that whether African-American speakers in all or some locations are diverging from European-Americans in their use of local features is a separate question from whether or not African-Americans in various locations are sounding more like each other, but this distinction is sometimes misplaced in studies attempting to trace patterns of convergence and divergence in AAVE.

The most comprehensive study of the issue of a supraregional AAVE norm is Wolfram and Thomas (2002), which follows the pattern mentioned above of considering this question in the context of convergence or divergence from European-American varieties. The researchers focus on one community of speakers in Hyde County, North Carolina, and trace trends between generations, looking at a variety of **morphosyntactic** and phonological features (an important methodological factor, since studies of isolated variables can be misleading). Wolfram and Thomas conclude that there is clearly "[an] alliance of the speech of younger Hyde County African-American speakers with contemporary AAVE norms . . . exhibited both in the change away from local dialect norms as well as the persistence and adoption of structures associated with contemporary AAVE" (2002:205–7).

Wolfram and Thomas present a table that clearly lists the morphosyntactic and phonetic features they looked at in assessing the shift toward a supraregional AAVE norm, as well as divergence from local European-American varieties (2002:206). The table lists a total of 11 phonological and 7 morphosyntactic features. If we focus on just those features that are a) changing, for young African-Americans, in the direction of urban AAVE norms, and b) not *also* changing in the same way among young European-American speakers, we find only 2 out of the 11 phonological features that fit the pattern: the loss of backing of the /ay/ **nucleus** and an increase in postvocalic *r*-lessness.

Similarly, 2 out of the 7 grammatical features fit the pattern: loss of *weren't regularization*, and use of habitual *be*. There are many other phonological and grammatical features consistent with urban AAVE in this community, but because they are also present among older speakers they don't indicate a trajectory of change. A few of the features actually show an alliance of the Hyde County African-American speakers with local European-Americans *against* the urban AAVE norm. For example, a **fronted** /o/ nucleus (in, e.g., coat) is shared by young Hyde County residents of both ethnicities, as is a variable use of raised, unglided /ɔ/ (as in *caught*).

In sum, the overall pattern does not provide strong evidence of changes towards a supraregional AAVE norm for young Hyde County African-Americans, although this pattern may be found in individual features. The use of habitual *be*, which is new to this community, might be a good candidate for a clear marker of ethnic identity, and possibly of affiliation with a larger transregional African-American identity.[9] But a salient feature of this type can serve as an ethnic marker without necessarily indicating a convergence of the dialect as a whole. Childs and Mallinson (2004), for example, show how lexical items can serve as ethnic markers, even when there is no evidence of convergence on general AAVE norms in other areas.

If we look at research on dialects in general terms, we find that the frequency of grammatical differences in the English of different regions (and even different countries) is small by comparison with the vast and varied body of phonological differences (Wald 1984:17). In the case of European-American vernaculars, for every instance of a regional structure like *He might could do it* or *The car needs washed*, there are numerous subtle vowel differences that distinguish, e.g., speakers from Atlanta, Georgia and Pittsburgh, Pennsylvania. Therefore, all other things being equal, we would expect AAVE varieties across the country to have relatively few morphosyntactic differences, especially in comparison with the number of phonological ones. Although Wolfram and Schilling-Estes (1998), in the citation above, assert that the regional differences in AAVE are much less significant than those of European-American varieties, at this point there is simply not enough empirical evidence to assess this claim, one way or the other. Because patterns of migration for AAVE speakers are relatively more recent than for European-Americans, we might expect a smaller degree of regional difference in AAVE due to settlement history (much as European-American dialects in the West show fewer distinctions than on the East Coast). This distribution would not require an explanation specific to African-American identity, though.

Considering Bailey and Thomas' (1998) comment above about phonology in AAVE as "the neglected stepchild," a number of regional differences in AAVE pronunciation could well be lurking out there, waiting to be catalogued. Green (2002), for example, mentions some specific AAVE phonological features throughout her study that she believes may vary by region: the substitution of *skr* for *str*, the use of [oi] for [oʊ] (in words like *coach*), and the lowering of the vowel in [ɛr] sequences (as in *prepare*). John Rickford (personal communication) confirms that *skr* for *str* is geographical, mainly reported for Savannah and portions of the South. Interestingly, Green also mentions a morphosyntactic variable, a particular use of *be done*, as possibly occurring more in some geographic regions than in others (2002:64). If it turns out to be the case that AAVE varieties are quite consistent in morphosyntactic features across regions, and share some phonological traits but vary in a number of others, then the pattern for AAVE will be much like the pattern for other English dialects. If this turns out not to be the case, in other words if AAVE varieties show little phonological variation by region, then this result would have interesting implications for the construction of ethnic identity. However, it seems premature to explore these implications until more data about what is actually happening are available.

3.7 ANOTHER POSSIBILITY: A BLEND OF SUPRAREGIONAL AND REGIONAL NORMS

The inescapable conclusion in all of this discussion is that we need more research focused on regional differences in AAVE. Only when research is conducted that collects data from different regions as part of a single study will we be able to answer confidently some of the questions raised here. A technique that seems very promising is the use of listener perceptions. Wolfram and Thomas, for example, elicited judgments of older and younger Hyde County speakers from listeners who lived outside the county (2002:190–1). They found that the ethnicity of an elderly African-American from Hyde County was correctly identified only about 10 percent of the time, while a younger African-American from the same area was correctly identified about 90 percent of the time, suggesting that the older AAVE speakers sound more like their European-American peers than the younger speakers do. The same type of experiment could be extremely fruitful in determining the extent to which African-Americans from a particular region can distinguish the origins of African-Americans from other places. Interestingly, while a young African-American from the mainland was identified correctly 100 percent of the time, for the young Hyde County speaker this figure dropped to 89.7 percent. One interpretation of this result is that there continue to be some perceptible features distinguishing different regional varieties of AAVE, even within North Carolina.

Until more data are available, we should be cautious in extending claims about the similarities in AAVE dialects too far. However, there is an explanation consistent with the patterns in the data we do have, besides the explanation of shifting toward a supraregional AAVE norm. It may be that in most African-American communities speakers balance supraregional and **regional norms** in their construction of identity. Specific communities might undertake this process in different ways, and certainly we would expect different features to be used. The general pattern, though, would fit well with what we know about the construction of identity in general, and the ways in which it occurs at multiple overlapping and intersecting levels, a theme that recurs throughout this book.[10]

The data from Wolfram and Thomas (2002) are perfectly consistent with this analysis, possibly more so than with a shift towards general AAVE features. If we see the young Hyde County speakers as performing both local and ethnic (non-local) identities, then the mix of patterns across individual features makes sense. They reflect their identification with a larger African-American identity by using habitual *be*. They reinforce their local Hyde County identity by using a fronted /o/ nucleus in words like *coat*. This theoretical approach coincides nicely with the results of some other studies as well. Childs and Mallinson (2004), for example, conducted fieldwork in a community of African-Americans in Appalachia. They found that, while young African-Americans showed certain distinct AAVE features, they also had features in their phonology (such as pre-voiceless /ai/ glide weakening) that clearly aligned them with white Appalachians. In fact, some of these features showed an increase among younger speakers. At the same time, these young African-Americans used lexical items associated with hip-hop as part of their construction of ethnic identity. As Childs and Mallinson note, the dialect of these speakers represents a confluence of regional and ethnic norms.

There are other studies (e.g., Fridland 2003, Edwards 1997) that show the use of features of local European-American varieties by African-Americans. I am not suggesting that these studies indicate that AAVE varieties are converging with those of European-American speakers generally; in fact, Wolfram and Thomas (2002) among others show convincingly with their perception experiment that older AAVE speakers in Hyde County sound more like their European-American peers than younger AAVE speakers do. However, the data available so far do suggest that different patterns of variation and change can be found in different communities. We need to continue gathering data on how ethnic identity is constructed in the social context of specific communities; in particular, we should be attuned to the multiple overlapping identities in a community, and to the possible blending of regional and supraregional norms.

3.8 STANDARD AAE AND THE LANGUAGE OF MIDDLE-CLASS AFRICAN-AMERICANS

The early studies of AAVE tended to focus primarily on the language of working-class African-Americans. In particular, the language of working-class teenage boys was privileged as being of primary interest, a perspective which has been criticized in more recent work (e.g., Morgan 1994). A number of recent studies refer to a "**Standard African American English**" (e.g., Spears 1998, Mufwene 2001, Rahman 2002), but overall this variety has been neglected in pursuit of what Wolfram (2001) calls the "vernacular obsession." While studies focusing on middle-class African-Americans are less copious than those focusing on working-class communities, this line of research also has the potential to address intriguing issues in the study of language and ethnicity. It is possible for working-class African-Americans to grow up in segregated areas where a strong majority of their interactions, and consequently the influences on their culture and speech, involve other African-Americans (cf. Baugh 1983:5). On the other hand, middle-class African-Americans are more likely to have a variety of contacts with people of different ethnic backgrounds. They are also more likely to encounter pressure to assimilate to mainstream norms, including language norms, as part of their participation in various professional fields. Among other effects of this pressure is the fact that most of them will need to command some version of "standard" English as a professional or personal resource.

This is not to say that working-class speakers are free from this type of pressure – far from it. Particularly in the school system, these pressures may be acute, as will be discussed in Chapter 9. However, it is possible in theory for some working-class speakers to fulfill all the regular functions of their lives in AAVE, shifting in style between, e.g., informal and formal occasions, but always within a variety that includes at least some of the features associated with AAVE grammar. To many middle-class speakers, this option will not be open.

For some middle-class speakers, use of a completely standard and unmarked variety of English may have begun early in life, and may be supported by others in the immediate network so that there is little internal conflict involved in using the standard. In fact, for them, it may be the acquisition of AAVE that comes later, with varying degrees of success (Baugh 1999:123ff.). Other middle-class speakers, though, may experience a tension from the beginning between the language norms associated with mainstream middle-class culture in the USA (based strongly in European-American culture) and language norms traditionally associated with African-American communities, the "ethnic pride versus assimilation" dichotomy discussed in Chapter 2. How, then, does an individual in this latter group display ethnic loyalty, while simultaneously gaining access to those resources for which assimilation to mainstream language norms is a prerequisite? The resolution of this type of dilemma provides crucial insights into the construction of ethnic identity.

To begin with, it may be helpful to clarify one potential problem for middle-class African-Americans: to sound "white" can be very negatively valued. Rickford, for example, gives the example of a black teenager in California who comments, "Over at my school . . . first time they catch you talkin' white, they'll never let it go" (1999:275). Fordham and Ogbu (1986) discuss in detail how young speakers particularly feel a need to distance themselves from the standard variety because it is associated with whiteness (see Chapter 6 for more on this issue). The challenge, then, is to find ways of speaking that achieve all the necessary aims in terms of standardness and so forth, while avoiding potential accusations of ethnic disloyalty, selling out, or being "an Oreo."[11] There are, of course, speakers who do not address the issue at all, who simply speak exclusively either AAVE or a variety that is indistinguishable from the varieties of other ethnic groups, but never attempt to incorporate the two in any way. Nonetheless, it is the other African-Americans – including, I assume, a fairly large proportion of the middle class – who are the focus of this discussion.

The research that has been done so far suggests, not surprisingly, that middle-class African-American speakers resolve this dilemma in a number of ways. Weldon (2004) is one of the most comprehensive studies to date of the language of middle-class African-Americans. She analyzed twelve speakers participating in a political symposium that gathered African-American intellectuals from a variety of regions and professional fields; the symposium was broadcast nationally to a presumably diverse audience. While it has sometimes been taken for granted in the literature that middle-class speakers in a somewhat formal public setting such as this would not use features of AAVE, Weldon shows that this assumption is incorrect. Several of the speakers in her study used AAVE grammatical, phonological, lexical, and rhetorical features.

The most diverse range of AAVE features was displayed by Tavis Smiley, a popular US television and radio personality and the organizer of the symposium. Weldon reports that his verbal strategy fell clearly into a pattern of switching between dialects, so that at some points he was also using a variety that could clearly be identified as standard. Though Weldon does not comment on this fact, in the "standard" sections Smiley nonetheless uses some AAVE phonological or intonational elements. One possibility for middle-class speakers, then, is to switch between a more standard variety (which will be discussed more below), and a variety that encompasses many of the key AAVE features. Furthermore, in contrast with what has sometimes been implied in the literature, these two varieties need not be saved for different occasions, with the AAVE variety relegated to the closet in any event that might be classified as either "formal" or "interethnic." Even in a formal setting, some middle-class speakers elect to use a variety that encompasses non-standard features, and concomitantly makes a strong statement about ethnic affiliation.

Other speakers in Weldon's study used fewer AAVE features, ranging along a continuum of sorts. One very common pattern was for speakers to use a wide range of phonological features, including some that might be stigmatized (e.g., stopping of interdental fricatives), but very few grammatical elements. This is highly reminiscent of the pattern found for middle-class speakers in Wolfram's (1969) study, discussed above. It also coincides with Lippi-Green's (1997) observation above that, while non-African-Americans may criticize phonological features of AAVE, the debate among African-Americans is focused almost solely on grammatical issues. Another option for middle-class speakers, then, is to eliminate most marked grammatical elements from their "standard" variety, but continue to use the full range of phonological elements that mark the variety as specifically African-American, so that they still "sound black," in even their most standard style. The same speakers might or might not also use a variety incorporating AAVE grammatical features on other occasions.

A related but slightly different strategy is discussed by Smitherman (2000b:Chapter 14), who presents an analysis of the Clarence Thomas–Anita Hill hearings that took place in the USA in 1991. She found that Thomas, a judge, and therefore unquestionably middle class, did not use grammatical or phonological features of AAVE (Smitherman 2000b:197). He did, however, use a combination of African-American rhetorical strategies (including "signifying," which will be discussed further in Chapter 8), to mark his ethnicity. Smitherman terms this "African-American Verbal Tradition" (AVT); it constitutes yet another way of "sounding black," one that in essence is not about the sound itself, but about language use and discourse patterns.

A final way of resolving the class–ethnicity dilemma is to use a variety of Standard English that is indistinguishable from that of European-American speakers, and allow the style-shifting function itself to count as the sign of ethnic affiliation. The speaker, then, would be known as a person who cannot be identified as African-American when speaking Standard English, but who can also use AAVE when the occasion requires it. Presumably, this is the type of speaker that Rachel Jones, author of the personal essay cited earlier, is. She reports both that her roommate told her she "sounded white" over the phone, and that she uses *ain't* and *he be* only around family and friends (Jones [1982] 1998). Lanehart (2002) also compares and contrasts a number of these different choices across several generations of African-American women. Even though I have focused on ways of "blending" identities, there also exists, of course, the option of using a standard variety, indistinguishable from European-American varieties, all the time, without shifting.

I have presented the various strategies used by middle-class African-Americans, one after another, without attempting to evaluate them in any way. It is clear, though, that within particular African-American communities, there are, in fact, evaluations and judgments associated with choosing one or another of these options. The last two options, for example, could leave a speaker open to the criticisms, ridicule, or charges of "selling out" that go with "sounding white" (see also Chapter 6). Morgan argues that those who exclusively use Standard English can even "risk losing community membership" (2002:67). On the other hand, the association of using a standard variety with "selling out" is itself a type of subordination, not categorically different from the imposition of use of the standard variety on children in school, for example. The claiming of a standard variety (by using it) as part of the repertoire of an African-American community can be seen as an assertive, rather than assimilationist, move.

We can return now to Smitherman's analysis of the Thomas–Hill hearings. While Thomas infused his standard grammar and phonology with elements of African-American Verbal Tradition, Hill, who is also

African-American and middle class, used verbal strategies and behaviors associated with European-Americans. Smitherman identifies this difference as the source of many negative opinions about Hill among African-Americans, who claimed, among other things, that they did not trust her (2000b:264). The implication is that one needs to command at least the *style* associated with African-American ways of speaking in order to have credibility within African-American culture. As discussed in Chapter 1, the attitudes of others, particularly ingroup others, play a key role in the construction and maintenance of ethnic identity.

3.9   AAVE IN THE MEDIA

An area that is just beginning to be explored, but that shows promise for the future, is the study of AAVE in the mass media. Several recent works on AAVE include chapters on rap and hip-hop (e.g., Smitherman 2000b, Morgan 2002), detailing how these genres draw on African-American verbal traditions. Baugh (2000) includes a chapter on the role of editorial cartoons and internet parodies in reaction to the Oakland Resolution. Another study of "Ebonics humor" on the Internet is found in Rickford and Rickford (2000:203ff.). Rickford and Rickford also look at the use of AAVE and other varieties by stand-up comedians (2000:57ff.). Rahman (2003) is another study of the stand-up routines of African-American comedians. These studies will be explored in more detail in Chapter 6.

There have also been a few preliminary explorations of representations of AAVE on television and in films. Green (2002:200ff.) traces the history of representations of African-American language in films. She finds that AAVE features play a significant role in the presentation of black characters, including grammatical forms (e.g., multiple negation, habitual *be*), phonological forms (stress on the first syllable of *police*) and lexical items, particularly those associated with adolescents or young adults such as *dawg* and *cheese*. In addition, she discusses the representations of speech events associated with African-Americans, such as call and response and signifying (see Chapter 8). Green shows how these features are used (not always accurately) to construct certain images of African-Americans with respect not only to race but also to other factors such as socioeconomic class.

One of the very few quantitative studies of AAVE in the media is Fine and Anderson (1980). This study focused on US television shows from the late 1970s that featured primarily African-American casts.

The researchers counted occurrences of eleven features of AAVE, and found, interestingly, that the most frequently used features on the shows tended to be those that also occur in the non-standard dialects of other ethnic groups, so that they were not as intimately tied to ethnicity, such as negative concord or the use of *ain't*. There was very little use of features like habitual *be* or deletion of plural *-s* that are specifically associated with African-American ethnicity. In addition, when Fine and Anderson compared the scripts for the shows with the actual taped versions that aired, they found that a number of AAVE variants were added between working scripts and final broadcasts. In fact, from 36 to 81 percent of AAVE variants on the television shows they looked at were not scripted. In their conclusions they say:

> By rarely introducing the variants of BEV [i.e., AAVE] which almost exclusively are used by blacks, television presents BEV not as a dialect with linguistic integrity, but merely as the high density of otherwise widely occurring, and usually stigmatized, forms. (1980:405)

Fine and Anderson call this the general strategy of "black but not too black" (1980:406).

Fought and Harper (2004) conducted a quantitative study to see if the pattern identified in Fine and Anderson also applied to more recent television shows, as well as in other aspects of the media such as feature films and stand-up comedy routines. They found strong support for this pattern. In each of the media types analyzed, non-standard syntactic or morphological features of AAVE shared by other dialects (such as multiple negation) were significantly more frequent than those that were specifically associated with African-American ethnicity (such as possessive *-s* absence). Fought and Harper also identify a "continuum of conservativeness" in the media, such that the number of AAVE features found is lowest in commercials, then television shows, then feature films, and finally stand-up comedy routines, which have the highest frequency of AAVE features.

To date there are only a few quantitative studies of this type on AAVE in the media. This is a promising area for future research, however, particularly since the number and range of media productions geared toward and featuring African-Americans is increasing, slowly but steadily. One reason why sociolinguists might want to conduct more studies of this type is that there are people in less diverse communities who may be getting their ideas about other ethnic groups (African-Americans and others) partly or primarily from media representations. Mike, the European-American boy discussed in Chapter 2, may be a good example of someone in this situation. Therefore, it is important for us to know how accurate these representations are, and what sorts of ideologies about language and ethnicity they are presenting.

In general, sociolinguistic research on AAVE has a number of implications for the study of language and ethnicity. Many of the patterns, attitudes, conflicts, and solutions found in African-American communities are likely to apply in other cultures as well, particularly in settings where one variety of a language is dominant, but a minority variety, tied to ethnicity, exists in the same community. In the end, just as it is hard for ethnicity to be a neutral topic, it is hard for language use related to ethnicity to be viewed neutrally by communities. Without needing to read Le Page and Tabouret-Keller (1985), communities automatically view the language choices of their members as acts of identity, and these acts have social consequences on many levels. In particular, the tension between indexing ethnic loyalties and the pressure to assimilate is one that many individuals in minority ethnic communities will have to negotiate and resolve.

DISCUSSION QUESTIONS

1. Are there any characteristic words or phrases you would add to those listed in the discussion of AAVE? Why do you think AAVE is such a fruitful source for new words?
2. Why do you think there has been less sociolinguistic study of middle-class African-Americans? Why do you think there has been relatively little study of regional differences among African-Americans? Can you think of anything else that seems to be relatively neglected in looking at the speech of African-Americans?
3. If you are familiar with a black community outside the USA, can you list some features that are associated with this group? How do they compare with the types of language features characteristic of African-Americans?

SUGGESTIONS FOR FURTHER READING

Just a selection of many excellent books in this area:

Green, Lisa. 2002. *African-American English: A Linguistic Introduction.* Cambridge: Cambridge University Press.

One of the most recent and comprehensive works on AAVE, covering all aspects of structure and use, and including exercises and discussion questions.

Labov, William. 1972a. *Language in the Inner City: Studies in the Black English Vernacular*. Philadelphia: University of Pennsylvania Press.

A classic study of AAVE in New York City, presenting one of the first variationist analyses of AAVE structures, as well as discussions of narrative patterns and other features of AAVE use.

Lanehart, Sonja L., ed. 2001. *Sociocultural and Historical Contexts of African American English*. Amsterdam: John Benjamins.

A collection of chapters by numerous prominent researchers in the study of AAVE, focusing both on classic themes and on newer perspectives such as uses of AAVE by women.

Rickford, John. 1999. *African American Vernacular English: Features, Evolution, Educational Implications*. Malden, MA. Blackwell.

A collection of Rickford's essays on AAVE, from his earliest studies to his more recent research. Good for an overview of AAVE structure and use, as well as for application of AAVE studies to other areas such as style, or language in the educational system.

Rickford, John Russell and Russell John Rickford. 2000. *Spoken Soul: The Story of Black English*. New York: Wiley.

A book geared towards a general audience presenting many aspects of research on AAVE. Particularly strong in looking at AAVE as a crucial part of USA culture, in fiction, the mass media, and other areas.

Smitherman, Geneva. 2000b. *Talkin that Talk: Language, Culture, and Education in African America*. London and New York: Routledge.

A collection of Smitherman's essays on a number of themes, drawing on her long tradition of research on AAVE, as well as her personal experiences, to give an insightful overview of the politics of AAVE in America (particularly with respect to education).

4   Latino groups

Two languages sounds better for us Mexicans. (David, a 17-year-old
Mexican-American speaker from Los Angeles, talking about
code-switching, from Fought 2003:209)

While the construction of ethnicity by African-Americans generally
involves choices related to different dialects or possibly styles of
English, for Latino groups[1] in the USA, as for many ethnic groups
around the world, the relationship of language to ethnicity can also
encompass an entirely separate language, in this case, Spanish, as well
as the use of code-switching. In looking at ethnic identity among Latinos and Latinas, then, we must look not only at the range of dialects
and discourse styles available to them, but also at how bilingualism
(or monolingualism) fits into the picture that the community has of
what it means to be Mexican-American, Puerto-Rican American, and so
forth. Both bilingualism or multilingualism and code-switching have
been the focus of a great deal of study in sociolinguistics, although
most of the research that relates them to ethnicity has focused on
communities as a whole rather than on how these factors fit into the
individual construction of ethnic identity. The Latino groups discussed
here serve as good case studies for the exploration of issues related to
ethnic identity that arise in specifically bilingual settings.

   With that said, it is also important to note that the linguistic expression of identity for Latinos and Latinas in the USA is not only or even
primarily signaled by an ability to speak Spanish. A large number of
the speakers born here, especially from the third generation and later,
are completely monolingual in English (Veltman 1990, Schecter and
Bayley 2002, Fought 2003), so they must mark their ethnicity with
resources other than the use of Spanish. In the sociolinguistic literature on Latino groups, which is less extensive than the existing
research on African-Americans, there has historically been a focus on
issues of bilingualism and code-switching and relatively little study of

how individuals who are not in fact bilingual construct their ethnic identity. I want to focus here on both of these important facets of language in US Latino communities. Particularly interesting are some of the most recent studies, which look at groups that have not been studied much before (e.g., Dominican-Americans) and at the emergence of new contact dialects in areas such as North Carolina, where there has been a rapid increase in the Latino population. The research that has been done on these communities has broad implications for the field of sociolinguistics as a whole.

4.1 THE COMPLEXITIES OF IDENTITY IN LATINO COMMUNITIES

Latino communities in the USA provide a good lens for observing the multiple and overlapping layers of identity, and how these are reflected and reproduced in language. To begin with, speakers in these communities often have some level of direct access to their heritage culture. While elements of African culture, and particularly ideologies of this culture, may form a key part of African-American identity, most speakers in the African-American communities of Los Angeles, for example, have not been to Africa. However, almost all the US-born Mexican-American speakers I interviewed in Los Angeles (Fought 2003) had spent at least some time in Mexico. Similarly, Zentella (1997) discusses the many trips that US-born Puerto-Rican Americans made to the island. At the same time, contact with these cultures is intermittent and can sometimes be in conflict with the cultural norms that prevail in US settings.

In addition, there is often a division in the community between speakers born in the USA and those who are recent immigrants, and sometimes the tension between these groups can be intense. For example, US-born Latinos sometimes refer to Mexican immigrants as "wetbacks," an extremely derogatory ethnic term (Fought 2003:54). In my research, I also encountered an incident in which Mexican-immigrant students and Mexican-American students at a local high school had a conflict over the type of music to be played at an assembly, which led to their meeting behind the school with the intention of having a fight (Fought 2003:39). There are, then, multiple cultural groups available within which (and against which) Latino speakers can define and enact their identities, including: a) the heritage culture of other countries (e.g., Mexico), b) the immigrant Latino culture in the USA, c) the second-generation (and later) Latino culture in the USA, and d) other US cultural groups, including the dominant European-American culture, and the cultures of other ethnic minority groups such as African-Americans.

Studying Latino communities also can illuminate issues of race and ethnicity, because of the variety of phenotypes that individuals in the community represent, and the varying perspectives on race (what Urciuoli [1996] calls "racializing discourses") of the different cultures mentioned above. Dominican-Americans and Puerto-Rican Americans, for example, may exhibit a range of phenotypical features. Some of them may look "black" from the perspective of the dominant US culture, while others will tend to be classified physically as "Latino." Phenotype and issues of ethnic ascription are overtly discussed in these communities, as we saw in the example from Chapter 1 of the young Puerto-Rican American mother in Zentella's (1997) study who kept pointing out physical differences between her two sons to the researcher. Similarly, a Dominican-American man from Bailey's Rhode Island study noted "a lot of people confuse me for an African American most of the time . . . You can confuse a lot of Dominicans as African American by their color" (2000b:565).

The presence of African-descent phenotypes in Latino communities is particularly salient in racial ideologies, given the strong privileging of a black–white dichotomy in the USA, as discussed in Chapter 1, but there are also other important racial and ethnic distinctions. To begin with, types outside of "white," "black," or "Latino" are also a possibility. For example, there are Latinos and Latinas of Asian descent, whose parents come from Asian-immigrant communities in the Caribbean and South America. In addition, as with most communities in the USA, there is a certain proportion of people of mixed race. In my fieldwork in Los Angeles, for example, I interviewed speakers with one Latino parent and one European-American parent, and a speaker with one Latino parent and one Native-American parent (Fought 2003). Gordon (2000), in his study of the Calumet region of Indiana, includes speakers with one Mexican and one European-American parent, as well as a speaker who has one Mexican and one Vietnamese parent. One of the speakers in Urciuoli's (1996) New York City study had a Puerto-Rican American mother and an African-American father. Finally, in many of these communities there is an overt discussion of the issue of skin tone, which has numerous ramifications in Latino communities, as in many others. As with culture, the picture of "race" in Latino communities can be diverse and complex.

In addition to issues of race and culture, numerous other factors play a role in the construction of ethnic identity by Latinos and Latinas.

Many of these are relevant to other groups as well. Gender, for example, plays a role in the construction of identity generally, but also in specific use of languages and varieties, as well as the interpretations given to these uses by the community. Bucholtz (1995), for example, discusses how elements of gender identity such as clothing and hairstyles are interwoven with language issues in defining Mexican-American female identity. Social class is another crucial element that shapes the construction of ethnic identity. As with other groups, middle-class Latinos and Latinas do not speak in exactly the same way as working-class Latinos and Latinas (see, e.g., Fought 2003). In addition, ideologies about class interact with ideologies about language. As Urciuoli articulates it, with reference to her research in New York:

> "Puerto Rican" or ("Hispanic") is conflated (fused together) with
> "poor" or "lower class" and both conflated with "Spanish" or
> "Spanish interference in English" or simply "bad English." Thus, what
> seems at first glance a simple classification of language turns out to
> be fundamentally a classification of people. (1996:2)

These factors interact with the historical and political context of particular places as well, such as the amount of time a Latino group has been present in a particular area. In some parts of the Southwest, for example, Latino settlement predates settlement by European-Americans, while in parts of the Southeast and Midwest, there are Latino communities growing in areas that had almost no Latino populations a generation back. Finally, particular Latino communities may have factors crucial in defining identity that are specific to the community (e.g., the various gang affiliations in Mendoza-Denton 1997).

4.2   REPERTOIRES: MULTIPLE CODES FOR MULTIPLE IDENTITIES

In all the Latino communities that have been studied systematically by linguists, there are multiple linguistic codes available for the indexing of ethnic and other identities. Language in Latino groups is often simplistically reduced by the dominant culture to "English" and "Spanish," but the actual number of linguistic varieties available is much more extended, as is appropriate to the voicing of multiple identities that such communities require. Drawing on a number of studies (Urciuoli 1996, Mendoza-Denton 1997, Zentella 1997, Bailey 2000b, Fought 2003), I present here a list of the types of codes that can be found in Latino communities in the USA:

"Standard" English. I put the word "standard" in quotes because the concept itself is so difficult to define; entire books are available on this topic (e.g., Bex and Watts 1999). However, it is definitely the case that, for example, middle-class Latinos in the communities that have been studied often use a variety that contains few or no vernacular grammatical structures. Also, there is pressure to use a standard variety in the school setting, and at least some children will use a different variety there than they do at home.

A variety of Latino English. Examples include Chicano English, Puerto-Rican English, Cuban English, and so forth, of which Chicano English is the most intensely studied (see below). These are non-standard varieties that show the influence of language contact from Spanish (and potentially other varieties), particularly in the phonology. Often they develop as elaborated and regularized native-speaker versions of what were historically non-native-speaker varieties.

Other local varieties of English. These include any local non-standard varieties marked for geographic region, such as Appalachian English or California European-American English.

Non-native Spanish-influenced English. This is the typical "learner" English, used by immigrants from Spanish-speaking countries who learn English after the **critical age**. It is often confused by outsiders with the local Latino English variety, but in fact the two are quite distinct (see Fought 2003:80ff.).

"Standard" Spanish. This variety may not be widely available in some communities, but where it is it is usually associated with the use of Spanish in professional situations, e.g., a speaker who writes for a Spanish-language newspaper. In some places, this variety may include a few regional markers in the spoken form, but the grammar is universally "standard."

A regional variety of Spanish. In contrast with the previous variety, this type of Spanish contains features that are clearly marked for a particular geographic area of origin, some of which may be considered non-standard. An example would be the use of [l] as a phonetic variant of /r/ in Puerto-Rican Spanish, or the non-inversion of subject and verb for questions in Dominican Spanish.

A variety of Latino Spanish. Paralleling the nature of "Latino English," there is usually a variety of Spanish in US communities that differs from the regional variety spoken in the heritage country of the community. This variety generally includes a large number of English **borrowings** and **semantic**

extensions, and may also show direct or indirect influences in grammatical patterns, such as the conflation of *ser* and *estar* found in Los Angeles Spanish by Silva-Corvalán (1994).

Non-native English-influenced Spanish. Parallel to the learner English variety, this one is found among US-born Latinos and Latinas who have some bilingual ability, but are not fully fluent speakers of Spanish. The continuum of levels of fluency, of course, is quite complex, so the term "fully fluent" is vague and unscientific. But I've chosen it to identify a certain part of the continuum that includes speakers who can converse in Spanish only with some difficulty, and who make numerous errors that are not found in the speech of native speakers, even when those speakers are using a variety that includes English loanwords.

Code-switching. This includes the alternation of languages within a single discourse or a single utterance. Of course, it is really the alternation of language *varieties*, so that when we hear a blending of English and Spanish numerous combinations of the above varieties may be involved. In most Latino communities, code-switching plays a crucial role.

AAVE.[2] This variety may not be found in all Latino communities, but in a large number of them, there is regular contact with African-Americans due to shared socioeconomic conditions and residence patterns. In these groups, AAVE is a further code on which Latino individuals, even those who do not themselves have primary African-American contacts, can draw. AAVE can also have an influence on the structures of Latino English varieties.

4.3 ATTITUDES, CHOICES, AND THE CONSTRUCTION OF IDENTITY

Before looking in more detail at the structure and features of various codes, it is worth discussing the role (or roles) that each of them has in the indexing of ethnic identity by speakers in the Latino communities that have been studied. The varieties and styles discussed so far are associated with a range of attitudes and evaluations in the community, and different community members may draw on these ideological perspectives in different ways. To begin with, as noted above, not all of the varieties discussed are available in every community, and in addition a variety may be available to some community members and not others. Standard Spanish is a good example of a variety that might be available to a relatively small group. The availability of AAVE is extremely variable. In the Puerto-Rican American community studied by Urciuoli, contact with AAVE speakers was quite frequent; in fact, she claimed that there was "no fixed boundary between Puerto Rican and African American social life in this neighborhood" (1996:65). On the other hand, speakers in the Mexican-American community of Los Angeles had less contact with African-Americans due to high interethnic tensions (Fought 2003:95–6). Nonetheless, each member of a Latino community will have some range or subset of these codes available to him or her.

Standard Codes

The usual patterns with respect to standard and non-standard varieties are evident in the Latino groups that have been studied. At some level, "correct" English or "pure" Spanish are privileged in the ideology over non-standard varieties of either, code-switching or AAVE. This does not mean that the other varieties are not valued by at least some community members, but they are often subject to overt criticism both within and outside the community. The standard varieties are seen by many as a way to "get ahead," yet they can also carry negative connotations of their own. To begin with, standard varieties of English are often associated with European-Americans. Puerto-Rican American listeners, in an experiment conducted by Urciuoli (1996) associated speech samples that contained standard grammar with European-Americans, and those that contained non-standard grammar with Puerto-Rican Americans or African-Americans. Ironically, although Urciuoli does not comment on this fact, in many cases the Puerto-Rican listeners themselves used perfectly standard forms in giving their assessments.

Standard Spanish may be less controversial simply because it is less frequent. Urciuoli (1996:91) gives an example of two children in her study who derived much amusement from looking up words in a Spanish–English dictionary and comparing the standard Spanish forms with the (often borrowed) ones they were accustomed to (e.g., the standard *melocotón* instead of *piche* for English "peach"). Urciuoli notes that it was clear that these children privileged in some sense their own, English-influenced variety as being the "real" or most relevant Spanish. On the other hand, some first-generation speakers may express negative attitudes toward the English-influenced varieties of Spanish found in local communities. A middle-class first-generation Mexican speaker in Northern California, for example, commented that local Spanish television does not help her daughter learn Spanish because it is full of "barbarisms" like the use of the word *ganga* for "gang," instead of the original Spanish word *pandilla* (Schecter and Bayley 2002:57). Within communities, then, there may be a tension between standard and non-standard varieties of Spanish as having the greater claim to being the "real" language associated with ethnicity.

Spanish, bilingualism, and language shift

Attitudes towards Spanish in general (and, for most speakers, this means the local variety of Spanish) are often mixed. A number of speakers in Zentella's study identified Spanish as crucial to Puerto-Rican identity; one young woman said, for example, "If you Puerto Rican, you SHOULD know [Spanish], because that's their blood, because that's what they are" (1997:146). A young Mexican-American speaker in Los Angeles expressed very similar sentiments about speaking Spanish: "I think it's very important. Very. Cause, you know, you're Mexican, you have it in your blood" (Fought 2003:200). In Chapter 2, the crucial role of Spanish in establishing Dominican-American identity was also discussed. Speakers in Fought (2003) also pointed out the practical benefits of speaking Spanish, such as being able to translate for others in the community or to communicate with monolingual grandparents.

At the same time, though, increasing language shift to English suggests that, despite the positive affirmations of the role of Spanish in Latino ethnic identities, little progress is being made in fighting the dominant US ideology that values English and associates Spanish with the poor and uneducated. Despite the recent lip service by US politicians, who have sometimes attempted to deliver speeches in Spanish to reach Latino voters, attitudes about Spanish in the USA continue to be undergirded by deep prejudices and fears. The US media promote, as Zentella notes (in the foreword to Schecter and Bayley), "metaphors of 'immigrant hordes' and 'alien floods'" in which Spanish speakers are "portrayed as unwilling or unable to use English" (2002:ix–x). The use of Spanish in the public sphere is particularly perilous. For example, a couple in Schecter and Bayley reported that they had switched to using mainly English when they were young because of fear of "punishment if overheard using Spanish on school premises" (2002:73). Urciuoli concludes that, "[w]hen people use languages other than English in public and in ways that are not tightly scripted or framed by an unequivocally middle-class presentation, they are seen as dangerously out of order" (1996:38). Unsurprisingly, Spanish-speaking parents may receive this message clearly, with the result that many of them are reluctant to teach their children Spanish at home, fearing that they will be subject to the very real prejudices that exist in US society.

The result is that in most of the Latino communities that have been studied, retention of Spanish beyond the second generation is uncommon (Veltman 1990, Zentella 1997, Fought 2003). Where Spanish is maintained, this maintenance is not a one-time choice made by the family, but rather, as Schecter and Bayley (2002) observe, necessitates a process of continuing recommitment to Spanish maintenance. Even speakers who initially acquire Spanish may lose it through attrition later. A Puerto-Rican American speaker from Zentella's study who strongly linked Puerto Rican ethnic identity with the ability to speak Spanish nonetheless admits that her own Spanish has gotten "a little rusty" (1997:154). Similarly, a speaker in Los Angeles says, "Before I used to know perfect Spanish, everything, I knew. But when I talk Spanish now it's like I get confused" (Fought 2003:197). As a result, in many communities, ethnic identity is being reinterpreted so that language is no longer a crucial element. Zentella, for instance, reports on a study of attitudes that asked whether it was possible for someone who only speaks English to be Puerto Rican; 91 percent of the Puerto-Rican American respondents said that it was (1997:53). In sum, then, while Spanish still seems to have an important symbolic role in established Latino communities, its use as a specific index of ethnic identity may decline with each generation. On the other hand, as Schechter and Bayley (2002) illustrate, within individual families these patterns can vary greatly.

Code-switching

Attitudes toward code-switching are perhaps the most complicated of all. A speaker in the Puerto-Rican community studied by Urciuoli summed the conflicting attitudes up nicely: "Don't mix, it's awful – well, it don't sound to *me* awful, but it would sound awful to a teacher" (1996:97). Similarly, a speaker in Zentella's study criticized her own "bad habit" of mixing Spanish and English because she felt it could be "confusing" (1997:154). On the other hand, a number of young speakers in many communities also have positive attitudes about code-switching, and see a specific link between this practice and ethnic identity. There was an example in Chapter 2 of a young speaker from Fought (2003) who felt that code-switching was what distinguished the ethnic identity of Mexican-Americans like himself from that of immigrant Mexicans – two groups which, as discussed above, exist in a tense relationship. A number of other speakers in Fought (2003) expressed positive attitudes about code-switching as well. Similarly, a Puerto-Rican American speaker from Zentella's research in New York City articulates her association between ethnic identity and code-switching (which she calls "Spanglish") very explicitly. She comments, "Sometimes I'm talking a long time in English and then I remember I'm Puerto Rican, lemme say something in Spanglish" (1997:114). Although I am focusing only on Latino groups in the USA, many of the attitudes and patterns discussed here are also found in other settings in the world where code-switching is prominent.

AAVE

A classic study of the role of AAVE in a Latino community is Wolfram's (1974) study of Puerto-Rican Americans in New York City. Wolfram found a significant influence of AAVE on the English of young Puerto-Rican speakers, particularly young men. In terms of attitudes, using AAVE features was often viewed negatively, and subject to the same interpretation we find with many instances of use of an outgroup code; namely, that the speaker is trying to be something that he or she is not. Wolfram also gives an example of a speaker who was "smacked" by his father for using AAVE; the father told him, "You *can* talk English, but normal English" (Wolfram 1974:42). Interestingly, speakers often were not aware of how much AAVE had influenced their own speech. One boy in Wolfram's study was startled when he heard his own voice played back on the tape and commented with surprise on how much he sounded like an African-American (1974:41).

4.4 THE STRUCTURE OF DIALECTS IN LATINO COMMUNITIES

By far the most extensively studied dialect of a Latino group is Chicano English, the dialect spoken by Mexican-Americans (and others) in the Southwestern USA. Beginning in the mid-1980s and continuing up until the present, this variety has drawn the interest of sociolinguists. In talking about the structure of dialects in Latino communities, then, I will begin by describing Chicano English, and will add information about other dialects where this information is available. As noted earlier, the role of this dialect (and others like it) in the community is crucial, because for many monolingual speakers their ethnic identity is expressed through use of Chicano English rather than use of Spanish.

Historically, Chicano English is the result of language contact between Spanish and English. When groups of Mexican immigrants arrived in California and other areas through the early part of the twentieth century, many of them learned English as a second language. The variety they spoke was a learner variety of English, as described above, heavily influenced by phonological and other patterns from Spanish. Children of these immigrants born in the USA, however, generally grew up using both Spanish and English. The non-native English of the community became the basis for a new dialect of English, Chicano English, now spoken natively by those born in the community. Wald (1984) draws a parallel between the development of such varieties and the elaboration of a **pidgin** into a creole by the next generation. Besides the contact of Spanish and English, other varieties in the geographic area probably influenced the development of Chicano English, including local African-American varieties, and local European-American varieties (see Fought [2003:86–92] for more discussion). It should also be noted that, as mentioned earlier, the learner varieties of English continue to be spoken by more recent adult immigrants to US Latino communities.

4.5 CHICANO ENGLISH PHONOLOGY

There are more salient differences between Chicano English and other dialects in the area of phonology than in the area of grammar, and it is these differences that are most likely to be used by speakers outside the group in identifying a speaker as Latino or Latina. In comparison with the phonetic differences found in AAVE, though, many of these distinctions can be hard to identify precisely. Often they involve a very slight shift in quality towards a corresponding Spanish sound, although it is too simplistic to say that Spanish influence accounts for all of the differences (cf. Godinez 1984). One very important factor in how Chicano English "sounds" to outsiders is the presence of intonation and stress patterns from Spanish that give it a unique rhythm and prosody among English dialects (Fought and Fought 2002, Fought 2003:70ff.). This quality can be highly salient to outsiders, even in the absence of many phonetic or grammatical differences. In an early study of Chicano English, for instance, we find the following comment: "intonation continues to be a problem even among adults with an otherwise flawless command of English" (González 1984:39). Reflected here, unfortunately, is the long-standing myth that Chicano English is just a stage on the way to acquisition of Standard English. But in addition, this statement illustrates the salient nature of Chicano English intonation and, most important for the theme of this book, the ways in which suprasegmental features might reflect ethnic identity, even among speakers whose dialect is otherwise very standard.

To begin with, here are a few of the more salient features of Chicano English vowels and consonants (see Fought [2003] for a more complete discussion):

- *Less frequent **vowel reduction**.* Most American English dialects are characterized by a pattern where unstressed vowels tend to be reduced to **schwa** [ə], or something similar. Overall, there is much less of this type of reduction in Chicano English. For example, the first vowel in *together* would usually be schwa [ə] in many dialects, but in Chicano English this word might be pronounced [tʰugɛðɚ]. Santa Ana (1991) found that Chicano English speakers tended to reduce vowels in unstressed syllables less often than European-Americans, and also that the direction of movement for unstressed vowels was sometimes quite different.
- *Frequent lack of glides.* The **high vowels**, [i] and [u], tend to be realized as [ij] and [uw] by speakers of many dialects of English, but Chicano English speakers often have more monophthongal versions of these vowels, similar to the corresponding vowels in Spanish (Santa Ana 1991). This can also happen with the **diphthongs** [ej] and [ow].
- *Tense realization of /ɪ/.* In certain contexts, Chicano English speakers use [i] as a phonetic variant of /ɪ/. In particular, this tends to occur in the **linguistic environment** of the **morpheme** *-ing* (Mendoza-Denton 1997), so that *going* is pronounced [gowin]. It is important to note that in many other contexts, however, Chicano English shows a clear **contrast** between the **phonemes** /i/ and /ɪ/, in contrast with the English spoken by Spanish-speaking learners, who do tend to neutralize the distinction.
- *Stops for interdental fricatives.* As with AAVE and a number of other dialects, Chicano English frequently substitutes **alveolar** stops [t] and [d] for the interdental fricatives [θ] and [ð], so that *then* becomes [dɛn], for example. Fought (2003:68) found that this feature occurred even among speakers whose dialect was very standard overall in terms of grammar and other features.
- *Loss of final consonants.* As with all dialects of English, Chicano English tends to reduce consonant clusters, and like AAVE it shows quantitatively more reduction than comparable dialects spoken by European-Americans (Wald 1984, Santa Ana 1991). Perhaps more significant is that fact that, unlike European-American dialects, Chicano English can delete final consonants that are not in a cluster. For instance, the word *night* can be pronounced [naj]. AAVE also can exhibit this type of reduction (Bailey and Thomas 1998), but it may be even more frequent in Chicano English (Fought 2003:69). **Voiceless** final stops that are not deleted in Chicano English may be glottalized instead (Fought 2003:69–70).

In addition to the segmental features listed above, Chicano English, as noted earlier, sounds very distinctive in terms of its prosody. As with the segmental features, some of this distinctiveness reflects the historical influence of Spanish on the dialect. To begin with, stress patterns on isolated lexical items or on phrases may differ slightly from their placement in other dialects (Fought 2003:70ff.). The pattern of less frequent vowel reduction discussed above also combines with a tendency toward syllable timing (versus the **stress timing** typical of Standard English). Fought and Fought (2002) found that there was a difference between Chicano English speakers and European-American speakers in California, such that the Chicano English speakers produced a more even-timed rhythm pattern, particularly at the beginnings of utterances.

The combination of these features (prosodic and **segmental**) has a tendency to make Chicano English sound more like Spanish, especially in the quality of the vowels, the preference for open syllables created by the loss of final consonants, and the syllable-timed rhythmic patterns. This effect has certainly contributed to a mistaken idea that people often have when they hear Chicano English; namely, that the speaker must be a native Spanish speaker who is just "learning English." In fact, these exact features are found among monolinguals with almost no knowledge of Spanish.

Looking at this misperception from another angle, there are a number of features clearly characteristic of Spanish learners of English that never occur in Chicano English, as long as this latter term is reserved only for the speech of native English speakers. Non-native learners, for example, collapse certain phonemic distinctions in English such as between [i] and [ɪ], between [ɛ] and [æ], between [tʃ] and [ʃ], and between [ə] and [ɑ] (Fought 2003:81–3). Chicano English speakers have clear distinctions for all these pairs. Therefore, it is not accurate to say that Chicano English is simply a "Spanish **accent**." While it may sound superficially similar to the English of non-native speakers, especially for those outside the community, in fact the two varieties are distinct.

4.6   CHICANO ENGLISH GRAMMAR

As mentioned above, the features of Chicano English morphology and syntax are not nearly as distinct as its phonological features. In comparison with AAVE, there are fewer grammatical structures specifically associated with Chicano English, although there are some. There are also many non-standard features that Chicano English shares with other vernacular dialects. Listed here are some of the main morphological and syntactic features associated with Chicano English, along with a few semantic features; examples are from Fought (2003) unless otherwise noted. (See Fought 2003 for more detail, including discussion of the influence of Spanish.)

Features specific to Chicano English:

- *Extended use of modals*: In Chicano English, **modals** may be used with stative verbs in the present, which is often disfavored in other dialects, as in the following example from Wald (1996:520):

  If he'd be here right now, he'd make me laugh.

There is also a high frequency of the modal *would* in *if*-clauses, more so than in other dialects, as in this example from Fought (2003:99):

  If I woulda been a gangster, I woulda been throwing signs up.

Finally, although this is more a semantic rather than syntactic difference, the modal *could* can be extended to mark competence or ability, in environments where other varieties of English would generally use *can*, as in:

  I learned that people that are left handed could draw better than people who are right handed.

Here, the speaker is describing a general ability of left-handed people.

- *Non-standard use of prepositions*. Many speakers of Chicano English use prepositions other than those used in other varieties of English. Examples include: *We're really supposed to get out of here <u>on</u> June. We all make mistakes <u>along</u> life. They got <u>off</u> the car.* Often, these uses are traceable to the influence of Spanish. This fact is worth noting, because the majority of grammatical and semantic features of Chicano English are not so clearly related to Spanish influence.
- *Use of* tell *to mean "ask."* For example, *If I tell her to jump up, she'll <u>tell</u> me how high.*
- *Extended semantics of* barely (to mean "just recently" or "a short time ago"). For example, *These were expensive when they barely came out. He just barely got a job you know back with his father.*

Features associated with AAVE:

- *Habitual* be: For example, *The news be showing it too much. Me and my mom be praying in Spanish.*

- *Use of existential* it (for *there*). For example, *It's four of us, there's two of them.*
- *Use of preterite* had: For example, *The cops had went to my house. . . . Before we had fought, she had came up to see me* (see Rickford and Théberge-Rafal 1996 for more on this feature).

Features common to many non-standard dialects:

- *Subject–auxiliary inversion in embedded questions.* An example of subject–**auxiliary inversion** in an **embedded question** is: *Then they asked them where did they live* (Wald 1984:25). This feature occurs in AAVE, but might also occur in some European-American varieties (Green 2002:88–9), so I have listed it here.
- *Regularization of agreement patterns*: Examples of regularized **agreement** include *Everybody knew the Cowboys was gonna win again. Otherwise, she don't know Brenda.*
- *Use of* ain't. For example, *My name ain't exciting either.*
- *Non-standard reflexive pronouns*: For example, *theirselves* as the **reflexive pronoun** in *[They] have to start supporting theirselves at early ages.*
- *Resumptive pronouns.* For example, *they* as the **resumptive pronoun** in *The guy that um, that they knew he was doing it.*
- *Negative concord.* For example, *Things ain't gonna never change in LA no more. I don't think that nobody really knows anything.*

Looking at the various influences involved in the structure of Chicano English is a good illustration of how language indexes identity. The tapestry of forms reflects influences from the speech of Spanish-dominant immigrants, African-Americans, and European-Americans, as well as innovations, features that signal the unique identity and creativity of Chicano English speakers.

4.7   THE STRUCTURE OF OTHER LATINO ENGLISH DIALECTS

Comprehensive studies are still needed for many varieties of Latino English across the USA. Very little has been done, for example, on the English of Cuban-Americans in Florida, even though they constitute a large and important ethnic group in the region (see, e.g., MacDonald 1996). One of the few groups besides Chicano speakers in the Southwest for which we have significant data on the Latino English variety spoken is Puerto-Rican Americans in places like New York City and

Philadelphia. Wolfram's (1974) study, mentioned earlier, documents the presence of AAVE grammatical and phonological features as a significant factor in Puerto-Rican English in New York City. Some of the features incorporated by Puerto-Rican speakers included negative inversion (e.g., *Didn't nobody do it*), habitual *be*, realizations of /θ/ as [f], and monophthongization of /ay/. Zentella's (1997) study also lists the use of preterite *had* as an influence from AAVE. In addition, Zentella notes that, as with Chicano English, syllable timing is characteristic of Puerto-Rican English.

An interesting development in sociolinguistic research on language and ethnicity is the study of new dialect formation in areas that until recently had few Latino residents, but that have experienced a rapid increase in their Latino populations. One main area for recent studies of this type is North Carolina. The study of emerging dialects provides us with a rare opportunity to see how elements of language in contact settings, such as those that will be discussed in Chapter 7, are woven together over time to create new varieties. In particular, the varieties in question will be tied to ethnic (Latino) identity, and so they have important implications for the study of language and ethnicity.

In their study of two developing Latino communities of this type in North Carolina, Wolfram et al. (2004) focus on the degree to which second-language speakers of English acquire local dialect traits, traits which might then be transmitted to future (native) varieties of English. As in other cases of dialect accommodation that have come up, the various components of the linguistic system seem to play different roles in the formation of new Latino English dialects and their assimilation to local varieties. In terms of phonology, Wolfram et al. (2004) explored the production of the /ay/ diphthong, since monophthongization of this vowel is characteristic of the local European-American variety. Though neither community showed widespread assimilation to the local /ay/ variant, some speakers in the more rural community they focused on did show incipient (and gradient) accommodation to the local norm. One adolescent boy produced 63 percent of his diphthongs as unglided, a factor which Wolfram et al. trace to his strong identification with the local "jock" culture. With respect to the lexical component, on the other hand, they found widespread adoption of forms that signaled local identity, such as the use of second person plural *y'all*, and the auxiliary *fixin' to*. These highly symbolic social forms were used even by heavily Spanish-dominant speakers, whose phonology and grammar showed little adaptation to local norms. As the dialect develops and stabilizes, new permutations of these patterns may emerge, reflecting the integration of ethnic and local identity in different ways.

4.8 LATINO DIALECTS OF SPANISH

Much of the sociolinguistic research on Spanish in the USA has focused either on interference effects from English or on code-switching, both of which are part of the use of Spanish in most Latino communities. Zentella (1997:182ff.) gives a summary of the grammatical features that have been found to be typical of Spanish as spoken by younger generations born in the USA, including:

- more marking of the imperfect on the auxiliary verb (*estaba buscando* = "was searching") rather than on the main verb (*buscaba* = "search" + imperfect)
- absence of a variety of subordinate clauses
- increasing absence of use of the **subjunctive**

Silva-Corvalán's (1994) study of Mexican-Americans in Los Angeles is probably the most comprehensive study of effects of the English system on Spanish grammar. She focuses particularly on the tense–**mood**–aspect system, and finds attrition generally in the number of distinctions that are maintained by young bilingual speakers. She analyzes the corresponding effects that these losses have on other language areas, such as oral narratives. In addition, she looks at borrowings and loan translations in Spanish, including literal translations of English phrases, e.g., *tener un buen tiempo* for "to have a good time," or *cambia su mente* for "(he or she) changes his mind." Nonetheless, not every grammatical feature of US Spanish varieties can be attributed to English influence. Bayley and Pease-Alvarez (1997), for instance, found that the overt expression of subject pronouns (which are optional in Spanish) correlated with generational status among Mexican-descent children in California. However, the US-born children whose parents were also born here or emigrated from Mexico at a young age actually expressed these pronouns *less* often than those born in Mexico – exactly the opposite of what we would expect if English influence was a factor. Lipski (1996) finds a similar lack of correlation between strength of English and expression of subject pronouns for Cuban-Americans. As this summary suggests, the vast majority of the research on US Spanish has focused on grammatical and lexical features. There has been very little work on phonological patterns in the Spanish of Latino communities.

4.9   THE LANGUAGE GAP: DIFFERENCES AMONG GENERATIONS

One issue that is prominent in Latino communities, and in bilingual immigrant communities generally, is the differences among generations in terms of language use. Interestingly, in these communities we may find that different generations are actually constructing different ethnicities in a sense. The immigrant generation may see their ethnicity as straightforwardly "Mexican," for example, while the second-generation speakers see their ethnicity as a combination of their Mexican descent and the US culture of the country in which they were born, different from and even in conflict with the ethnicity of their parents. Often, as we saw in a number of examples, code-switching may be taken as the linguistic symbol of this complex identity.

Another interesting facet of the intergenerational relationship is language competence. As was discussed, attrition of Spanish in most established Latino communities means that the younger generation's competence in this language may be fairly low. On the other hand, most of their immigrant parents may speak English only as a second language, with varying ranges of competence depending on their individual experiences. This can lead to a situation in which parents and children within the same family do not share a language for communication in which they both feel completely at ease. A teenage Mexican-American boy in Los Angeles explained it this way:

> I like my parents, but um, sometimes we just don't, we don't really get along cause we don't talk to each other. Cause I can't really explain to 'em how I feel in Spanish, and I would– and I wouldn't be able to explain to them in English. (Fought 2003:199)

The idea of a language barrier between generations in the same family has not been explored much in the literature. It seems likely, though, that it would play a role in the construction of a separate ethnicity by younger speakers in bilingual communities, and would be worth exploring further. Like many other issues discussed in this chapter, this one probably is relevant in a number of bilingual and multilingual settings around the world.

DISCUSSION QUESTIONS

1. Looking forward fifty years, what changes might we expect to find in the parts of North Carolina where there has been a large influx of Latinos and Latinas, especially with respect to language?

2. What are some similarities and differences that emerge in looking at the construction of ethnic identity by African-American
   groups versus Latino groups in the USA?
3. Code-switching is often the topic of overt commentary in communities where it occurs, and is often viewed as humorous, but
   can also be seen as an important component in ethnic identity.
   What factors do you think might influence how positively or negatively a particular group (or individual) views code-switching?
   If you are familiar with a community that code-switches, discuss
   the attitudes about it that you have observed.

SUGGESTIONS FOR FURTHER READING

Fought, Carmen. 2003. *Chicano English in Context*. New York: Palgrave/
Macmillan Press.

The most comprehensive modern work on Chicano English, presenting
phonetic, syntactic, and semantic features, sociolinguistic patterns, and
an analysis of the role of bilingualism in Chicano communities in the
USA.

Santa Ana, Otto. 1991. Phonetic simplification processes in the English of
the barrio: a cross-generational sociolinguistic study of the Chicanos of
Los Angeles. University of Pennsylvania dissertation.

One of the first studies to look in depth at phonetic features of Chicano
English and to distinguish speakers of different generations, who had
often been grouped together by previous researchers.

Schecter, Sandra R., and Robert Bayley. 2002. *Language as Cultural Practice:
Mexicanos en el Norte*. Mahwah, NJ: Lawrence Erlbaum.

A very recent study of two different Latino communities in the USA,
looking at the politics of ethnicity, and the role of language in the
construction of cultural identities by communities and individuals.

Zentella, Ana Celia. 1997. *Growing Up Bilingual*. Malden, MA. Blackwell.

One of the most comprehensive studies of patterns of bilingualism in a
US Latino community in the USA – Puerto Ricans in New York City. This
book explores the linguistic and cultural ramifications of political and
social policies, as well as including a detailed study of code-switching
in the community.

5 Linguistic variation in other multiethnic settings

Some Cajuns are ashamed of their nonstandard English, but most are not . . .
Male college students have told me that they consciously exaggerate their
accents when vacationing at resorts outside of Acadiana, in order to attract
the attention of non-Cajun women, who are allegedly fascinated by the Cajuns'
unconventional style of speech. (Gutierrez, cited in Walton 2004:107)

In any community that encompasses people of multiple ethnic backgrounds, we might expect to find interesting sociolinguistic variation
related to ethnicity. In a majority of countries where research related to
language and ethnicity has been done, though, the focus has been on
bilingualism and language choice issues as part of ethnic or national
identities. Studies that look at variation within a language, on the
other hand, can provide a different sort of window into the construction of ethnic identity. Not everyone in a community may have access
to the heritage language associated with it, so that bilingualism versus monolingualism might not ever come up as a choice for some
speakers of a particular ethnicity. On the other hand, most or all of
the speakers in a community may have some access to the dominant
language, so that variation within or across dialects is more available
as a signal of ethnicity. This chapter brings together sociolinguistic
research from several multiethnic areas around the world, focusing
on variation (particularly dialect variation) related to ethnicity. The
role of heritage languages will also be touched on, particularly where
it plays a key role in ethnic identity. Rather than attempting to cover
all the areas where sociolinguistic research has been done, I've chosen
to present three very different multiethnic settings in detail, looking
for common patterns and notable differences related to the linguistic
indexing of ethnicity. In each case, I have focused on the construction
of ethnicity by minority ethnic groups in the area (I will return to
ethnic identity in majority groups in Chapter 6).

The geographic locations I discuss in this chapter are: 1) Southern Louisiana (US), with a focus on two distinct minority ethnic groups, Cajuns, and Creole African-Americans; 2) South Africa, with at least four relevant ethnic groups in contact; and 3) New Zealand, looking at contact between the dominant European-descent group, and the indigenous Maori group. All of these places share the fact that English has been one of the politically dominant languages historically, but in other ways they are quite different. In some settings, there is extended interethnic contact among at least three different groups, which provides a particularly interesting context for the construction of language and ethnicity, while in others only two groups are central. In Louisiana, two languages (French and English) plus a creole play important roles historically. In South Africa, two languages associated with dominant groups (Afrikaans and English) are present, while the languages associated with other groups are too numerous to list. In New Zealand, the Maori language has come to a point of near extinction, so in a sense there is only one language playing a major role in day-to-day life: English. The sociopolitical histories of these places are also strikingly different; among them they cover slavery, legalized oppression by race into the late twentieth century, reshuffling of ethnic groupings and terms, code-switching, language revival movements, and the use of ethnicity as a tourist commodity. These locations provide three very different windows into the indexing of ethnic identity through language.

5.1   CAJUNS AND CREOLES IN LOUISIANA

The social, political, and ethnic history of Louisiana is quite complex, involving slavery and its abolition, immigration from many parts of the world, and a shifting economy, all corresponding to shifts in both ethnicity and language. I will give a brief summary of the key points related to the history of the two ethnic groups discussed, but a number of other references can provide more background on Louisiana's history (see, e.g., Dubois and Horvath 2003b). In terms of language, Louisiana's history includes Acadian French, other dialects of French, a French-based creole, Spanish, Native-American languages, and several dialects of English. Overall, however, the shift from French and other languages to English has been fairly widespread. A particularly interesting factor in the ethnic setting of Louisiana is that one of the most salient minority ethnic groups is of European descent (the Cajuns). This fact provides an opportunity to explore in more detail some of the issues raised in Chapter 1 about ethnic versus racial differences. Of course, technically the Creoles are of European descent as well, given that one element in the definition of someone as "a Creole" is French ancestry (Dubois and Melançon 2000). However, because they are also of African descent, and because of the ideology in the USA by which people with any African ancestry are characterized as "black," they are not viewed (nor do they view themselves) as "white." The Cajuns, on the other hand, are seen as white, and always have been (Dubois and Horvath 2003a). This allows them to claim "optional identity," as described by Waters (1990), a factor that we might expect to see reflected linguistically.

Cajuns

The Cajuns are descendants of French-speaking immigrants who came to Louisiana from Nova Scotia in Canada in the mid-eighteenth century. Initially, the group maintained a fair amount of isolation and separateness, but over time economic and social changes brought them into more contact with the dominant English-speaking community, leading to more assimilation (Dubois and Horvath 1999). In the late 1960s, a "Cajun Renaissance" began, which generated renewed interest in and appreciation of Cajun culture from inside and outside the group. Among other things, Cajun identity became a commodity, packaged for tourists in the form of musical performances, tours of the bayou, and large numbers of products with the label "Certified Cajun" (Dubois and Horvath 1999, 2003a). Generally speaking, French as a marker of cultural identity has been lost among the younger generation of Cajuns (Dubois and Horvath 2003c). While the Cajun Renaissance has led to some language revival efforts, such as the offering of Acadian French at Louisiana State University (Walton 2004), in general English is the language in which most Cajuns live their lives and construct their identities. The dialect known as Cajun Vernacular English (CVE) has been the subject of a sudden burst of sociolinguistic research in recent years. Below are some characteristics associated with this dialect (from Dubois and Horvath 1998, 1999, 2003c, Walton 2004).

Phonology

- monophthongization of /ay/, so that *time* is pronounced [taːm] (like "tahm")
- stopping of interdental fricatives [ð] and [θ]; in particular, the lexical items *this* and *that*, pronounced "dis" and "dat," are part of the stereotype of Cajun speech; stopping occurs medially as well in words like *brother* (distinct from other non-standard varieties

of English with fricative stopping, where it tends to be only initial)

- heavy nasalization of vowels before nasal consonants, e.g., *man* is pronounced [mæ̃ n]
- **unaspirated** initial stops /p/, /t/, and /k/
- dropping of /h/ in word-initial position
- phrase final stress

Grammatical structures

- verbal –s absence (*She go with it.*)
- absence of past tense marking (*She wash my face.*)
- copula absence (*She pretty.*)
- past tense *be*-**leveling** (*You was lucky last night.*)
- negative concord (*They didn't want no schooling.*)
- non-standard past tense marking of verbs (*She brung it.*)

Cajun Vernacular English is also characterized by the use of particular lexical items, often borrowed from French, such as *cher* ("my dear"). Like other varieties that grew out of a bilingual setting (e.g., Chicano English, which was discussed in Chapter 4), CVE has many features that can be traced to **transfer** from a heritage language (French). Also like these other varieties, however, it is now spoken by people who are monolingual in English, so the features cannot be attributed directly to influence of another language.

What role, then, does CVE play in the construction of ethnicity by its speakers, especially in light of the "Cajun Renaissance"? And is the "optional" nature of Cajun identity indexed in any way by language use? Dubois and Horvath, in a series of articles (e.g., Dubois and Horvath 1998, 1999, 2003a), explore the trajectories of change in CVE by looking at speakers from older, middle, and younger age groups in a Cajun community. They report on an interesting pattern for a number of the phonetic variables linked to Cajun identity, including nasalization, /ay/ monophthongization, and stopping of fricatives. For each of these, they found that use of the variable was generally highest in the oldest age group, declined sharply in the middle group, and then showed a rising trend in the youngest group. Dubois and Horvath refer to this shift among the youngest group as "recycling"; previously stigmatized features that were declining in use are picked up again by the youngest generation as an expression of renewed ethnic pride.

For some variables, both young men and young women are participating in the shift, but in other cases the recycling of the variable was strongly differentiated by gender, with men leading significantly.

Dubois and Horvath link this gender effect to the fact that the activities most associated with the expression of Cajun culture tend to be male-dominated; these include fishing, performing Cajun music (although this may be changing), and preparing special holiday meals. As one of Dubois and Horvath's informants explained, "Women in Cajun culture cook food for sustenance. When it was a special occasion with many people coming, my father cooked" (1999:306). Men are also more likely to interact with tourists, by taking them on tours of the bayou, for example. In addition, young men with "open" networks, who were more likely to have contact with tourists, led everyone in the use of stopped /ð/, producing it at a rate of about 90 percent, more than even the oldest generation (Dubois and Horvath 1999). In contrast, for young women, those in "closed" networks, who mostly interacted with others in the community, used more Cajun features.

Again, these data are a good reminder that ethnicity is not indexed in the same way by every member of a community. Gender, network, social class, type of employment, and many other factors can affect how ethnicity is constructed. The trajectory of change in the Cajun community over the generations also may be related to a question raised earlier: Does the "optional" nature that goes with a minority ethnic (but not racial) identity affect its linguistic expression? These data suggest that it does. As the middle age group began to have more access to the outside world and other dialect patterns, they were able to downplay, hide, or disclaim Cajun ethnicity during the period when it was more stigmatized. Dubois and Horvath found evidence in both questionnaires and sociolinguistic interviews that historically "both middle aged men and women moved away from a Cajun identity" (1999:305). They enacted this identity shift partly by minimizing use of Cajun features. For nasalization, and /θ/-stopping, for example, the values in this group range from 5 percent to 20 percent at most (Dubois and Horvath 1999). This trend itself is not unusual. But the extremely rapid "recycling" is more noteworthy. For the young men, /θ/-stopping occurs at about 50 percent, and nasalization jumps to almost 100 percent (Dubois and Horvath 1999). Although theories about the motivations for shifts can be hard to prove definitively, it seems likely that the renewed taking up of an "optional" ethnic identity is what allows such a rapid shift to significant use of a formerly stigmatized feature.

Another theoretical contribution from the Cajuns and their linguistic situation is a better understanding of the role of boundaries in ethnic identity. As discussed in Chapter 1, interethnic boundaries are central to how ethnic groups define themselves. The specific effect of increased interethnic contact across boundaries, though, is not clear, especially in terms of language. In situations of increased contact, will the two groups tend to become more alike linguistically, or more different? This question will be addressed further in Chapter 7. The results from the Cajun community studied by Dubois and Horvath, though, suggest that (and I hope this is unsurprising to you by now) the picture is a complex one. It would seem that increasing contact with outside ethnic groups may have led to a decline in use of ethnic features by the middle age group. For the younger group, women seem to follow a similar pattern, where those with more contact with outsiders use fewer Cajun features, and those in traditional roles within the community use more features. For young men, however, it is precisely a high degree of contact with outsiders (particularly tourists) that triggers a strong indexing of Cajun identity through linguistic features. The conclusion, then, must be that interethnic contact can have different effects for different community members, depending on the context.

Creole African-Americans

For the second ethnic group in Southern Louisiana that will be discussed, I will use the term Creole African-Americans, following Dubois and Horvath (2003a), who note that African-Americans with some French heritage may refer to themselves either as "Creoles" or as "African Americans." The term "Creole" itself has been the subject of shifting definitions historically. In the eighteenth century, there was a social tolerance of interethnic relations, usually between French-speaking white men and black (slave) women, which led to a high population of mixed-race individuals. These people of color were called "mulattos" and recognized as legally free by the Louisiana courts in 1810 (Dubois and Melançon 2000). In the nineteenth century, before the Civil War, people of mixed race were distributed throughout the economic system, with some of them becoming wealthy landowners on the same tier as the white social elite, while others were tenant farmers, or field hands (toward the lowest end of the socioeconomic hierarchy). After the Louisiana Purchase in 1803, large numbers of Anglo-American immigrants began to replace the French at the top of the social pyramid. This development led to a stronger separation of populations by race, especially after the Civil War ended in 1865 (Dubois and Horvath 2003b).

Originally, the term "Creole" referred to the people who lived in the French colony that became Louisiana, regardless of race. Later the term narrowed to focus on just those who could claim French ancestry, and in particular the terms "White Creole" and "Colored Creole" came into use, referring particularly to the socioeconomically higher groups, with the Creole identity now tied to ancestry and language (French), as well as religion (Catholic), particularly after the Anglo-American influx of the early nineteenth century (Dubois and Melançon 2000). Later, however, a more dichotomous view of "white" versus "black" in opposition developed, and the group that had been defined as colored was now combined with the black population in the dominant ideology of the white majority. In addition, "White Creoles" began to merge with the Anglo-American population. Dubois and Melançon found that currently the term "Creole" is associated strongly with African-Americans who have Creole French-speaking ancestors. Despite the massive shift from French to English in Louisiana as a whole, they note that a certain core group of black speakers continue to speak Creole French fluently. In one of the communities they studied, they even found a few families that had "children who are monolingual in Creole French until they attend school and receive instruction in English" (2000:248). In terms of the definition of Creole identity, Dubois and Melançon found that the most important criteria were having Creole ancestors or having ancestors who spoke Creole French; speaking French and speaking Creole French themselves were identified as important by some respondents but not others.

Much less research has been done on Creole African-American Vernacular English (CAAVE) than on Cajun English. However, some recent studies have attempted to trace the role of this variety in the complex sorting out of Creole identity. Dubois and Horvath (2003b) describe CAAVE as sharing features of Southern dialects in general, and also of Cajun Vernacular English, though they do not list specific features. What they focus on is the unusually high amount of glide absence on diphthongal vowels in CAAVE, which occurs for the vowels /ay, aw, oy, iy, uw, ey, ow/, all of which tend to have a diphthongal quality in many American dialects. While some of these vowels, such as /ay/, are undergoing monophthongization in other Southern speech communities, no other community applies this process to such a large number of vowels. In addition, there was no evidence that these vowel variants were being lost by the younger generation, except for those who were college-educated. Dubois and Horvath note that the persistence of this pattern when it has been lost in other dialects is striking. They explain it with reference to the relative isolation of Creole African-Americans from other groups, because of socioeconomic and racial barriers.

In comparing these two groups to each other, we find linguistic differences that can be tied to the social and historical context. Dubois and Horvath (2003a) conducted a quantitative study of the use of two locally marked variables, /ay/ monophthongization and stopping of the fricative /ð/, among both Creole African-American and Cajun speakers. They found that Cajun speakers from the youngest generation who had "open networks" – that is, interacted more with others outside the local community – showed a marked increase over older speakers in the use of these once-stigmatized variables. The younger generation of Creole African-Americans with open networks, however, showed a marked decrease in the use of these variables. Dubois and Horvath suggest that this pattern may be tied to the fact that the cultural renaissance has benefited Cajuns more than Creoles, and they speculate about whether, as Creole culture becomes even more central in the ethnic revival, Creole African-Americans might begin to use more of these local features as well. Another possibility, it seems to me, might be that these features which formerly marked "local" identity are now shifting to mark Cajun or "white" identity. If so, we might see an even more marked decrease in their use among Creole African-Americans. In either case, the difference between a minority group distinguished by race and one distinguished by ethnicity appears to have linguistic repercussions.

5.2 SOUTH AFRICAN ETHNIC GROUPS

Of the three geographic locations presented here, South Africa provides the most complex opportunity for the study of language, race, ethnicity, and culture, and I have devoted a large section of the chapter to it. South Africa spent most of the twentieth century clinging to policies of racism and brutality that were legally institutionalized at every level, through apartheid. Its dominant group was an "ethnic minority," and other groups were physically forced into specific geographic locations. The government had a complex system of racial classification in which self-identification was irrelevant, and there were laws against various types of interethnic contact. In 1994, this system of institutionalized oppression was dismantled, and a new era for the country began.

It is difficult to wrap one's mind around this level of change and what it meant to the cultural identities of South African citizens. Would groups that had been formally separated before now have more interaction? Would the ways in which culture was expressed by, for example, Black South Africans change in the context of new freedom? And with all of this, inevitably, come linguistic questions. Under apartheid, language was intimately tied to ethnic segregation, a key factor in the ascription of ethnic identity by the government (Kamwangamalu 2001). The classifications made by the government included Whites, Blacks, Indians, and Coloured. But within these groups there were also subgroupings related to language: Black individuals were classified by the African language of their heritage, White people were divided according to whether their mother tongue was Afrikaans or English. Would people in formerly oppressed groups continue to use languages associated with the oppressor? Would more status be accorded to African languages, or to the dialects of English influenced by these?

Not surprisingly, a number of linguists both inside and outside South Africa took up the challenge to explore these issues. At least one of them (McCormick 2002a, 2002b) conducted fieldwork both before and after apartheid, and provides a comparison of changing attitudes. Often, the image we associate with apartheid involves two ethnic groups: one black and one white. An interesting element of this setting, however, is the number of different ethnic groups that are present, all of which have had to work out their cultural and linguistic identities in the new South Africa. There are also a large number of languages present. Eleven of these are recognized by the government officially: English, Afrikaans, Zulu, Xhosa, and seven other African languages (Kamwangamalu 2001); language planning and policy, though, are still in a period of adjustment and uncertainty. This section presents some of the sociolinguistic research that has been done so far on South Africa in an attempt to address at least some of the issues related to language and ethnicity in this complex context.

Blacks in South Africa

The ethnic groups for which the end of apartheid meant the biggest changes are clearly those that were classified as "Black." This is also the group in which individuals are most likely to have a language other than Afrikaans or English as their mother tongue. Gough (1996) reports that one frequent pattern for many speakers is to use either an African language or a mix of that language and English in ordinary encounters. For most Black students, he notes, it is common for schooling to begin in the relevant African language, after which a sudden transition to immersion in English is made. Recently, however, a growing number of Black students have begun to attend completely English-medium schools, and some studies cited by Gough suggest that at least a partial language shift has taken place, with the mother tongue declining in favor of English. Whereas English was previously a functional language for most Black speakers, used in formal public situations or as a lingua franca for those who did not share another language, this new trend has led to an increased use of English across more settings, even at home.

The dialect of English spoken by most Black South Africans, then, is one that grew out of a setting where most speakers were second-language learners, much like Chicano English, discussed in Chapter 4. As with Chicano English, though, the dialect is now a first language for a growing number of speakers. The characteristics of this dialect are described in some detail by Gough (1996). Below are a selection of the features he identifies as typical of Black South African English (BSAfE).

Phonology

- overall, vowel systems characteristic of the local African languages, which have either a five- or seven-vowel system
- contrasts found in other dialects of English are lost, so that for example /ʌ/, /æ/, and /ɑ/ are all merged as [ɑ]
- **short vowel** and **long vowel** contrasts, e.g., /i/ and /ɪ/, may also be lost (merged as [i])
- loss of glides, with [ej] and [ow] realized as [e] and [o]
- no reduction of unstressed vowels; schwa realized as a full vowel (often [ɑ])
- stopping of interdental fricatives [ð] and [θ]
- "r" realized as a trill, rather than a liquid
- final stop **devoicing**
- variations in stress on multisyllabic words
- tendency toward syllable timing rather than stress timing

Grammatical structures

- **mass nouns** treated as **count nouns** (*a luggage*)
- omission of articles (*He was good man.*)
- resumptive pronouns (*The man who I saw him . . .*)
- unexpected gender on pronouns (*she* used for a male)
- absence of plural –*s* marking (*all our subject*)
- absence of third singular –*s* marking (*The survival of a person depend on education.*)
- use of present for past tense (*In 1980 the boycott starts.*)
- extension of contexts for prepositions (*They were refusing with my book.*)
- inversion in embedded questions (*I asked him why did he go.*)
- use of particle *nè* as a tag question (comes from Afrikaans)

There are discourse patterns and stylistic norms that characterize BSAfE as well, and the discussion of these will be picked up in Chapter 8.

The key question here is this: What role does BSAfE play in the construction of ethnic identity for Black South Africans? The answer is a complicated one. Gough (1996) notes that, among those who have been educated entirely in English, there is a tendency to view it as a symbol of elite status. Historically, English was also viewed by some as a symbol of black unity, providing a common language for speakers of diverse African language backgrounds, without the oppressor-language connotations of Afrikaans. Others have expressed concerns about English, particularly the ways in which access to it can be unequal through the educational system. Nonetheless, in either case, the views are tied to some standard variety of English. Gough cites several studies showing that the local, non-standard variety described above is stigmatized, as is the case in so many other places. Interestingly, another trend Gough mentions is the positive evaluation of American English (particularly AAVE) by urban black speakers.

It is not easy to predict what will develop linguistically among Black South African speakers in the future. Their situation is a unique and challenging one, in that they do not have, a priori, a single clear language tied to their ethnicity. For those who speak an African language, the mother tongue may be a symbol of ethnicity, but there are signs that younger speakers may be in the process of language shift. Even if certain African languages are strengthened and revitalized, the particular political history of South Africa has left a desire in at least some Black speakers for a code to represent unity across the Black ethnic groups, who have shared the history of oppression and now share in the governing of the country (de Klerk and Gough 2002). It may be that, as more time passes and more speakers grow up with English as a first language, BSAfE will increasingly function in that role, despite the negative attitudes associated with it as a non-standard dialect.

In addition, Gough found a growing presence of both code-switching (English and one or more African languages) and urban slang in the media, especially in magazine articles on topics related to township life and black identity. Similarly, Makhudu (2002) discusses the increasing use of a mixed code, Flaaitaal, based on Afrikaans and Bantu languages, used by black males in urban centers. It may be that elements of Flaaitaal, or even elements of AAVE as mentioned before, will be incorporated along with BSAfE to construct the new black South African identity.

Indian South Africans

There is a long history of migration of workers from India to South Africa. The Indians who immigrated, according to Mesthrie (2002b), were not speakers of English, but in the mid-twentieth century, schooling in English led to a rapid increase in English fluency. At the current time, a strong language shift has taken place, such that a large percentage of Indian South Africans are now monolingual in English (Kamwangamalu 2001, Bharuthram 2003). Like many of the other English dialects that have been discussed, Indian South African English (ISAE) shows the effects of having developed in a language contact situation, even when used by completely monolingual speakers. Its distinctiveness is probably also attributable in part to the lack of interethnic contact with speakers of standard varieties imposed by apartheid. One of the key aspects of ISAE is the variation within it, so that some speakers use a variety that is similar in some ways to the South African standard varieties, except for the phonological system, while others incorporate a wider range of non-standard features (see Mesthrie [2002b] for a discussion of parallels with the creole continuum). A selection of the main characteristics of ISAE, as listed in Mesthrie (1996) and (2002b), is given below, with the caveat just mentioned – that speakers vary immensely in terms of how many features they use (in general, or across specific situations):

Phonology

- many similarities to Indian English (as spoken in India), but less of some features, e.g., **retroflexion** of consonants
- a syllable-timed rhythm

Grammatical structures

Most common features
- use of *y'all* as second plural pronoun
- copula after *wh–* in indirect questions (*Do you know what's roti?*)
- extended use of partitive *of* (*He's got too much of money.*)

Other features
- **topicalization** (<u>Banana</u>, *you want?*)
- sentence-external placement of certain elements (<u>Lucky</u>, *they never come. <u>I like</u> children must learn our mother tongue.*)
- coordination without markers, or with markers specific to the variety (*She was calling, she was telling . . . I made rice too, I made roti too.*)

- double marking of clause relations (*But it'll come, but too late.*)
- *stay* and *leave* used as aspectual markers for habituality and completion, respectively (*They used to fight an' stay*, meaning "They used to fight all the time." *She filled the bottle an' left it*, meaning "she filled the bottle completely.")
- resumptive pronouns (*I'm a man I don't go church an' all.*)
- copula deletion (*Where that place?*)
- extension of contexts for prepositions (*He's got no worries of anyone.*)
- intonation rather than *do*-support for yes–no questions (*You bought cheese?*)

There are also a number of specific lexical items and semantic extensions of items that characterize ISAE.

Overall, then, English currently has a much more pervasive and entrenched role among Indian ethnic groups than it does among Black South Africans, given that a large percentage of Indian South Africans have no other language they can use to signal their ethnic identity. Since ISAE is considered a colloquial or vernacular variety (Mesthrie 2002b), many of the usual issues about standardization and dialect prejudice are relevant, and some speakers may experience pressure, in school or elsewhere, to learn a more standard-like variety. On the other hand, as with Black South Africans, English provides a link among people who may not share the same linguistic heritage. In the post-apartheid era, the sense of "Indian South Africans" as a group may be more important than association with a specific group (e.g., "Tamils"), with a unique variety of English serving to index this pan-Indian identity.

"Coloured" South Africans

In addition to the ethnic groups discussed so far, some interesting research has been conducted on speakers living on the Cape Peninsula. These speakers were classified under the apartheid system as "Coloured," although the term now may have strong negative connotations. As mentioned in Chapter 1, this group was designated by the government as neither white nor black, and included mixed-race speakers, but also some people of single ethnic origins, such as Malay slaves. Socially, this group shows some parallels with communities in other places that have been viewed politically as being in the "border areas" of ethnicity. The geographic region that is currently referred to in the literature as District Six, where much of the research was conducted, was originally settled by a highly diverse group of immigrants, including Europeans (Dutch, Eastern European Jews, and others), former slaves, people from other parts of Africa, and so forth. In this linguistically diverse climate, Afrikaans and English became the dominant languages, the latter propagated in great part through the school system (McCormick 2002b). Under the system of apartheid, much of this area was systematically destroyed. Only a small area was left intact (District Six), to be inhabited by people who were classified as "Coloured" by the government.

Unlike the other groups discussed, this one did not have a particular language that could clearly be identified as part of its heritage (even one no longer spoken much, as with Indian South Africans). Instead, what developed was a unique (and quite rich) range of vernacular varieties, which are currently evolving in interesting ways as part of the ethnic identity of this group. To begin with, the English spoken in this area was mostly a second language, historically, although there is some evidence that young people today are acquiring more (and more standard-like) English in school than their parents (McCormick 2002b). The more significant variety in the community is a non-standard variety of Afrikaans, one that evolved out of contact with English, and contains a large percentage of English lexical items. McCormick (2002b) argues for a third vernacular variety: code-switching between the English and Afrikaans varieties. There are clear motivations for this classification in the sociopolitical attitudes of the speakers themselves, which I will return to in a moment. The local term *kombuistaal* is used for both non-standard Afrikaans and the code-switching variety. McCormick lists some features of the non-standard varieties of Afrikaans and English in this community, focusing especially on linguistic convergence between them. In addition, Malan's (1996) study focuses just on linguistic features of the English of the area. The features identified by these studies include the following.

Non-standard Afrikaans

- different rules for verb order; speakers tend to keep modal or auxiliary verbs adjacent to the main verb in situations where Afrikaans would have an intervening element
- semantic extensions from English, e.g., use of *daai* ("that" demonstrative adjective) as a pronoun, paralleling English pronoun *that*
- significant numbers of lexical items borrowed from English

Non-standard (or "Cape Flats") English

- non-standard subject–verb agreement (*It fall down. They makes a lot of sense.*)

- use of "did" to mark simple past (*He did eat his food.*)
- deletion of auxiliary verbs (*We five in the family. I got two uncles.*)
- extension of contexts for prepositions (*He get a lift by his father. She went with the aeroplane.*)
- different placement of adverbs (*My daddy bring me tonight chips. I want also a lift.*)
- topicalization (*My friend he ride home.*)
- multiple negation (*I didn't catch nothing.*)
- loan translations involving word for word translations from Afrikaans

I have focused here on morphological, syntactic, and semantic elements, but Malan (1996) also discusses phonological features characteristic of some varieties of English in this community.

Apart from the varieties of Afrikaans and English that are spoken, McCormick (2002b), as mentioned earlier, argues for the identification of code-switching as a third variety in the community, separate from the already "mixed" varieties above. In theory, one could treat code-switching in this way for any community where it is prominent. But there is evidence that such an analysis is particularly appropriate here, in terms of the attitudes of the speakers themselves and their construction of identity. Because McCormick's research was conducted partly in the 1980s during apartheid, and partly in the 1990s after it ended, she is in a good position to track changing attitudes.

In the majority of communities where non-standard dialects and code-switching have been studied, these forms are viewed very negatively by speakers, and the standard varieties are more likely to be accorded **overt prestige**. At least among some District Six residents, though, the "pure" varieties of the two languages can also provoke overt criticism, at least in the context of informal neighborhood interactions. When one older resident in McCormick's study was asked how he would feel if one of his neighbors spoke to him in "pure English" or "pure Afrikaans," he responded in the local Afrikaans variety, "Then I would say to him, 'Hey, you must talk properly now!'" Another responded in English that he would say, "What's wrong with you? Keeping yourself high and mighty?" (2002b:224). There are also instances where a speaker claimed not to understand the "pure" variety: "The Afrikaans like the white nationalist Afrikaners speak – that pure Afrikaans – I can't understand that either. I can only understand the way we speak it" (McCormick 2002a:99). Accusations of snobbery associated with the use of a particularly educated-sounding variety, especially in specific situations, are not unusual, but the degree of overt criticism for the standard variety in general seems heightened in this community.

The explanation for these attitudes, and for the role of both the "mixed" non-standard Afrikaans and code-switching as varieties in the community, lies in the social and political history of this ethnic group. To begin with, District Six, by accounts in oral records, seems to have been a place where a very diverse group of residents were knit together as a community, interacted at deep levels (including inter-marriage), and supported each other economically through difficult times. McCormick (2002a:49) claims that the kind of economic inter-dependence described by residents, with a great deal of bartering and extending of credit, would have required "flexibility and creativity" linguistically as well.

The value of the mixed codes available in the community, though, is not just practical; it is also highly symbolic in the construction of ethnic identity. The people in District Six were marginalized by the apartheid government, denied the rights and privileges accorded to whites because of their (presumed) racially mixed ancestry. It is not surprising that they would view attitudes about "linguistic purity" with the same suspicion accorded to notions of "racial purity." As McCormick notes, "In District Six, a concern for linguistic purity came to be seen as the province of those whites who had declared them 'other' and rejected and often humiliated them" (2002b:222). On the other hand, people in District Six generally did not have heritage family languages to which they could turn for identity, as the Black South Africans did. In this setting, the mixed codes, particularly the local vernacular Afrikaans, acquired **covert prestige** and have come to be symbolic of "mixed" people, a way of subverting the marginalization of this border area identity. The long history of District Six as a place where a diverse group of people lived together in relative harmony left this legacy in the linguistic system, which survived even after the laws of apartheid imposed a physical and geographic separation of groups. In the New South Africa, this heterogeneous ethnic group uses a set of linguistic codes that reflects their identity and heritage in a strikingly appropriate metaphorical way.

This is not to say that there are no negative attitudes toward the vernacular varieties. Vernacular Afrikaans, particularly in the 1980s interviews from McCormick's research, was often labeled negatively as stupid, bastardized, and so forth. These attitudes could also be found with respect to code-switching, which was described as confusing, silly, or messing up the language (McCormick 2002a:97–101). But even in the apartheid era, not all community residents shared this view, and these codes were still seen as valuable signs of community membership, intimacy, and solidarity.

McCormick (2002a) tracks certain trends in attitudes as part of the current situation of this ethnic group. To begin with, there are more positive values associated with Standard English. For example, one speaker claimed that she tries to speak only English with her children, saying (in the local vernacular Afrikaans), "You go far in life with English now . . . even if you are now a brown girl but if you speak English then you get a job really easily" (McCormick 2002b:225). Note, however, the very clear separation of functional value from identity; ethnicity with respect to English is presented almost as an opposition. Even though English is used for many functions in the community, such as schooling or formal meetings, it is not at this point associated with ethnicity in the way that vernacular Afrikaans or code-switching are. In fact, there is stronger evidence that English is associated with whiteness by this community.

The most significant trend is probably the growing acceptance and positive evaluation of the vernacular varieties. Speakers overtly counter the negative attitudes cited earlier, with comments like "I don't think it's stupid. Look here: we coloureds grew up speaking kombuistaal, right? Which is Afrikaans and English mixed" (McCormick 2002a:93) – note that this citation itself is translated from the mixed code. One speaker in McCormick's study who had only recently returned to the local area expressed regret that his children knew mostly English and had not had the opportunity to learn vernacular Afrikaans (2002a:131). In fact, many community members had a strong negative reaction to those who did not know or refused to use the vernacular codes, following the general pattern that was discussed in Chapter 2. One woman said of people who refuse to use the mixed code, "That makes me angry . . . They totally deny themselves where they come from" (2002a:131-2). It seems that, despite its controversial role historically in South Africa, Afrikaans is destined to survive among people in District Six, in this adapted form which so iconically indexes ethnic identity for the community.

5.3 MAORIS IN NEW ZEALAND

The situation of Maoris in New Zealand is different in a number of ways from the other settings that have been discussed so far. The majority population of European descent is called by the ethnic term *Pakeha* (a Maori term, the significance of which will be discussed in

Chapter 7). The Maori, the indigenous people of New Zealand, are the largest minority population by far in the country (at about 14 percent, according to Bell [1999]), although there are also Pacific Islanders who have immigrated there, as well as a few other small groups of European or Asian descent. One factor that sets the situation in New Zealand apart, then, is the relatively binary quality of interethnic relations, in contrast with the multiple ethnicities found in the other two places. According to Holmes, these two ethnic groups "mix freely in almost all domains in New Zealand society" (1997a:67), which also contrasts with a number of the other settings that have been explored. Nonetheless, socioeconomic differences between the groups mean that in practice there is more interethnic contact in working-class and lower-income groups than in the middle class. Bell (1999) notes that to some degree the boundary between Pakeha and Maori is not sharp, since many Maori now also have Pakeha in their ancestry. Nonetheless, ideologies about ethnic differences remain.

Another interesting facet of this particular setting is that, as Bell and Holmes put it, New Zealand is "one of the world's most monolingual nations," with English as the only language of 90 percent of the population (1991:153). For the Maori, the loss of the heritage language is more complete than in any of the cases that have been discussed so far, except for Indians in South Africa. Even though Maori is one of New Zealand's official languages, it is clearly endangered. Bell (1999) notes that Maori is now spoken natively by only a few thousand people, most of whom are elderly, despite a number of revitalization efforts (see Benton 1991, Holmes 1997a). Since English is the dominant language for almost all Maori, it makes sense to look for the construction of ethnic identity in English, apart from any role that attitudes toward or use of Maori may play. If South Africa, then, represents an extreme of ethnic and language contact – multiple mixed and unmixed ethnic groups, numerous languages and codes – New Zealand represents the other end of the continuum. Here we have just two salient groups and only one main language to work with. How will the construction of ethnicity be similar or different?

While other groups that have been discussed clearly have their own distinct varieties of English or another dominant language, whether or not the Maori have such a variety has been a matter of debate. A book on English varieties in different parts of the world includes a chapter entitled "Maori English: a New Zealand myth?" (Benton 1991). Benton surveys a number of studies comparing Maori and Pakeha speakers and concludes that there is no clear indication of a set of phonological and grammatical features distinguishing such a variety. Some studies found a quantitatively higher presence of non-standard syntactic forms among Maori schoolchildren, but since all the forms were also used by Pakeha children of similar socioeconomic status they could not be considered distinctive markers. Nonetheless, a quantitatively higher use of non-standard forms could itself be an ethnic marker. Benton's conclusions about the existence of "Maori English" are pessimistic, although he suggests that English might be used "semantically and figuratively" in a different way by Maori speakers (1991:195).

It would certainly be fascinating to find that a distinct ethnic and racial group of significant size, subject to prejudice and cultural oppression (such as the historical banning of Maori), did not index ethnicity in any way through language. But, as my including them in this chapter may have hinted, further research has shown that in fact Maori speakers *do* index their ethnicity through language. Holmes (1997a) suggests that there are a number of linguistic features that came up in earlier studies that may distinguish Maori English. A few of these may be used only by Maori speakers; potential candidates include:

- stopping of interdental fricatives
- plural marking on count nouns, as in *We collected the fire-woods*
- use of *went to* as a past marker, i.e., *They went to make a house* for "They made a house"

Overall, however, the majority of differences seem to be quantitative. For example, one study that Holmes cites found that Maori women used irregular past tense forms (*He seen it*), marked –*s* inflection on verbs other than third singular (*They goes there*), deleted auxiliary *have*, and used negative concord. These forms were used far less by Pakeha women of the same age and socioeconomic background. Holmes' summary of what previous studies suggest about Maori English is that there exists a variety used by people in lower social classes with certain differences in vocabulary, grammar, and phonology, and also a higher-status variety that retains only some pronunciation features. This description sounds remarkably like the use of AAVE in many situations in the USA, where certain non-standard features are used primarily by working-class speakers, while middle-class speakers often speak Standard African American English, a variety that differs from other dialects mainly in phonetic features.

Holmes (1997a) conducts her own acoustic analysis of three phonetic variables, all of which were found to be significantly more frequent among Maori as compared with Pakeha of the same age and social class. The variables Holmes analyzed were:

- unaspirated initial /t/ (used seven times as often by Maori)
- devoiced final /z/, e.g., *was* pronounced [wəs] (used four times as often by Maori)
- use of full rather than reduced vowels in unstressed syllables (used almost twice as often by Maori)

All of the speakers in the study were classified as middle class, which suggests that even higher uses of these features might be found in other social groups. In addition, the features can all be traced to patterns in Maori, even though the people who used them were not necessarily Maori speakers themselves. As with other situations, the heritage language can leave an imprint on dialects associated with ethnic identity, even when use of the language is no longer widespread. Holmes suggests that the symbolic value of features like these as identity markers actually becomes more significant when the heritage language is less available as an ethnic marker. She predicts that "the use of at least some features of ME [Maori English] is likely to increase with the decline in the numbers of native speakers of Maori" (1997a:83). This type of pattern also fits the trajectories of language change in many of the other groups that have been discussed, such as the Cajuns, above, who are recycling features of French-influenced English as French usage declines. On the other hand, Bell (1997) found that young Maori speakers are shifting toward more use of the centralized /ɪ/ variant that characterizes the speech of Pakeha New Zealanders, and away from the more close front variant used by older Maori speakers, so the pattern of change is complex and not unidirectional.

Looking beyond phonological and syntactic features, we find that Maori English has particular pragmatic features that serve as ethnic markers as well, again in a quantitative rather than qualitative way. Meyerhoff (1994) explored use of the discourse particle *eh* among working-class Pakeha and Maori New Zealanders. She found that this marker was used much more often by Maoris, who generated about 85 percent of all the tokens used. Interestingly this same proportion was found for Maori *interviewers* in the study as well. Young and middle-age group Maori men in particular had extremely high values for this feature. Meyerhoff notes that *eh* has clear similarities to the Maori tag particle *ne*. Interestingly, some of the young working-class Pakeha women used more *eh* than other Pakeha speakers. In particular, three of the five young women in the study had Maori or Pacific Islander partners, and these women had a higher use of *eh* than the other two, suggesting that interethnic contact and identification with the Maori ethnic group plays a key role in this pattern.

Other differences in the speech of Maori versus Pakeha New Zealanders may occur at an even more abstract level. Stubbe (1998), for example, examined the use of **backchanneling** (listener feedback to the speaker) in a corpus of conversational New Zealand English. The participants were middle-class speakers aged 40 to 60. Stubbe found that, overall, Maori listeners used about a third fewer verbal feedback responses than Pakeha speakers, a result that was statistically significant. She also found that the use of explicitly supportive verbal responses was linked closely to gender. Maori still used these particles less than Pakeha overall, but Maori women were more similar to Pakeha women, and used more of these responses than the men. Again, we see that gender interacts with the expression of ethnicity. Stubbe also suggests that Maori may be more tolerant of silence than Pakeha are, and that they may prefer to convey meaning in a more implicit way than Pakeha speakers, relying more heavily on context.

As with some of the other minority ethnic groups that have been discussed, the speech patterns among young Maori seem to show a combination of elements indexing ethnic identity and larger national identity. Some features of older varieties of Maori English, like front /ɪ/, are being lost in a shift toward markers of general New Zealand identity. Other features are increasing among younger speakers, such as the use of *eh* (particularly among men). In terms of the sociohistorical context, Maori culture appears to be experiencing a renaissance somewhat like that which was described for the Cajuns. Bell (1999), for example, discusses the widespread use of Maori cultural symbols in nationally oriented advertising. In addition, the attempts to revitalize Maori continue to be salient in the national consciousness, regardless of how successful they are in preventing the extinction of the language. In the context of this cultural renaissance, it will be interesting to observe whether certain Maori-marked phonetic features that seemed to be less frequent in the younger generation, such as unaspirated /t/ (Holmes 1997a), become "recycled" in the way that the Cajun features were.

DISCUSSION QUESTIONS

1. In what ways is using another language in the construction of ethnic identity different from using a separate dialect of the

dominant language? In what ways are these two phenomena similar?

2. It has been noted that the construction of ethnic identity occurs in the context of other social factors such as gender, age, social class, and so forth. How do the case studies presented here illustrate this pattern?

3. For each of the three multiethnic settings in this chapter, a number of social and political trends were discussed. Try to project these trends into the future, in terms of how they might affect language. What do you think will happen to the languages and varieties in each of these places? For instance, will they become more similar or different? Do you think any varieties will die out altogether?

SUGGESTIONS FOR FURTHER READING

Cheshire, Jenny, ed. 1991. *English around the World: Sociolinguistic Perspectives.* Cambridge and New York: Cambridge University Press.

A collection of chapters by prominent linguists on variation in English as it is used in a number of different countries, focusing on structural features as well as social and political contexts.

De Klerk, Vivian, ed. 1996. *Focus on South Africa.* Amsterdam, The Netherlands: John Benjamins.

This book collects chapters by a number of authors focusing on linguistic features and patterns among different ethnic groups and geographic areas in South Africa.

Dubois, Sylvie; Horvath, Barbara M. 2003a. Creoles and Cajuns: a portrait in black and white. *American Speech* 78:192–207.

One of a numerous series of articles by these two authors, exploring various aspects of language in Louisiana, and focusing particularly on the role of language variation in the construction of ethnic and cultural identity.

Holmes, Janet. 1997a. Maori and Pakeha English: some New Zealand social dialect data. *Language in Society* 26:65–101.

One of relatively few quantitative articles on ethnicity and language in New Zealand, looking in depth at particular sociolinguistic variables and their distribution among different ethnic groups.

Mesthrie, Rajend, ed. 2002a. *Language in South Africa.* Cambridge: Cambridge University Press.

A modern collection of chapters on linguistic variation in South Africa, focusing particularly on the changing historical and political context and how that has affected the numerous varieties available to South Africans in different ethnic and regional groups, including issues of language contact and language policy.

6 Are white people ethnic? Whiteness, dominance, and ethnicity

"[clear throat] Oh goodness! [clear throat]"
"What's the matter, Chance?"
"[clear throat] I don't know, Schuyler. [clear throat] I have a scratchy sensation
I am not familiar with. [clear throat] I better schedule an MRI [clear throat]."
(George Lopez doing "white" characters, *Right Now Right Now*, 2001)

I discuss issues of racial identity, including what it means to be "white," with my colleagues and students all the time. But my first experience with this particular concept outside the academic setting occurred when my husband and I were having dinner at a Mexican restaurant (a big chain type) near our home in Southern California. We got into a conversation with the waiter, who was European-American, on the topic of beers. My husband, for reasons known only to himself, asked, "What's the first beer you remember drinking?" The waiter answered, "Budweiser," but he followed up with a comment that interested me. "You gotta understand," he explained, "my family is all white people, you know? I don't mean to be racist or anything, but it's true. And that's what they drink: Budweiser, Miller Genuine Draft, or Coors." Many things struck me about this response: his stereotyping of whites as a group, his apology and identification of the stereotype as potential racism, and his willingness to discuss issues about his family's construction of ethnicity with two total strangers. I asked for his permission to include his comments in this book, because it seems to me that discussions of "whiteness" outside of academia generally occur in the context of contrasts with other groups, rather than in the abstract, making this interaction somewhat unusual, at least in my experience.

Many people might look at the title of this chapter and find the question absurd. Of course white people are ethnic; there is no such thing as a lack of ethnicity, just as there is no such thing as a dialect without an "accent." Everything is relative, and being a member of the dominant group will certainly change one's day-to-day experience of ethnicity, but that does not mean that ethnicity is absent. Nonetheless, there is good evidence that being "white" is not just another ethnicity, one neutral side of a neat boundary that divides, e.g., "White–Black" or "White–Latino" or "Pakeha–Maori." In places where people of European descent are the dominant group (which includes a majority of the places for which we have sociolinguistic studies of ethnicity), such ethnic boundaries are never neutral, because the two sides are not equal in terms of political power or influence on the dominant ideology.

One of the repercussions of this difference, in practice, is that their own whiteness can be invisible to members of the dominant culture, as highlighted in the emerging field of whiteness studies within sociology and anthropology. Hill (1998), in her discussion of white public space, identifies a set of contexts in which white people are seen as "invisibly normal" while other groups are both visible and marginal. Similarly, Bell comments, "Pakeha [white New Zealanders] are the dominant ethnicity and culture within New Zealand, but we tend to be identified by default, by what we are not rather than what we are . . . not Maori, not Polynesian, not Australian, not British, not European" (1999:539). In their introduction to a special issue of the *Journal of Linguistic Anthropology* focusing on whiteness studies, Trechter and Bucholtz sum up this view: "[i]deologically, whiteness is usually absence, not presence: the absence of culture and color" (2001:5). It is this type of cultural invisibility for whiteness that made my conversation with the waiter seem notable. (As a number of scholars have pointed out, however, whiteness is much less likely to be invisible to members of other groups.)

In the dominant US discourse, it is not unusual for people of European descent to view themselves as lacking ethnicity, either partly or completely. A European-American friend said to me recently, "I wish I were more ethnic," as though, for her, ethnicity existed along a continuum, as something of which you could have a greater or lesser quantity. I perceive something similar among my European-American students, many of whom borrow clothing or hairstyles from African or Indian cultures, a sense among them that they are culturally empty in some way, and need to borrow from other cultures to fill that gap. One of the things they borrow is language, as will be discussed more in Chapter 10.

Even if we begin with the quite reasonable (to social scientists, at least) assumption that whiteness is a constructed ethnicity, like all ethnicities, *how* it is constructed must be viewed in the context of ideologies about dominant ethnic groups. A number of questions relevant to this context must be addressed, particularly with respect to the role of language in the construction of white ethnic identity. To begin with, stereotypes of minority groups may be easy to locate in the culture, while stereotypes of the dominant group (like those of the waiter, quoted above) may be more hidden or subtle. What stereotypes, particularly linguistic ones, might be associated with dominant groups, such as European-Americans, and where can we locate them? Also, is it possible to distinguish elements that characterize some more general category such as "educated" or "middle class" from the specific racial category of "whiteness" with which these categories might be conflated in public discourse? Furthermore, if a dialect of the dominant group is treated by society as unmarked or neutral in some sense, how can that dialect serve as an expression of ethnicity? (This is the same question that was raised in the discussion of the *Urban Invaders* documentary about the New York City residents, presented at the beginning of Chapter 2.) Finally, what are the consequences for members of other groups of using linguistic (and other) features associated with whiteness, a practice that might seem useful or necessary in a society where the dominant group sets the norms for public arenas such as the school system, government, multinational corporations, and so forth?

As scholars in the area of whiteness studies are careful to emphasize, the experience of being white is not monolithic, any more than the experiences of members of other groups. In some countries, the racial label "white" can apply to both majority and minority ethnic groups. Canada is a setting of this type, and a great deal of sociolinguistic research has been done on Francophone and Anglophone Canadians (e.g., Poplack 1989, Heller 1992, Thibault and Sankoff 1993, Blondeau et al. 2002).[1] In addition, the same group can be classified as "white" or "not white" differently over time. There are numerous discussions, for example, of European immigrant groups to the USA in the nineteenth century, particularly Italians and Irish, and how these groups were reclassified historically in terms of race, becoming what Zelinsky (2001) calls "unhyphenated whites." Zack, in her discussion of mixed race and the construction of race generally, comments, "before the 1920s white Anglo-Saxon Americans believed that Italian, Irish, and Polish immigrants were distinct races. No one would suggest that now" (1993:165). Perhaps the most famous study of this process is Ignatiev's *How the Irish Became White* (1995), which looks at a single group in the USA over time, in a political and historical context. In addition, a number of studies (e.g., Brander Rasmussen et al. 2001) have pointed out that certain members of white communities, such as gay individuals or those from low socioeconomic groups, may not be accorded the same types of privileges as others. Therefore, explorations of what it means to be "white" must be interpreted as being not about some essential quality of individuals, but about the dominant ideologies of race in a particular culture at a particular moment in time, in the same way that all explorations of race must be interpreted.

6.1 THE SOCIAL CORRELATES OF BEING WHITE

In general, ideologies concerning the social correlates of being white that we find in the discourse of societies like the USA follow directly from the dominant social position of white speakers and the privileges that being the dominant ethnic group affords. Whiteness is often associated with the middle class, for example. In Urciuoli's (1996) study of working-class Puerto-Rican Americans in New York City, this theme emerged frequently among the speakers she talked to, who often saw becoming middle class as inextricably linked with becoming more white. One man articulated this view in the following way:

> I'm doing this, I'm doing that. I'm gonna get to the middle class. What do I do with my skin color, do I go and dye my color? Do I go and dye my hair? Do I try to speak fluent English, use these sophisticated words? . . . [you] bring the same economic problems, the same racial problems, the same language problems. (1996:143)

The very first thing that strikes me about this excerpt is that the speaker mentions his own "language problems," and refers to them in other places, but it is clear from the excerpt that he is quite articulate and additionally commands a very standard variety of English. I will return to specifically language-related associations with whiteness below. But this serves as a good example of the association of whiteness with the middle class. Similarly, the African-American drag queens studied by Barrett (1999) often indexed white personas as part of performing female gender. One individual specifically referred to herself as a "white woman," and talked about a life of privilege, including shopping, lunch in restaurants, owning expensive jewelry, and so forth. Barrett points out that the term "white woman" when used in this way refers primarily to a class distinction rather than an ethnic distinction. In other words, the drag queens he studied indexed whiteness as a way of indexing a middle-class identity.

Whiteness is also often associated with education and/or intellectual orientation (Trechter and Bucholtz 2001). A Puerto-Rican American woman in the experimental part of Urciuoli's study, for example, who was asked to describe a speaker whose voice she heard on a tape, said, "she's white. She's very educated and chances are she could be a teacher" (1996:116). The listeners consistently linked educated-sounding voices to whiteness, although not all the speakers identified this way were in reality white. Similarly, Clark (2003) found that African-American high-school students identified a rhetorical style which he calls "abstract/speculative inquiry," and performed parodies of it in class, evoking "white linguistic stereotypes" among their inter-locutors. Bucholtz (2001) also found an association of whiteness with a scientific **register** among European-American "nerd" teenagers in California. While all the ideologies discussed here can be dangerous in their social repercussions, this link between education and whiteness seems particularly pernicious in the message it sends to people of other ethnic groups (which I will discuss more below). A similar but slightly different pattern is the association of whiteness with rationality and calm. For example, the teenage European-American boy in Bucholtz (1999b) uses a narrative involving both himself and several African-American participants to index his whiteness. In this narrative, as Bucholtz notes, he constructs himself as "nonconfrontational, reasonable, and *white*" (1999b:451). This ideology is also explored in the work of Kochman (1981), which will be discussed in Chapter 9.

One ideological pattern that seems a bit more complex, and does not follow directly from a social position of dominance, is that whiteness does not seem to be associated with masculinity. In the US racial ideology, which tends to dichotomize race as white versus black, for example, masculinity is more closely associated with "blackness." In the narrative from Bucholtz's (1999b) study, mentioned above, when the narrator emphasizes his whiteness, he is consistently linked to homophobic and misogynistic challenges to his masculinity, but when he begins to borrow AAVE features and introduces an interlocutor who links him symbolically to African-American culture, his masculinity (as portrayed in the narrative) is strengthened. Fordham and Ogbu (1986) found that the African-American high-school students in their study linked doing well in school not only with whiteness but also with homosexuality. Even the "white men can't jump" stereotype exploited in the movie of the same name seems to be an instance of this unphysical, unmasculine view of whiteness.

Finally, one key characteristic of the ideology of whiteness is that whiteness is "not cool," or "unhip" (and I use this latter term deliberately, with full knowledge of its African-American and ultimately African origins). For example, Bucholtz (2001) found that the youth culture in the California high school she studied associated coolness with the black students at the school. In contrast, the deliberately "uncool" stance taken by the nerd group was associated with being "too white." One consequence of this perspective is the constant borrowing of slang terms from AAVE into white varieties. As Smitherman points out, these terms are discarded by AAVE speakers once they move into the "white mainstream" (2000b:61).

I have not attempted to differentiate systematically here between ideologies held by communities of speakers who identify themselves as white and those that do not. In many cases there seems to be overlap, and the examples above come from studies of speakers of European-American ethnicity (e.g., Bucholtz 1999b, Bucholtz 2001) as well as studies of other groups. However, it seems probable that ingroup and outgroup views will differ in some respects. I will be discussing some specifically outgroup views of whiteness below.

6.2 THE LINGUISTIC CORRELATES OF BEING WHITE

The ideologies associated with linguistic aspects of whiteness often correlate with the social aspects discussed above in predictable ways. Three basic perspectives on language and whiteness seem to be dominant in the communities that have been the focus of recent anthropological and sociolinguistic studies:

1) Anything standard is associated with white speakers; for example, speaking standard varieties of English (which may be hard to define, but play an important ideological role).
2) A level of standardness that is somehow beyond the "basic" level is associated with white speakers, e.g., **superstandard** grammatical forms (see Wolfram and Schilling-Estes 1998:12–13) or highly specialized vocabulary.
3) Stereotyped (often stigmatized) varieties associated with a particular geographic region are seen as "white" e.g., Valley Girl dialects, New York City dialects.

Not all ideas about language and whiteness fall clearly into one of these categories, but they do encompass many of the perspectives found in sociolinguistic studies of language and ethnicity.

The first perspective is the one presented in Ogbu's (1999) study of African-Americans in California; Ogbu comments that "both voluntary and involuntary minorities consider standard English to be 'White language' and a symbol of White identity" (1999:154). In general, the African-Americans in his study believed that white Americans spoke "proper or correct English" and black Americans spoke "slang English." Fordham and Ogbu (1986) list "speaking standard English" as one of the characteristics that the African-American students in their study associated with "acting white" (in fact, it is the first item that the authors list, although this may not be significant). The same perspective can be found in the Puerto-Rican American community studied experimentally by Urciuoli (1996). Many of the listeners in the experiment linked standard grammatical forms to whiteness. One commented of a speaker on the tape (who in fact was white), "she's white . . . Because she knew where to put the letters where they belong, her English, her grammar was so good" (1996:116). Another man in Urciuoli's study said about a white Jewish male speaker on the tape, "He used the proper English, like 'ran'. If a Hispanic person would say that, he would say 'run'" (1996:116). His comment makes clear not only that he associates Standard English with whiteness, but in addition that he does not feel a standard variety could also potentially be associated with other groups, such as Latino speakers.

In other cases, whiteness seems to be associated not with *any* standard linguistic forms but rather with those that count as somehow at the extremes of the standard. This includes what have been called superstandard forms (Wolfram and Schilling-Estes 1998, Bucholtz 2001) such as "to whom" or "It is I," and overly careful phonetic articulations. It can also include lexical items that sound particularly technical or literary. This is the perspective on whiteness represented by the European-American "nerds" in Bucholtz's (2001) study, who use these sorts of features to construct identities that are seen by other European-Americans as "too white" in comparison with the language of their peers. The African-American students in Ogbu's study associated white speakers with, among other things, "a better vocabulary" (1999:163).

Lexical items also featured prominently in the ethnic characterizations of voices as white by participants in Urciuoli's (1996) experiment. About one speaker, listeners picked out words and phrases such as "rather" and "the new breed of sanitation" in classifying him as white. One listener said of the same person, "He talks English like a little bit of high-class, like when he says 'congestion'" (1996:115). Interestingly, the speaker being described is not white, but rather Puerto-Rican American. In another case, a listener gave this description of a woman (who was, in this case, white): "She's good, she is good . . . She's white, she's well-educated . . . very articulated, and she uses very very good words, like 'chronically'" (1996:115). What strikes me about this last example is not only the reference to certain lexical items, but also the very clear value judgments being expressed. The presumably white speaker is "good" and her words are also "good"; it seems highly probably that this listener has a corresponding "bad" category as well. This is language ideology at its most naked.

The final perspective on whiteness and language is in some ways the most interesting. It involves the association of whiteness with linguistic varieties that are regionally marked. The African-American students in Ogbu's (1999) study listed "valley talk" (presumably the stereotyped dialect that originated with California teenagers) as something they associated with white people. Similarly, a Korean-American boy from Chicago in Chun's (2001) study identified the Southern US item *y'all* as a white term that he felt he should resist using. This example illustrates the mismatch that can occur between perceptions of the language associated with a particular ethnicity and reality, since *y'all* is in fact used by people of many ethnicities in the South (as the two Texan Korean-Americans in Chun's study later point out). Another question that this example raises is how regional varieties can be associated with white ethnicity in places where the regional features are also shared by members of other groups. One answer appears to be that regional features may be parceled out, so that some features mark region, regardless of ethnicity (like *y'all*), and others are tied to a particular ethnicity. Wolfram and Schilling-Estes (1998:180) note with respect to the Southern US process of /ay/ monophthongization, for example, that only European-Americans apply the process before voiceless consonants, so that, for instance, *tahm* for "time" is considered just Southern, but *raht* for "right" is associated specifically with white speakers. Although this association with regional dialects is found less frequently in the literature than the other two perspectives, as an interpretation of the relationship between whiteness and language, it will become important in the analysis of humor, below.

6.3 THE CONSEQUENCES OF ''SOUNDING WHITE''

Is it bad to sound white? Despite all the privileges accorded to being in the dominant group, the answer at some level seems to be yes. Of course, speakers from other ethnic groups know that commanding a standard variety is a prerequisite for certain types of occupations, succeeding in the educational system, and more. And attitudes in various communities certainly reflect this reality at some level, despite the association of standard varieties with white speech. So, for example, the parents in Ogbu's (1999) study often encouraged their children to learn Standard English as a way of "getting into the system" and "learning the game." However, these same parents talked openly about the negative repercussions of being perceived as "talking white." One adult speaker in the study, for example, says of African-American members of his community:

> they would probably tend to be somewhat prejudicial of someone speaking very proper English, and they would probably make an assessment on that person's character as being "uppity" or . . . she is trying to be White, or something like that. (1999:170–1)

Similarly, Rickford gives the example of a black teenager in California who comments, "Over at my school . . . first time they catch you talkin' white, they'll never let it go" (1999:275). The most comprehensive study of this phenomenon is Fordham and Ogbu (1986), which looks in detail at the attitudes of African-American students, and ties attitudes about standard varieties and whiteness with difficulties in orienting towards success at school.

This critical view of sounding white occurs over and over in a number of different ethnic groups. For example, the Korean-Americans in Chun's (2001) study discuss the negative properties of sounding white, and express frustration about, among other things, Koreans adapting family names to a more Anglo-sounding phonetic form. The Puerto-Rican Americans in Urciuoli's (1996) study gave a long list of qualities associated with "acting white," and one of the most crucial ones was pretending not to know Spanish. They also mentioned trying to speak without "an accent," and anglicizing one's name as behaviors the community may view as undesirable. Interestingly, in Latino communities, "sounding white" may be seen as relevant to Spanish as well. One monolingual English speaker in Fought (2003) commented, "I have like a fear of speaking Spanish because I can't roll my r's and I don't want to sound like a white boy" (2003:203). I have focused here on the views of minority ethnic groups, but there are indications that this negative view of sounding white is sometimes shared by white speakers as well, as in Bucholtz's (2001) study of the "too white" nerds. Particularly in minority ethnic groups, though, these views set up a conflict for community members who want the privileges that speaking a standard variety affords, but do not want to be negatively sanctioned in the community for sounding white.

In Chapter 3, I discussed some of the ways that one group, middle-class African-American adults, resolves this conflict, including using a variety that is grammatically standard but includes non-standard or at least ethnically marked phonological forms. A different strategy was used by the low-income African-American students in Ogbu's (1999) study. The high-achieving students in this study countered the accusations of whiteness they drew from peers because of doing well in school or speaking a standard variety by emphasizing other traits in constructing their identities. The most frequent traits these students played up were athletic ability and acting "crazy" or being a clown. These choices are interesting in light of the ideologies about the social correlates of whiteness discussed above. The students used physicality and craziness to contrast with the intellectual orientation and rationality associated with whiteness.

6.4　HUMOR AND THE PORTRAYAL OF "WHITENESS"

As will be discussed further in Chapter 8, humor can be a crucial psychological resource, particularly among oppressed groups, and an important part of the construction of cultural identity. Humor based on stereotypes of the minority ethnic community that the comedian belongs to can serve a number of functions including political commentary, subversion of norms and expectations, and stressing of ingroup solidarity. Many of the same functions can be served by humor based on stereotypes of the outgroup, dominant community. In this section, I will look at two humor-based representations of "whiteness" by members of other groups: 1) Native-American "Whiteman" joking rituals and 2) the stand-up routines of US comedians. Each of these offers a slightly different view of the elements of whiteness, and how it is not, in fact, invisible or unmarked.

Portrayals of "The Whiteman" Among the Western Apache

Keith Basso, a European-American anthropologist, was working among the Western Apache in Arizona in the 1960s. At a certain point, well into his fieldwork, he witnessed an exchange that mystified him. An Apache man who had been speaking with a friend in Western Apache suddenly switched to English and began commenting loudly and angrily on the friend's health. After a few moments of this, everyone in the room except Basso began to laugh. When he asked the Apache man next to him what was going on, the man explained that it was a joke, specifically "He was just imitate a Whiteman. Pretty funny" (Basso 1979:7). Rather than becoming offended, as someone who was not an anthropologist might have, Basso seized the opportunity for research and wrote the now classic *Portraits of "The Whiteman"* (1979). The portraits tell us a good deal about how the Apache, at least at the time, viewed the white people with whom they had contact.

One of the ways Basso looks at this phenomenon is to take a single event of imitating the Whiteman and analyze the entire sequence in detail (1979:45–60). The focus of the joke is mainly on interactional norms, and the many ways in which typical European-American behaviors conflict with traditional Apache norms. In the sequence, the Apache joker enacts a "white" persona by doing a number of things:

- Using the term *my friend* frequently. Kinship and other relational terms are taken very seriously in Native-American groups, and it is perceived as offensive to use them lightly in this manner.
- Asking questions about the addressee's health. This topic is considered too personal by Apaches.
- Using ritual expressions that draw attention to another person, e.g., *Look who here! Look who just come in!* Generally, Apaches feel it is better not to draw attention unnecessarily to oneself or to others.
- Using the addressee's first name repeatedly. To Apaches, using someone's name indicates a close relationship. They explain this behavior in European-Americans somewhat jokingly as being an indication that they are very forgetful and must keep hearing something in order to remember it.[2]
- Touching the addressee. In public places, Apaches avoid physical contact if possible. They consider the type of back-slapping and patting and so forth done by European-Americans to be a violation of personal space.
- Giving direct commands, such as *Come in right now! Sit down!*, and so forth. These are a routine part of European-American hosting behaviors, but they are seen as rude and intrusive by Apaches, because they violate individuals' right to choose what they want to do.
- Using rapid-fire or repeated questions, without pausing for the addressee's response. *You hungry? You want some beer? . . . You want some crackers? Bread? You want some sandwich?* To me, this simply sounds like my Mediterranean mother and her food-offering rituals with guests, but Apaches find this behavior rude and unnecessarily repetitious. This example also illustrates the type of discourse pattern that can occur when two cultures have different norms for the appropriate length of pauses between turns (see Chapter 8).

- Talking about the future. Discussions of the future, especially on the topics of sickness or death are taboo to Apaches. European-Americans find this behavior unremarkable. There are even occasions, such as job interviews, where it is basically obligatory to talk about the future. This behavior is also encoded in many mainstream English-language departure rituals, e.g., *See you later*, or *Take care of yourself*.
- Making comments on the addressee's appearance. Like the health questions, Apaches see these as too personal and violating privacy.
- Using prosodic features associated with The "Whiteman," including a higher voice pitch, a much louder volume, and faster speed when talking. These features combine to produce an effect that Apaches associate with anger or scolding.

Certain themes recur across the elements of this portrayal that contribute to the overall picture of "whiteness" being enacted here.

One of the main issues is privacy and personal space. Native-Americans in general, across all the groups that have been studied, are on the low end of the continuum in terms of physical movement and taking up space (see, for example, Philips 1990). They tend to have what might be called a quieter physical presence: less movement when they are talking, less fuss when they enter or leave somewhere, less talking generally. In contrast, then, they view European-Americans as invading others' space by touching them, talking too loudly, or making eye contact (something European-Americans tend to view as respectful). The invasion of privacy can be metaphorical rather than physical, also: pointing someone out by commenting on their appearance, asking personal questions that they may not wish to answer, or telling them to sit down, whether they want to or not. These behaviors contribute to a view of European-Americans as feeling entitled to impose on others.

Another theme in the portrayal of the "white" persona is what might be termed carelessness. Matters which Apaches would take seriously, such as the use of someone's name or terms like *my friend*, are tossed off by European-Americans in a way that seems excessively casual. Talking about the future, which can be seen as a form of courting bad luck, is done frequently and without apparent hesitation. One sees portrayed in this and in some of the other categories a kind of naiveté about the world on the part of European-Americans, who don't seem to be aware of when they have crossed into serious territory in a conversation.

Finally, we see a certain level of impatience represented as a feature of "white" behavior. If a European-American speaker does not immediately get a response to a question, he or she repeats it right away or asks a different one, without allowing sufficient time, by Native-American standards, for an answer. Speech tends to be fast in general, as if European-Americans cannot wait to say whatever they are saying. Overall, the characteristics of European-Americans as presented in these performances reinforce the stereotype of a privileged group, imposing on others, taking up space, being careless in their behavior because as members of the dominant group, they do not need to be as careful as members of minority groups, who may feel their behavior is being scrutinized more carefully. These views coincide with ideologies about white speakers in other groups, such as Urciuoli's comment that speakers in her study sometimes expressed a view of white people as "naturally cold, controlling and greedy" (1996:27).

Stand-up routines of US comedians

In 1997, more than thirty years after Keith Basso witnessed his first Whiteman joke, Steve Harvey, an African-American comedian, produced *One Man*, a live performance of his stand-up comedy routine that appeared on a premium cable television network in the USA and was later released on DVD. This performance, too, contains a number of portrayals of whiteness. In addition, it is central to one of the first discussions of the role of comedians in the construction of ideologies about language and ethnicity, in Rickford and Rickford (2000). Specifically, the authors discuss one of Harvey's routines, which involves two office employees who are about to be fired – one European-American and one African-American. The boss doing the firing is also a European-American character. In giving voice to this scene, Harvey uses a number of features to represent white ethnicity, including the following (Rickford and Rickford 2000:60):

1. an "outlandish" nasal voice
2. Standard English grammar and phonology
3. corny slang/interjections: *Oh! Gee! Oh, Jesus!*

Although the authors don't mention them explicitly in the discussion, Harvey also uses other features in voicing his European-American characters that index stereotypes about the linguistic correlates of being white, which will be discussed more below.

Rahman (2003) conducts a study that is slightly larger in scope. She looks at the voicing of middle-class characters, both white and African-American, in fifteen monologues by African-American comedians. The characteristics that she finds are prevalent in the voicing of white characters include:

1. use of standard grammar (in marked contrast with African-American characters who are voiced with a heavy use of AAVE features)
2. standard phonology, e.g., including postvocalic *r*'s, sometimes overemphasizing them; initial interdental fricatives NOT stopped, *them* as [ðm]; /ay/ variable as a diphthong
3. *Brady Bunch*-type names, i.e., bland, conservative (e.g., *Bob, Becky, Amy*), in contrast with stereotypically African-American names (*Pookie, Tamika*)
4. corny, outmoded slang/interjections (e.g., *jiminy christmas, golly gee*)

In addition, I noticed in the excerpts she cites the frequent use of:

5. politeness formulas, e.g., *How was your weekend? Oh, I love your outfit!*

The features highlighted by both Rickford and Rickford (2000) and Rahman (2003) give a preliminary view of how whiteness is performed, and can be tied in with some of the ideologies mentioned above. Before doing so, however, I want to add some further data to the analysis.

For my own informal study, I decided to focus on two comedians who frequently incorporate the performance of white characters into their routines: Steve Harvey (an African-American male) and George Lopez (a Mexican-American male). I included Steve Harvey because I was interested in looking at his entire routine in a bit more detail than the brief analysis given by Rickford and Rickford (2000). I included George Lopez because it is important to look at portrayals by comedians who are not African-American, to see which characteristics of whiteness appear to be widespread. For Steve Harvey, I used the entire performance of *One Man* (1999), which runs for about ninety minutes, keeping track of any features that occurred in the portrayals of white characters. For George Lopez, I used the performance *Right Now Right Now* (2001), which was about eighty minutes, again keeping track of features associated with white performances. In both cases my analysis was qualitative. I did not attempt to count the exact number of occurrences of each feature, although such an analysis could also be done. I also listened to a number of other comedians who perform white characters, just to get some idea of the degree of consensus. These included: Eddie Murphy (an African-American male), Carlos Mencia (a Latino male), and Margaret Cho (a Korean-American female).

Steve Harvey has performed a number of comedy routines now available on DVD, had his own television show for a while (it lasted six seasons), and is currently a talk show host. He was also featured in the film *The Original Kings of Comedy* (2000). Below is a brief excerpt from *One Man* to provide some sense of what Harvey's performances of white personas entail:

> ["white" voice] "Hey, Bob? Bob, can I see you in my office for a moment please?"
> [AAVE] Bob says, "Sure thing, Tom." Bob stood right up, walked right into Tom's office and said,
> ["white" voice] "Uh, Tom? You wanted to see me?"
> [AAVE] What the hell do you mean does he want to see you? He just walked out to yo desk and said, Bob, can I see you in my office for a minute. What is this bullshit about? It's denial. He don't see it comin'. And Tom proceeded to firing Bob right by the book.
> ["white" voice] "You know Bob, at the board meeting this past week, and after going over the board, we were kinda lookin at your evaluation. And well, to tell you the truth, you're just not cuttin it."
> [look of shock] "Tom, what are ya sayin?"
> [AAVE] You know good and hell well what he's sayin. Yo ass is almost outta here. You see what the hell's goin' on, but denial. [taps head] Tom said,
> ["white" voice] "Listen to me. Bob, you're makin this so difficult. I know you're gonna have a tough time explaining this to Becky. But we're gonna hafta let you go."
> [look of sadness] "Oh. Oh, Jesus. Oh, Tom, what am I gonna do? What about the mortgage? What about the children's college fund? Oh, Father God!"

Throughout *One Man*, Harvey employs AAVE as his baseline variety, the one he uses to address the audience directly most of the time. In some places he uses a more standard variety (Standard African American English; see Chapter 3). He also has what might be termed a "hyper-AAVE" register that he switches to in voicing some African-American characters, which includes an even greater use of AAVE features, particularly the most stigmatized lexical, grammatical, and phonetic features.

In contrast, the various white characters Harvey performs exhibit the following features:

1. nasal voice
2. Standard English grammar and phonology
3. corny expressions/interjections: *Oh! Gee, young Tim, For Pete's sake!*
4. religious interjections: *Oh Father God!, Jesus!*
5. politeness formulas that are specifically empty. [To boss] *You wanted to see me?, To tell you the truth . . .*
6. conservative names: *Tom, Becky* (in contrast with African-American names *Willie* and *Willamena*); also frequent use of names by characters in addressing each other
7. formal language: *a service* (for "church")
8. higher pitch in voicing European-American than African-American characters
9. animated, happy affect: *This is great!, Warm days and sunny rays*
10. hedges/intensifiers: *kinda, well, you know, so*

The first three are the elements mentioned by Rickford and Rickford (2000). The others involve elements of both linguistic form (**hedges** and **intensifiers**, prosodic features) and discourse features (politeness formulas, happy affect). In general, I would describe the dialect selected by Harvey for most of his white characters as "Midwestern," if I had to assign it a regional origin. I will return to this below.

George Lopez is a Mexican-American comedian who currently has his own television show, a situation comedy somewhat like Steve Harvey's. In another parallel, he appeared in *The Original Kings of Latin Comedy* (2003), which attempted to capitalize on the success of the older film. Like Harvey, Lopez voices a number of white characters; in fact, I would say that he performs even more of them, involving a wider range of personas, than Harvey does. The excerpt that began the chapter involves two such characters. Here is an additional excerpt from *Right Now Right Now* that illustrates some of the characteristics of his "white" voices:

> [Chicano English] Other people are happy when they see somebody. You know, they save seats for them.
> ["white" voice] "Oh my gawd, this is Brian's chair, alright? When Brian comes this is his chair, I got a email, he is coming. He confirmed earlier through an email."
> [Chicano English] And when they see 'em they wave 'em over.
> ["white" voice] "Oh my gawd! Brian, oh my gawd! We're totally over here! Oh my gawd!"
> [Chicano English] They'll call you on the cell phone.
> ["white" voice] "Oh my gawd! I am totally in front of you, oh my gawd!"

Lopez, like Harvey, exhibits some variation in terms of his "regular" voice, used to address the audience. It is usually Chicano English, a non-standard variety, though in other places he seems to switch to a fairly standard variety with only a few Chicano English phonetic features.

The linguistic features Lopez uses for white characters overlap somewhat with those used by Harvey. They include:

1. standard English grammar and phonology (but see below)
2. corny expressions/interjections: *Oh goodness!*, *The third time's the charm!*
3. religious interjections: *William, Joseph, and Mary! Jesus Christ!*
4. politeness formulas: *Excuse me, sir*
5. conservative/preppy names: i.e., *Chance, Mason, Hillary, Schuyler* (and frequent use of these names by the characters in addressing each other)
6. formal language, including:
   a) superstandard grammar, *Does anyone care for an orange?*
   b) formal or technical terms, *MRI, electrolytes*
   c) literary style: *He confirmed earlier, There's an incline, within our realm*
7. deep, low-pitched voice (for educated speaker)
8. animated, happy affect: *The third time's the charm!*, *Give me a hug!*, *We're totally over here!*
9. regional stereotypes (California Valley Girl or surfer personas, using, e.g., /u/-fronting)
10. incorrect Spanish: *carne estrada* (for *carne asada*, a traditional meat dish)

One issue that is clearly addressed by the data presented so far is the question of whether whiteness is simply synonymous with neutrality and everything unmarked, or whether there exists a positive "white" stereotype with regard to language. A feature such as the use of Standard English grammar might in theory be considered neutral (although we have seen earlier in the discussion that often it is not, being linked clearly with whiteness). However, many of the other forms used by these comedians are clearly marked: corny expressions, a nasal voice, superstandard grammar. Clearly from the perspective of these two comedians of color, whiteness is in no sense invisible.

In the brief survey of other comedians that I conducted, many of these features recur. Literary or formal language, for example, is used by both Carlos Mencia (e.g., *flabbergasted, fathom*) and Eddie Murphy (e.g., *tremendous, peculiar*). Murphy also uses a high-pitched, nasal voice for his white characters. Regional stereotypes seem to vary a great deal from comedian to comedian. The characters used by Steve Harvey, for example, don't seem to have a clear regional origin. On the other hand, many of George Lopez's white characters are Californian, surfers, or Valley Girls. Though Rahman (2003) does not specifically list "regional persona" as a factor in her study, her analysis includes an "Ethnic Italian" character, and in introducing another character she describes her as sounding like a "Valley Girl." Several of Eddie Murphy's characters are like Harvey's, middle-class-sounding but regionally unmarked. On the other hand, Murphy has several routines that include highly stereotyped Italian-American characters who exhibit most of the linguistic features used by Sylvester Stallone in the *Rocky* movies. Margaret Cho performs both Valley Girl/surfer personas (exaggerated for white people, although her own baseline dialect is Californian to begin with), and a Southern redneck stereotype. Mencia's white characters are sometimes unmarked for region and sometimes Southern. One trend seems to be for comedians to make use of white stereotypes associated with the region in which they live. Cho and Lopez are both Californians. Murphy is from New York, where Italian-American ethnicity is much more salient. It seems common for everyone to make fun of working-class Southern whites, however.

How do the performances of white characters by comedians from various ethnic groups fit with ideologies of whiteness? In general, it seems that many of the beliefs about whiteness mentioned above are indexed and reproduced in these routines. For example, the connection between whiteness and standard linguistic forms is clearly evident. In addition, the use of superstandard forms and literary language reinforces the association of whiteness with education, intellectual orientation, and the scientific register. The use of hedges and intensifiers and the use of "empty" politeness forms both seem to go with the somewhat feminine (or at least "unmasculine") view of whiteness that was discussed earlier. The use of corny expressions reinforces the ideology of whiteness as "unhip," and this quality may also explain the use of exaggeratedly happy affect. One area of disagreement in the stereotype of whiteness seems to be pitch. A number of comedians voice white characters with higher pitch, perhaps again drawing on the less masculine view. George Lopez, though, actually drops his pitch for some characters, usually the upper-middle-class, professional characters such as doctors, where the pitch seems to go with the stereotypical "voice of authority." Interestingly, the three different ideologies about the linguistic correlates of whiteness are all represented here:

standard language use, superstandard language use, and use of regional varieties.

The regional nature of portrayals of whiteness is interesting in other ways as well. In the same way that all performances of ethnic identity are simultaneously performances of gender identity (see, e.g., Bucholtz 1995), it seems that all performances of regional identity may also be performances of ethnic identity. We can return now to the question raised at the beginning of Chapter 2, about how the white New Yorker in *Urban Invaders* expresses his ethnicity. Although we may see the most stereotypical features of the dialect of a particular geographical area as primarily marking "region," in fact many of these may also be marking white ethnicity in the language ideologies of those outside the region. This may be true for those within the region as well, or these speakers may have a more carefully differentiated system where particular elements can be distinguished as regional versus ethnic, as in the case of /ay/ monophthongization in the South, discussed earlier.

The performances used by African-American comedians are not unique to the stand-up genre, but are related to the community practice of **marking**, a phenomenon where the speaker imitates and exaggerates the tone and mannerisms of another person in a reported quotation, in order to comment indirectly on something about that person, such as his or her personality or perceived motives (Mitchell-Kernan 1972). A variant of this practice is found in Clark's study, where African-American high-school students would engage in "marking white," which Clark defines as "the parodistic verbal performances of linguistic and paralinguistic features . . . commonly recognized to be stereotypically white" (2003:306). In some cases, a single sound, e.g., an exaggerated postvocalic /r/, was enough to call forth this stereotype. Perhaps most striking is the use of a style like this by Delilah, the European-American woman discussed in Chapter 2, who had grown up using AAVE as her primary linguistic variety. Sweetland (2002) notes that Delilah does not use a "white" variety in any of the settings of her daily life. However, occasionally she switches to a "white voice" in joking contexts. It seems, then, that Delilah's command of AAVE includes the entire range of appropriate speech styles, including a "marking white" register.

Interestingly, there is some overlap in the portrayals of whiteness in comedy routines and the "Whiteman" performances. The boss and employee in Steve Harvey's routine, for instance, repeatedly use each other's first names (*Sure thing, Tom.*). The people saving a seat for "Brian" in George Lopez's routine call attention to his presence by shouting his name and waving. The couple in the routine at the opening of the chapter openly discuss health matters. Despite the very different time periods, cultures, and settings in which these performances occur, some features of the ideology of whiteness seem to persist.

DISCUSSION QUESTIONS

1. If you are familiar with another speech community in which a socially and economically dominant group coexists with other substantial social, ethnic, and linguistic minorities, can you compare and contrast it with the discussions of the USA in this chapter?
2. Are there any features you think are characteristic of "Standard American English" that are not mentioned in the chapter? Features of "white" speech?
3. The linguistic ideologies of multiethnic communities often link the use of standard varieties to the dominant ethnic group. Can you think of any strategies for "uncoupling" this link (i.e., associating the use of standard varieties with a wider range of people)?
4. Think about some places, such as Ireland or Canada, where there are two groups that consider themselves to be of different ethnicities but that could both currently be categorized as "white." Do you think language variation in these settings might be different from what we find in places where there is a "white" dominant group, and a number of other groups that do not consider themselves "white"? If so, how?

SUGGESTIONS FOR FURTHER READING

Basso, Keith H. 1979. *Portraits of "The Whiteman": Linguistic Play and Cultural Symbols Among the Western Apache*. Cambridge and New York: Cambridge University Press.

A classic early study of linguistic performances of the "other." Basso presents and analyzes in detail the linguistic construction of white outsiders by members of an Apache community in Arizona.

Brander Rasmussen, Birgit, Irene J. Nexica, Eric Klinenberg, and Matt Wray, eds. 2001. *The Making and Unmaking of Whiteness*. Durham, NC: Duke University Press.

A recent collection of papers in the field of "whiteness studies," looking at white ethnicity in the USA from a number of sociological perspectives.

Fordham, S. and J. Ogbu. 1986. Black students' school success: coping with the burden of acting white. *Urban Review* 18:176–206.

A crucial article exploring the role of associations between the use of a standard variety and connotations of "white" ethnicity among African-American students.

Ignatiev, Noel. 1995. *How the Irish Became White*. New York: Routledge.

A classic book analyzing the mutability of concepts of ethnicity and race over time, focusing on Irish immigrants to the USA in different historical contexts.

Ogbu, John U. 1999. Beyond language: Ebonics, proper English, and identity in a Black-American speech community. *American Educational Research Journal* 36:147–84.

Like the earlier Fordham and Ogbu article, this one explores the connotations and meanings of different linguistic varieties, including standard ones, in African-American communities.

Trechter, Sara and Mary Bucholtz. 2001. White noise: bringing language into whiteness studies. *Journal of Linguistic Anthropology* 11(1):3–21.

This is the introductory article to an entire volume of the *Journal of Linguistic Anthropology* devoted to the emerging field of whiteness studies. All the papers are interesting, but this one lays out some of the basic concepts and questions in the field.

7 Dialect contact, ethnicity, and language change

[D]ialect adoption is not a simple matter of who you interact with under what circumstances – it's a matter of how you perceive and project yourself – much more capturable in cultural identity schemes than interactional reductionism. (Walt Wolfram, cited in Hazen 2000:126)

7.1 DIALECT CONTACT AND ETHNIC BOUNDARIES

What happens when two or more ethnic groups, each with its own linguistic variety, are in contact in a geographic area over long periods of time? In some ways, it seems evident that this prolonged contact would lead the dialects in question to influence each other. On the other hand, we saw in the case of Muzel Bryant, presented in Chapter 2, that ethnic boundaries can be extremely strong, even in contexts where assimilation seems most likely, and that these boundaries have corresponding linguistic effects. In order to study dialect contact issues, then, we cannot begin with a priori notions of how much linguistic convergence there will be in a particular multiethnic community. Each setting must be explored individually in the context of its own history, and particularly in terms of the specific categories and beliefs that are most relevant to how speakers in that community view their own ethnicity and that of other groups.

One issue that has frequently been raised in research on dialect contact is the question of convergence or divergence. That is, are the varieties in an area influencing each other in such a way that they become more alike, are they influencing each other in such a way that they become more different, or do they develop and change as two (or more) completely independent entities? There has been a particularly large body of research dedicated to addressing this question in the case of AAVE and local European-American varieties of English. There is not room in this chapter to do it justice, but two good sources of information on the debate are the special issue of *American Speech*

(Fasold et al. 1987), and Bailey and Maynor (1989). Although these studies focus on the USA, many of the issues raised are equally relevant to any multiethnic community.

Both Rickford's (1987) and Wolfram's (1987) articles in the journal issue (Fasold et al. 1987) give diagrams showing the many permutations of convergence and divergence patterns that are possible between European-American and African-American dialects. They focus particularly on the direction of changes – for example, are both dialects changing to become more alike (or more different), or is one dialect responsible for this increase/decrease? These questions have important ramifications, and we would expect the answers to be tied to the role of ethnic divisions in local contexts, and to attitudes about ingroup and outgroup members. Interestingly, none of the diagrams represent the possibility that some varieties of AAVE may be converging with local European-American varieties, while others are diverging. Hazen (2000), however, found exactly this type of division within the group of African-Americans he studied in North Carolina, so we must keep it in mind as a possibility. There will be more discussion of these issues later in this section.

Another point to keep in mind is that the occurrence of a feature in two different dialects does not necessarily mean that there is convergence, or that such a feature cannot be tied to ethnic identity. To begin with, the quantitatively higher use of a feature in a particular variety may be associated with ethnic identity. Hazen (2000:105), for example, found some degree of copula absence among European-American speakers in his sample (8 percent), but much less than for African-Americans in the same area (38 percent). In Edwards' (1997) study of Detroit, African-Americans had postvocalic /r/ absence at an overall rate of 37.8 percent, while for working-class European-Americans in the same area the rate was only 5.6 percent, indicating a clear ethnic difference. In addition, the rules constraining the use of particular variants may differ across dialects. With respect to negative concord, for instance, which is a feature of many non-standard dialects, African-American speakers in some communities use constructions that are not found in similar European-American dialects that permit multiple marking of negation. Examples of such differentiating features are negative inversion (*Didn't nobody play in the sandbox*) and transfer of negation to a lower clause (*Ain't no cat can't get in no coop*) (Wolfram 1969, Labov 1972b), which are not found in vernacular European-American varieties. The transfer of negation to a lower clause is also found in Chicano English (Fought 1999b), although apparently not in Puerto-Rican English varieties (Wolfram 1974). In the area of phonology, Santa

Ana (1991, 1996) found that final consonant cluster simplification in Chicano English was governed by slightly different **constraints** from those found in the many European-American dialects that have been studied. Studies of this process in AAVE (e.g., Labov 1972b) also show different orderings of constraints.

One area that has not yet been discussed, but which is of tremendous importance here, is the role of interethnic contacts in the spread of linguistic features across dialect boundaries. Again, it is easy to jump to simplified conclusions – for instance, that the more interethnic contact there is in an area, the more the varieties will converge. But this assumption is not consistent with what we know about the construction of ethnic identity and the role of language. It is the individual's sociopsychological perspective that matters, in the end, particularly how a person views other ethnic groups versus his or her own group. This model of interethnic contact is the one encapsulated in the personal communication from Wolfram (cited in Hazen 2000) that opens this chapter, and it helps us account for the case histories discussed in Chapter 2. Mike, who has almost no African-American contacts, uses a variety that sounds like AAVE, and Muzel Bryant, who has almost exclusively European-American contacts now, still sounds distinctly African-American. In fact, in some situations increased interethnic contact may actually lead to less similarity in the dialects of the groups involved. Wolfram and Thomas, for example, provide evidence that there was actually a reduction in dialect accommodation by African-Americans in Hyde County, North Carolina, for the group most directly affected by court-ordered school integration (2002:200–1). Again, this serves as a reminder of the important role of boundaries between groups in the construction of ethnic identity, as well as the need to look at each situation of interethnic contact in the context of the social and political history of the specific region.

Also relevant to the discussion is a point that has already come up in a number of settings: different parts of the linguistic system may play different roles in the construction of ethnicity, because of their salience, symbolic value, or permeability. Rickford (1987) ties this concept specifically to the convergence/divergence issue, noting that different components of the various dialects must be looked at separately, since it is possible to have, for example, convergence in the phonology, and divergence in the grammar (1987:57). The impact of interethnic contact, then, might affect some linguistic features more than others. We have already seen an example of this phenomenon in the case of Muzel Bryant (Wolfram et al. 1999), who used some grammatical features of the European-American Ocracokers with whom she was in contact, but generally did not use local phonetic features or lexical items. Wolfram et al. attribute this pattern to the higher salience of phonetic and lexical variables in the construction of local "O'cocker" identity.

An interesting parallel case is the study by Rickford (1999:90ff.) of two older speakers, a European-American man and an African-American woman, in a rural community on one of the Sea Islands off the Southeastern coast of the US. Both speakers' personal histories involved contact with members of the other group, and Rickford hypothesized that this contact would have an influence on their dialect patterns, leading to some convergence. What he found was that this type of convergence turned up mainly at the phonological level. Both speakers, for instance, had stops for interdental fricatives, and also more local phonetic markers such as the palatalization of /k/ before /a/, so that *can't* is pronounce [kja:n]. Rickford reports that the European-American man clearly "sounds like a black Sea Islander" (1999:93). On the other hand, in the areas of morphology and syntax, the two speakers showed completely different systems. In particular, the European-American man showed a complete absence of any of the creole grammatical features (such as unmarked plural nouns) used by the African-American woman. It is striking that this convergence in the phonology coupled with the lack of assimilation of morphosyntactic features is an exact reversal of the findings from Wolfram et al.'s (1999) study of Muzel Bryant.

Rickford's interpretation of his data is that non-standard phonological features are part of a regional Sea Island identity in which both African-American and European-American speakers participate, but non-standard morphosyntactic features are associated with creole speakers, and serve as ethnic markers (1999:107). If we compare the two studies from this perspective, we see that the results are not inconsistent at all. In each case, certain components of the linguistic system are more strongly associated with specifically ethnic identity (morphology and syntax on the Sea Islands, phonology and lexicon on Ocracoke). In each case, despite sharing their socioeconomic background with other residents and despite a personal history of interethnic contacts, certain key linguistic boundaries tied to ethnicity are not crossed by the speakers in these communities.

Although many of the studies cited so far in this section have focused on small, rural settings, the same types of patterns turn up in larger urban areas as well. Ash and Myhill (1986), for example, looked in detail at the dialects of African-American and European-American speakers in

Philadelphia, focusing particularly on individuals with a large number of interethnic contacts. African-Americans showed more linguistic influence from contacts outside their ethnic group than European-American speakers, although both groups showed some convergence. Again, the particular linguistic component made a difference in the permeability of the speakers' dialects. For European-American speakers with African-American contacts, phonological features seemed much more permeable than grammatical ones. Interestingly, Labov and Harris (1986) found a mirror image of this linguistic asymmetry in looking at the same two groups. African-Americans with many contacts in the Philadelphia European-American community showed shifts away from AAVE variables in their grammar, but did not adopt the phonological variables characteristic of local European-Americans. Edwards (1992) also found contact with European-Americans to be a significant factor which correlated with a relatively lower use of AAVE variables by young African-American speakers in Detroit. Of course it is difficult to be sure whether it is the contact itself that produced this effect, or whether the same factors that led speakers to use fewer AAVE variables also made them more likely to have interethnic contacts.

Most of the discussion has focused on contact between two different ethnic groups. But what happens in situations where more than two groups (and more than two ethnic boundaries) are involved? An interesting case of this type is the Lumbee, a group of Native Americans living in North Carolina, in an area where there has been a long period (almost 300 years) of tri-ethnic contact among Lumbee, African-American, and European-American groups (Wolfram and Schilling-Estes 1998, Wolfram and Dannenberg 1999). Because there is no clear evidence of a particular heritage language for the Lumbee, they have often been denied the recognition and privileges accorded to other Native-American groups, a fact that has simply reaffirmed their strength as a group and their calm assertion that "we know who we are" (Wolfram and Dannenberg 1999). Socially, the Lumbee have worked towards an identity which goes beyond the white/black dichotomy that is the focus of the surrounding culture, through petitions to the government for recognition, the establishment of a teacher training school, the revival of regular powwows, and other cultural events (Wolfram and Dannenberg 1999).

Research on the linguistic aspects of identity among the Lumbee has yielded some intriguing results. Studies such as those cited above have found that certain features index Lumbee identity specifically, and are not shared by other varieties in the local area. These include the regularization of *was* to *were*, and the use of perfective *be*, as in *I'm been to the store*. The Lumbee also use features from the local variety of AAVE, but with a slightly different distribution, such as the extension of habitual *be* into non-habitual contexts, as in *I hope it bes a girl*. There is evidence, though, that younger Lumbee speakers may be assimilating to AAVE norms, since they show an increasing tendency to use *be* mostly in habitual constructions (Wolfram and Schilling-Estes 1998, Wolfram and Dannenberg 1999). This combination of shared and distinct forms was found in the Lumbee phonological system and lexicon as well. The Lumbee use regional phonetic features that are shared by everyone in the area, but also features not found in the other two ethnic groups, such as /ay/ raising and backing. Clearly, despite the loss of an ancestral language, the Lumbee construct their ethnicity in a unique way through language. In particular, the use of variables from other ethnic varieties in distinctive ways may serve to reinforce both local ties and a specific and separate ethnic identity.

The results of research on interethnic dialect contact and accommodation raise a further question: What does it mean to be a member of a community? In small rural settings, for example, such as the island in Rickford's study, which had about a hundred residents, we might expect there to be "one community." We see from the data, however, that even where there is extensive interethnic contact and integration on the surface, the study of linguistic variation can reveal the underlying preservation of identities divided along the lines of ethnicity. The same can be true in urban settings. Henderson's (1996b) research in Philadelphia, for example, showed the lack of local linguistic features, even among African-Americans who seemed completely integrated into European-American communities. Recently, the notion of "speech community" has been re-evaluated in many ways (see, e.g., Bucholtz [1999a] for an interesting critique of this concept). It seems that the only way to make sense of the variations we have seen so far in the linguistic patterns of speakers is to conceptualize their context as something broader (or narrower) than a single community. For each individual, a series of identities and ingroup–outgroup boundaries flows around them on a daily basis and over the course of their lives. In constructing their identities through language, they draw on the resources to mark these different groupings: gender, ethnicity, local identity, style, and any number of other factors, some of which may be opaque to outsiders.

7.2 INFLUENCES OF MINORITY ETHNIC DIALECTS ON THE DOMINANT DIALECT

There has been relatively little research on the possible influence of varieties associated with minority ethnic groups on the dominant local variety. Given that varieties associated with minority ethnic groups are generally of lower prestige in a society than those associated with the majority group, we would expect the linguistic influence to be stronger on the minority variety, rather than in the other direction. For example, we might expect that, in contact between European-Americans and African-Americans, the uneven power relationship and the pressure to assimilate would lead to more, if not all, of the convergence coming from the African-Americans. Several of the studies cited above (Ash and Myhill 1986, Labov and Harris 1986) are consistent with this claim. Nonetheless, influence on the majority dialect is certainly possible, as is illustrated by some of the speakers in Ash and Myhill's study, or the European-American man who sounded like a black Sea Islander in Rickford's (1999) study.

One area where such influence has been clearly acknowledged is the lexicon (see Smitherman 1997, Baldwin 1997, Smitherman 1998). Lexical items associated with AAVE, for example, have historically expanded to general use in American English. Examples include *tote*, *gorilla*, *gumbo*, *jazz*, *cola*, *bad* (for "good"), and many others (Smitherman 1997). The issue of prestige discussed earlier is suspended here, because the lexical items borrowed are usually considered "slang" terms, an area where the covert prestige of urban cool associated with AAVE is much more relevant than the overt prestige associated with standard varieties. This is also one area where television and the media generally do seem to have an effect, spreading lexical items like wildfire, particularly among young adults of other ethnicities, who are in general more oriented toward the "coolness" of AAVE than toward the prestige of the standard. Of course, as each item passes into general usage, it loses some or all of its value as an ingroup ethnicity marker. As AAVE speakers create new terms, the entire cycle begins again.[1]

Although research on phonological or syntactic influence from the dialects of minority ethnic groups has been more sparse, there are a few studies that show that these types of influences are also possible. Several studies focus on contact between AAVE and local European-American varieties, particularly in the South. In the area of syntactic structure, Wolfram 1974, for example, found evidence that copula absence among European-Americans in the rural South came from

African-American speakers. Hazen (2000) also found some degree of copula absence among European-Americans in his study. In the area of phonology, Feagin (1997) concludes that non-rhoticity (lack of postvocalic /r/) in European-American dialects of the South was affected by the speech of African-Americans as well. Fought (2003:66) suggests that the tense realization of the vowel /ɪ/ as [i] in the morpheme –*ing*, which is very typical of Chicano English speakers, may also be spreading into the dialect of European-Americans in California. These types of influences represent a fruitful area for future sociolinguistic research.

One setting where there seems to be a clear influence from a minority variety onto a majority variety is New Zealand. There are a number of studies that show some influence of Maori speech styles on white New Zealanders. Holmes (1997b), for example, traces patterns of syllable timing in New Zealand to the influence of Maori English, particularly the variety spoken by middle-class Maori people. Holmes also suggests that Maori English may be the source of another change in New Zealand: the increasing use of final /z/ devoicing. In another study, Holmes (1997a), two more features were identified that seem to have developed first in the speech of Maori speakers and then spread to Pakeha (white) speakers' English: the tag particle *eh*, and the use of the high rising terminal contour (in intonation). Holmes also cites a comment from Bauer that "many of the features that are today attributed to Maori English will later become general features of NZE [New Zealand English]; we just don't know which ones!" (1997a:97).

Perhaps most interesting is the widespread use of a Maori term to designate the majority population of European descent: *Pakeha*. As noted in Chapter 5, it is the default term used in the sociolinguistic literature to indicate speakers who are white New Zealanders, mostly of British descent. Having a specific ethnic term for the white majority ethnic group is useful, in that it preempts a problem that can come up otherwise: the labeling of this group with the word that also indicates nationality. The Latino teenagers that I worked with in Los Angeles, for example, often referred to white people as "Americans," a term which I felt was ambiguous, but more importantly perpetuated a racist/xenophobic ideology. The use of Pakeha also reverses a historical trend by which dominant groups in so many places have put their labels on subjugated or otherwise oppressed populations. Using an "outgroup" label for the dominant group might simply be a matter of convenience, but it also can be seen as subverting traditional patterns of linguistic dominance.

In many places, modern multiethnic communities seem to be changing socially towards more tolerance and integration. We should not underestimate the very strong influence still of ethnic boundaries, prejudice, and so forth. But a number of the studies cited here find increasing interethnic peer contact among younger speakers in these types of communities, with accompanying shifts in attitudes about ethnic boundaries. Hewitt (1986) and Hazen (2000), among others, both found this sort of pattern. Holmes (1997a) notes that Maori teenagers who identify with a strong Maori peer group tend to use Maori English. If this increase in flexibility of social orientation toward ethnicity and language continues, we may find increasing influence from minority group varieties to majority group varieties in the future.

7.3 CONTACT AMONG ETHNIC MINORITY DIALECTS

Most of the studies discussed so far have focused on contact between a dominant variety, associated with the majority ethnic group, and a variety associated with a minority ethnic group. However, in areas where multiple ethnic groups are present, there also exists the possibility of dialect assimilation between two minority ethnic varieties. Many factors might favor this outcome. One is the fact that different minority ethnic groups may live in close proximity (often as a result of socioeconomic factors) and experience more contact with each other than with members of the dominant ethnic group. As we have seen, contact in and of itself is not sufficient to trigger assimilation. However, minority ethnic groups in some settings also may express an ideology that encompasses a sense of affinity with other oppressed groups. This view seems to hold for the African-American and Puerto-Rican American speakers in Urciuoli's (1996) study, for example, who often saw themselves as sharing exclusion from a white, middle-class-dominated world. One Puerto-Rican American man commented, "I'm more comfortable with blacks than with whites because blacks live in the same environment as us, they relate to us better than whites" (1996:66). It would not be surprising, in light of these views, to find speakers in a minority ethnic community assimilating features of dialects from other minority ethnic groups in the area. Note that the focus here is on widespread assimilation of features by large segments of the community, and not the occasional use of some features by isolated individuals (i.e., crossing, which will be discussed in Chapter 10).

A classic study of this type of contact situation is Wolfram's (1974) study of Puerto-Rican American speakers in New York City. In general, the (young, male) speakers in this study showed numerous influences from AAVE on their variety of English (Puerto-Rican English). What is interesting, in light of the discussions of race in earlier chapters, is that phenotype appeared to influence the amount of integration into African-American peer groups. According to Wolfram, Puerto-Rican immigrants whose phenotype was categorized as "white" tended to be more upwardly mobile, and more likely to assimilate into dominant white groups. Puerto Ricans with a darker skin tone and a more African phenotype were identified as "black" by the outside community, and often assimilated to African-American culture (1974:26–9). Not surprisingly, the strongest use of AAVE features tended to occur among those who had the most extensive contacts with African-American peers. These speakers were found to use certain AAVE grammatical forms, such as negative inversion (e.g., *Didn't nobody do it*) or habitual *be*, as well as numerous phonological forms, such as surface realizations of /θ/ as [f], and monophthongization of /ay/. In terms of attitudes about ethnicity and language, these speakers, according to Wolfram, tended to minimize differences between the two groups, even to the point of "deny[ing] that the ways in which blacks and Puerto Ricans speak English are different" (Wolfram 1974:37).

Again, though, we find that phonological and grammatical components play different roles in dialect assimilation. While Puerto-Rican speakers with many African-American contacts used both grammatical and phonological features of AAVE, those with few interethnic contacts were more likely to use only phonological features. Wolfram attributes this pattern to sociocultural attitudes within the community. Borrowing from AAVE is often viewed negatively, and Wolfram suggests that the "relative obtrusiveness" of grammatical features makes them less susceptible to borrowing than the phonological ones (1974:209). The various degrees and directions of borrowing, then, can be clearly linked to the social context.

Another interesting study of contact across minority dialects is Poplack's (1978) study of Puerto-Rican American children in Philadelphia. Poplack found that the children used variables characteristic both of the local European-American variety of English and of AAVE. The "white" Philadelphia variants were linked to prestige, and appeared more often in more formal styles (while within the European-American community itself, these variables would tend to be used less often in formal styles). The AAVE variants, on the other hand, were linked to covert prestige, and tended to be used more often by the boys in the study, a reminder that, as has been true throughout the discussion, additional social factors also affect the linguistic construction of identity.

Hazen (2000), looking at contact among three ethnic groups in North Carolina, finds a pattern that is in some ways strikingly similar to that found by Poplack. If we focus on just the Native-Americans in his study, we find that both European-American and African-American varieties are present in the region, and the Native-American speakers showed some assimilation to each of these two groups. Hazen identified a key factor beyond ethnicity, however, that was crucial to the patterning of variables in his study: *expanded identity* versus *local identity*. This variable refers to whether the speaker mostly maintains contacts within the local community or is oriented toward contacts and opportunities outside the community (for example, attending or planning to attend college). Local-identity Native-American speakers were more likely to assimilate to grammatical and phonological features characteristic of African-Americans, while expanded-identity Native Americans were more likely to assimilate to European-American features. Again, we see European-American varieties associated with generalized, overt prestige, and African-American varieties associated with local, covert prestige. Hazen also suggests that, because of the convergence between Native-American and African-American varieties in this community, certain AAVE features "may simply be marked as 'young, non-European American' in Warren County" (2000:141).

Sometimes the features of another group's dialect are borrowed, but with a slightly different distribution. This pattern seems to apply in the case of the Lumbee, discussed earlier, whose dialect of English incorporates the use of habitual *be* from AAVE, but extends it into non-habitual contexts. Hazen (2000) finds a similar pattern for the Native-Americans in his study, who adopt copula absence from AAVE, but apply it at a lower rate, and with slightly different constraints (e.g., type of verb not being a significant factor). As in other cases, then, borrowing features from another minority ethnic group as part of the construction of ethnic identity can lead to quantitative as well as qualitative differences among groups.

7.4   *ETHNIC MINORITY GROUP SPEAKERS AND SOUND CHANGE*

After several decades of sociolinguistic research, we know quite a bit about how **sound changes** in language take place. We know that they generally are initiated from interior social classes, for communities where numerous class stratifications are the norm (although other types of class distributions are possible, and will affect the patterning). We know that adolescents play a key role in initiating and perpetuating changes, and that in many communities women may be leading a change in progress. However, the vast majority of studies of sound change have focused on European-American speakers in large, urban US settings, with a smaller group focused on US rural areas. We still know relatively little about how change might be similar or different in markedly different communities around the world, and whether the principles that have been put forth above are truly universal.

While we have a large body of research on linguistic *variation* in minority ethnic groups at least for some groups, such as African-Americans (see Fought [2002] for a summary of these types of studies), there is relatively little research on language *change* within these same groups. Sociolinguists are only beginning to investigate the role of ethnic minority speakers in sound changes associated with dominant ethnic groups, and the processes of sound change taking place completely within ethnic minority communities really have not been explored at all. These areas will need to be investigated further in the future, but in this section I will discuss the implications of the research that has been done so far.

It has often been assumed that minority ethnic group members in the USA simply do not participate in sound changes characteristic of the dominant local ethnic group. A few of the early studies of sound change in the USA showed this lack of participation (e.g., Labov and Harris 1986, Bailey and Maynor 1987) and it was quickly picked up and extended as a generalization by later researchers, so that they *expected* to find an absence of participation by speakers of other ethnicities in sound changes associated with European-Americans. Some recent studies (e.g., Gordon 2000) also show this pattern, so it is fair to conclude that in some areas of the USA the assertion is valid, particularly for African-Americans. But, given the large range of types of communities that have never been explored, to generalize it to *all* minority ethnic groups in all geographic areas seems clearly premature. Yet the acceptance of exactly this type of generalization is prevalent in the sociolinguistic literature, as illustrated by the following citation from Labov (2001), considered an influential work of modern sociolinguistics:

> All speakers who are socially defined as white, mainstream, or Euro-American, are involved in the [sound] changes to one degree or another . . . But for those children who are integral members of a sub-community that American society defines as "non-white" – Black, Hispanic, or native American – the result is quite different. No matter how frequently they are exposed to the local vernacular, the new patterns of regional sound change do not surface in their speech. (2001:506)

This is perhaps the most wide-reaching version of the claim, but many variants of it surface in other studies (see Fought [2002] for a discussion of these). If this were, in fact, a universal truth about sound change, even just for US ethnic groups, it would of course have tremendous implications for the study of language and ethnicity. However, a quick look at current research suggests we should be cautious about jumping to such conclusions.

To begin with, these types of generalizations underscore how important it is for us, as sociolinguists, to ground the "socio" side of our research carefully, drawing on data from other fields such as sociology, anthropology, ethnic studies, and so forth. The definition in the above citation of a "sub-community" including African-Americans, Latinos, and Native-Americans, for example, seems unfounded, by any of the usual definitions of community. Secondly, the field of sociolinguistics is relatively young and there are large populations that have never been studied with respect to sound change. There are, as far as I know, no studies of sound change among Asian-Americans, and those involving Latinos are limited. Even African-Americans have not been studied everywhere, and, as mentioned in Chapter 3, phonology has tended to be a secondary focus. How can we know ahead of time whether a pattern that holds for black speakers in Philadelphia and Chicago does or does not apply in rural Kansas? Or Portland, Oregon? Or Portland, Maine? It is risky to guess whether *specific* ethnic speakers in *specific* regions will participate in any local European-American sound changes without studying them, especially given the fact that some data which contradict the generalization have already surfaced.

The classic early studies in sociolinguistics, if we analyze them carefully, actually show both patterns: ethnic minority group members participating and not participating in local sound changes. Labov (1966) showed in detail how Jewish, Italian, and Irish groups were involved in the various vowel shifts characteristic of New York City, such as the raising of /æh/ and /oh/, while African-Americans clearly did not participate in these same changes. On the other hand, in Labov's (1972b) study of Martha's Vineyard, the Portuguese and the Native-American groups on the island were participating in the centralization of (aw) and (ay) associated with local island speech. In fact, in the youngest generation, these groups often showed more of the local variables than their European-American counterparts.[2]

There is a similarly mixed pattern among the most recent studies. Gordon (2000), for example, conducts a careful study of the **Northern Cities Shift**, an important set of sound changes taking place in a large inland northern section of the United States. He looks at

European-Americans, African-Americans, Mexican-Americans, and a small group of mixed-race speakers (mostly Latino/white) in northwest Indiana. The inclusion of this last group in and of itself is noteworthy because so little has been done on speakers of mixed ethnicity, who make up a greater and greater proportion of the population. Their presence in this project represents an advance in the study of language and ethnicity. Gordon concludes that, overall, "the NCS [Northern Chain Shift] features are predominantly a characteristic of white speech" (2000:132), and in general this study can be counted as one that supports a lack of participation by minority ethnic group members in local sound changes.

Even so, there are a few nuances in the data that should be noted. To begin with, there were European-American speakers in the sample who also showed very little use of some of the NCS features (particularly ε-shifting), since the changes are relatively recent in this specific geographic area. This result shows that non-use of these features can be attributable to factors other than ethnicity, factors which may have affected the speakers from other groups as well. Second, several of the mixed-race speakers showed usages of these features that were comparable to some of the European-Americans in the sample. Finally, one out of the five Mexican-American speakers showed rates of all the features that were quite high – higher than some of the European-American speakers. Gordon explains that this speaker grew up in a predominantly white neighborhood, and mostly has white friends, in contrast to the other participants. This individual also did not emphasize the importance of Mexican ethnicity to her identity in the way that the other Mexican-American speakers did. As we have seen in other cases, then, individual life histories and contexts can affect the linguistic choices of speakers.

Another recent study, Fridland (2003), looks at the role of ethnicity in a completely different set of changes – the **Southern Vowel Shift**, occurring in the southern USA. A strength of this project is that it looks specifically at the construction of ethnic identity before attempting any correlations with language. Fridland discusses the historical and social context for African-Americans in the community of Memphis, Tennessee, and also develops an index for analyzing ingroup and outgroup ties, including measures of interethnic contact and network density. In general, Fridland found that the vowel systems of African-American speakers in her sample closely paralleled those of European-American speakers in terms of which vowels were and were not shifted. The study concludes that "it appears likely that black and white speakers in Memphis are displaying membership in the local community by adopting particular features of the SVS" (2003:16). Interestingly, the ethnic network integration scores did not have a strong overall effect on degree of participation in the Southern Vowel Shift. However, network ties did influence the use of more local, rural features, not associated with a general Southern norm.

Fridland interprets the data as being in some sense about locally bound identity rather than ethnicity:

> [L]ocal community membership and ethnic membership are not mutually defining, and selecting features to display local identity that happen to be shared by members of a different ethnic group does not negate the impact of other features that display ethnic identity. (2003:23)

This analysis fits well with the example discussed in Chapter 6, where /ay/ monophthongization in some contexts was associated with African-American ethnicity, and in other contexts was seen as simply Southern. Something similar in terms of local Southern identity seems to be going on with the fronting of **back vowels** as well, as found by Anderson and Childs (2003) and Fridland and Bartlett (2003). In sum, as important as ethnicity is, and we have seen the dramatic effects that ethnic boundaries can have, it is not necessarily the overriding factor in every linguistic "act of identity." The use of some variables to represent Southern identity, shared by speakers from different ethnic groups, shows that in a particular community regional identity may in some ways take precedence over ethnic identity. Fridland (2003) notes that the status of both AAVE and white Southern dialects as "less favored varieties" may also weaken the identification of the local white varieties as "dominant," as they are in the ideologies of other regions.

There are a number of other studies like these on the participation of African-Americans in local European-American changes, which individually and as a group show mixed results. Bailey (1993) assessed the use of European-American features of a Texan dialect by African-Americans, and found that blacks and whites participated equally in changes peaking before World War II but not in those that are more recent. Wolfram, Thomas, and Green (1997) looked at language change in the Outer Banks region of North Carolina, and found that some sound changes were in progress in both the black and white communities, including ungliding of /ai/ and the loss of front-glided /au/, although other changes originating among European-Americans were not picked up by African-American speakers. In general, older speakers showed more influence from the local European-American dialect than younger ones, who seemed to be mostly shifting away. Childs and Mallinson (2004), in contrast, found that younger African-American speakers in an Appalachian community displayed a number of key features of the Appalachian English variety characteristic of European-Americans in the region.

One interesting question is what the range of variation might be among individual African-American speakers. For studies which report averages or percentages for the group rather than individual values, interesting variation patterns may be obscured. It is possible, for example, that some segments of a particular African-American population are using as much of certain features as European-Americans, while others use none. Fridland (2003) summarizes some of the findings in this area of research, then comments:

> The interpretation of such research, however, often assumes a unanimity among African American communities, which may obscure the fact that there are competing norms within the community which demonstrate different levels of integration and contrast within the larger community. (2003:6)

This is an excellent point, one that has come up again and again in the discussion of language and ethnicity. Not all members of a particular ethnic community behave the same way (as illustrated, for example, by Hazen's study, discussed above). Also, as we saw in the Indiana study (Gordon 2000), even if most speakers in a particular group clearly are not participating in a sound change, some individuals may be. And if we want a full understanding of the construction of ethnic identity, we should not dismiss these people as "outliers," since their language is an important part of the puzzle as well.

If we broaden our focus to other ethnic groups besides African-Americans, we find a similarly complicated picture. Among Latino groups, for example, Gordon (2000), as reported, found little participation by Mexican-Americans in the Northern Cities Shift.

On the other hand, Poplack (1978) showed that among Puerto-Rican children in Philadelphia there was evidence of phonological influences from the European-American local community. Most notably, the children were participating in several Philadelphia vowel shifts, including the fronting of /ow/ and the raising and backing of the nucleus of /ay/ before voiceless consonants. Similarly, Fought (1997, 2003) found that young Mexican-American speakers in Los Angeles were participating in the fronting of /u/ and in the backing of /æ/, both known to be sound changes in progress in California (Hinton et al. 1986). Not all speakers participated in these changes, but the ones who did were not outliers or individuals who had no intraethnic contacts. They were core members of the community whose social networks consisted mostly of other Mexican-Americans (see Fought 2003:55–61). Whether or not they participated in the California vowel shifts was related to other social factors besides ethnicity, such as gender and social class, interacting in a complex pattern. This result is a useful reminder that ethnicity does not occur in isolation from other factors, as we have seen again and again.

There is much less information, unfortunately, about the participation of other ethnic groups in sound changes, which constitutes a key area for future sociolinguistic research. Some relevant studies do exist, however. Anderson (1999) found that speakers of Cherokee ethnicity in North Carolina used features associated with the local European-American variety (monophthongization of /ai/, and "upgliding" of /oi/). Their vowel realizations, though, were also influenced by ancestral language patterns, in certain ways that set them apart from other local groups, even for speakers who were not bilingual (as happens also with Chicano English, for example). So, as with a number of minority ethnic groups that have been discussed, their variety of English encompasses both accommodation to local features and variations in exactly how these features are patterned that set them apart slightly from other groups.

There is a notable absence of studies on the role of various Asian-American groups in sound changes. In fact, as Chun (2001) notes, studies of the language features of Asian-Americans have been largely neglected, except for studies of language maintenance issues or code-switching. The few studies that include Asian-Americans in analyses of sound change are inconclusive. Labov (2001:507) claims that Asian-Americans in Philadelphia do not show evidence of local dialect features; however, no data are provided to support the claim, which appears to be impressionistic. On the other hand, Hinton et al. (1986) and Luthin (1987) found that the Asian speakers in their sample were participating in the sound changes characteristic of European-Americans in the Bay Area. Nonetheless, their studies did not focus on Asian-Americans specifically. In fact, there were only two Asian-American speakers in the Hinton et al. (1986) study, for example. Clearly, more research is needed on these diverse and important US ethnic groups.

In general, then, we can conclude that in some areas of the USA, African-Americans, and sometimes members of other minority ethnic groups, do not participate in the local sound changes. Yet, in other communities, they do. Also, individuals within the group may participate to varying degrees, often in relation to other elements of their identity such as network integration. Therefore, we cannot draw one sweeping conclusion about minority ethnic groups in the USA and their participation in sound changes characteristic of the dominant (white) groups. The picture, as with so many other aspects of the construction of ethnic identity through language, is complex.

DISCUSSION QUESTIONS

1. Are there any cases of language contact among different groups in your community? How do the dialects or languages influence each other? Are there any areas where you see the potential for a new dialect to emerge?
2. Have you ever found yourself using features that you associate with an ethnic group other than your own? When? What do you think influenced you to use these features?
3. As discussed in the chapter, we now know that some speakers from minority ethnic groups do participate in sound changes characteristic of the dominant local community. What factors do you think might influence such participation? Do you think some types of ethnic groups or some types of individuals might be more likely than others to adopt regional changes?
4. What role, if any, do you think the mass media in the USA (or other countries) play in disseminating linguistic features from one group to another? Design a research project to study this phenomenon.

SUGGESTIONS FOR FURTHER READING

Ash, Sharon and John Myhill. 1986. Linguistic correlates of inter-ethnic contact. In D. Sankoff ed., *Diversity and Diachrony*. Amsterdam: John Benjamins. 33–44.

An early study looking at the role of interethnic contacts as a factor in language variation, charting the use of particular sociolinguistic variables by African-American and European-American speakers in a large US city.

Fasold, Ralph W, William Labov, Fay Vaughn-Cooke, Guy Bailey, Walt Wolfram, Arthur Spears, and John Rickford. 1987. Are black and white vernacular diverging? Papers from the NWAVE XIV Panel Discussion. *American Speech* 62:3–80.

A special issue of the journal *American Speech* devoted to the exploration of the question of whether African-American and European-American linguistic varieties in the USA are becoming more similar to each other or more different. Features articles by some of the most prominent researchers in the study of AAVE, discussing this question from different angles.

Hazen, Kirk. 2000. *Identity and ethnicity in the rural South: a sociolinguistic view through past and present be.* Publications of the American Dialect Society 83. Durham, NC: Duke University Press.

An excellent recent study of a community in the Southern USA, combining larger-scale quantitative methods with the exploration of identity construction by individuals. In the area of language and ethnicity, Hazen looks at African-American, European-American, and Native-American speakers in the region.

Labov, William and Wendell Harris. 1986. De facto segregation of black and white vernaculars. In David Sankoff (ed.), *Diversity and Diachrony.* Amsterdam: John Benjamins. 1–24.

As in the Ash and Myhill article, this one looks at African-Americans and European-Americans in the same city, addressing the question of how similar or different the dialects used are, and whether local variables prominent in one ethnic group are also found in the other.

Wolfram, Walt. 1974. *Sociolinguistic Aspects of Assimilation: Puerto Rican English in New York City.* Arlington, VA: Center for Applied Linguistics.

A classic early study of interethnic contact and its effects on language variation. Wolfram focuses on Puerto-Rican Americans in New York City and their use of AAVE variables, situating the discussion in a social and linguistic context.

Part III   The role of language use
in ethnicity

8 Discourse features, pragmatics, and ethnicity

Delilah: You look good!
Stella: That's cause you don't know good from spectacular! (from the movie *How Stella Got Her Groove Back*, 1998)

When my two cousins came from Spain to attend an American college for a year, they quickly became friends with other foreign students there. In particular, they told me, they had met two girls from Japan whom they liked very much. The funny thing, they reported, was how quiet the Japanese girls were. They were very nice, my cousins assured me, but they never seemed to hold up their end of the conversation. They just didn't have a lot to say. It was easy for me, as a linguist, to guess from this account that the norms for how long one should wait before taking a turn must be much shorter in Spanish than in Japanese. The Japanese girls were waiting for a pause of at least X milliseconds before they felt that it was OK for them to come in. My cousins were leaving the much shorter pause appropriate to the Spanish **turn-taking** system, and when the other party hadn't said anything yet, they went on to fill what would otherwise be an "awkward" silence. I imagined the Japanese girls at home talking to their own American cousin (*We met two Spanish girls. They're very nice, but they can't seem to stop themselves from talking! They never give anyone else a chance!*).

Ethnicity, as we have seen, is linked with culture, and culture encompasses our norms and beliefs about how to interact with others. When we think of an ethnic group other than our own, we may have in mind stereotypes of how the people in that group look, sound, and, (most important here), behave, e.g., "Asian people are quiet" (a view, incidentally, that is hard to sustain for anyone who has been in a crowded Chinese restaurant on a Sunday morning). Whether or not a particular individual exhibits any of the specific linguistic variables that have been discussed in connection with various ethnic groups, his or her language use and interactional style may nonetheless be very different from that of someone in another group. Some of these norms may stem from the source cultures of groups whose ancestors came from someplace else, while others may have developed independently, or perhaps as a response to particular social and cultural conditions. Morgan (1998), for example, has a thorough discussion of the connections between certain African-American speech styles and black–white interactions in the historical context of segregation and repression.

It's crucial to examine these discourse patterns associated with ethnicity, because, as will be discussed in more detail in Chapter 9, they can be the basis for misunderstandings and unwarranted negative evaluations. I will begin the discussion with some general areas in which interactional differences can often be seen: indirectness, turn-taking norms, joking, and complimenting strategies, looking at the role they play in the expression of ethnic identity. I will then address the question of how these norms are acquired, through the process of language socialization.

8.1   INDIRECTNESS

Indirectness is a prime example of the relativity of interactional norms. In the mainstream middle-class culture of the USA, ordering a coffee in a restaurant by saying, "It's quite cold outside; I wonder if it will be possible for me somehow to get a warm drink," would be perceived as excessively indirect. Translated into other cultures, this might sound fine. Kyoko Mori, an American woman who grew up in Japan, gives the following example:

> In Japanese, it's rude to tell people exactly what you need or to ask them what they want . . . Someone could talk about the cold weather when she actually wants you to help her pick up some groceries at the store. She won't make an obvious connection between the long talk about the cold weather and the one sentence she might say about going to the store later in the afternoon, the way an English speaker would. (1997:6)

In Spain, on the other hand, it is quite normal in a restaurant setting to address your server with a formula that translates as, "Are you going to bring me a coffee?," which to English speakers sounds rude. Additionally, what we mean by "indirectness" is somewhat ambiguous. A speaker might say something in a way that is completely clear to other members of the culture, who can identify the meaning of the utterance immediately and unambiguously, even if the words themselves seem "indirect" to a member of another group. Some cultures may also have ritualized occasions during which a particular type of indirectness is the norm.

Speakers within the same country and language might also exhibit differences in indirectness related to ethnicity, as research on the language of different ethnic groups shows. In many places where there are people of different cultural backgrounds in contact with each other, variations in indirectness are reported. In Black South African English, which has only recently begun to be the subject of sociolinguistic study, Gough reports a preference for indirectness over the "Anglo-Saxon norm" of getting to the point as quickly as possible (1996). Eades (1991), in her study of First Nations (Aboriginal) speakers in Australia, finds that their culture encompasses a number of strategies that seem "indirect" to European-descent Australians. For example, they often seek information by offering a general statement and then pausing to allow the listener to respond, rather than asking a question directly. A similar strategy of indirectness applies to requests. First Nations speakers will tend to avoid direct requests (*Will you give me a ride to town?*) in favor of indirect "fishing"-type questions (such as *What time are you leaving?*) (1991:88).

Patterns of "indirectness" have also been studied among Native-Americans in the United States and Canada. Though there is, of course, variation among specific tribes, there are also some commonalities in experience that seem to have produced similar discourse patterns. Leap (1993:86) notes that, among speakers of Northern Ute English, direct questioning is normally avoided, and there is a preference for more indirect formulations such as *I wonder how come he did that*. Scollon and Scollon (1981) discuss the Athabaskan cultural view that it is inappropriate to anticipate future good luck, or to speak highly of one's own accomplishments:

> The concept of *injíh* as it is expressed in Tanacross Athabaskan means that if you intended to go out hunting moose you would never say so directly. The most you might say is that you are going out and you hope you will not be hungry. (1981:20)

It is easy to see how such formulations would cause speakers from other ethnic groups – particularly white, middle-class American and Canadian groups – to believe that Athabaskans are unnecessarily indirect, and that it is difficult to know what they are "really saying." Basso (1979:53) notes the same kind of taboo among the Western Apache, with respect to talking about future misfortunes, especially sickness and death. In addition, they see direct commands to others as impolite (even in situations where other groups might consider them very polite, e.g., *Please sit anywhere, Help yourself to a cookie*). If Apaches do feel a need to extend a **directive** of some type, it ends up being so circumlocutional that other groups may find it hard to interpret (1979:50).

Similar "indirectness" norms may hold in other ethnic groups, sometimes even with the same cultural motivation behind them. Nhu (1994) gives a parallel example for Vietnamese-American groups in the United States. She says:

> In my family . . . if you loved someone, you would say the opposite. This can be quite confusing when taken literally, but as any Vietnamese can attest when a parent says to a baby, "I hate your little face," they're really telling them how much they dote on this precious child. (1994:4)

As with the Athabaskan example, Nhu attributes this practice to superstition associated with speaking about the future, and the possible courting of bad luck. She also talks about a general emphasis on indirectness in the expression of love, where overt and explicit declarations may be considered in some Asian cultures to devalue these emotions, and very subtle words or actions are seen as more meaningful.

What we might term "indirectness" can also take a quite different form. Unlike the examples above, which involve refraining from direct expression of certain things, indirectness can also involve a deliberate use of certain forms that have a particular meaning to the culture. African-American communities in the USA, for example, often have these types of resources. Mitchell-Kernan (1972) discusses *signifying*, a culturally specific way of conveying meanings indirectly, often in a humorous way (see also Smitherman 2000b:255–7). In contrast with the "avoidance" motivations discussed above, such as not inviting bad luck, Mitchell-Kernan describes the use of signifying as a deliberate, creative choice, saying that the use of this form is "selected for its artistic merit" (1972:315). She gives the example of two sisters, one of whom is pregnant but not ready to acknowledge it yet. In the exchange, the second sister, Rochelle, uses indirectness and metaphorical language twice to communicate that she knows her sister is pregnant:

> Rochelle: Girl, you sure do need to join the Metrecal for lunch bunch.
> Grace: . . . Yea, I guess I am putting on a little weight.
> Rochelle: Now look here, girl, we both standing here soaking wet and you still trying to tell me it ain't raining.   (1972:323)

Some examples rely on particular cultural knowledge for interpretation, such as references to the toast "The Signifying Monkey."[1] As well as signifying, Mitchell-Kernan analyzes the phenomenon of *marking*, which was discussed in Chapter 6, and also *loud-talking*, which I will not describe here, except to say that it also has an indirect focus. In fact, Morgan (1998), who also includes a discussion of various types of indirectness, asserts that a system of indirect language encompassing multiple levels of meaning "is the foundation of all African-American discourse" (1998:256).

The example of signifying between the two sisters also reveals the use of **metaphor**, a specific type of indirectness that is more widespread in some ethnic groups than in others. Heath (1983) talks about the importance of metaphors and similes in the working-class African-American community she studied, where these were a common element of ordinary conversations between adults. In addition, metaphors played an important role in the language socialization of children. Heath gives the example of an older man, respected as a leader in the community, who uses the parable of Solomon to stop a group of children from fighting over a tricycle (1983:50). Remarks comparing a child's behavior to something else – an animal, for example – were also frequent (1983:105–6).

Metaphors seem to play an important role in other African-American communities as well. Henderson (1996a) notes the use of metaphors in spontaneous compliments given by African-Americans in Illinois. Similarly, Foster (1995) found the use of complex, multi-level metaphors as a teaching strategy among middle-class African-American women teachers. This result highlights an important larger issue in looking at the role of discourse patterns in ethnic identity. Because the teachers Foster studied are middle class, they mainly used standard varieties of English, especially in the classroom. The use of interactional elements associated with African-American community norms allows them to express their ethnicity clearly apart from the use of specific linguistic variables, so that they can simultaneously project their dominance of standard varieties of English and their ethnic identity.

As with other features that have been discussed, both structural and interactional, variation in indirectness within an ethnic group can also be quite common. To begin with, other elements of identity may intersect with and affect these norms. Reynolds (1998), for example, illustrates how female speech in Japan is significantly more indirect and less assertive than male speech. Goodwin (1990, 1998), in her study of African-American children's play activities and discourse structures, shows that girls are more likely to use indirect forms for imperatives than boys, although, depending on the specific activity, direct forms are also available to them.

In addition, we cannot classify a particular ethnic group as simply "direct" or "indirect" overall. Not only are the meanings of these terms completely relative, but even relative indirectness may be valued by an ethnic group in some situations and not others. As an example, we have seen that a number of indirect strategies are common in African-American communities. However, Wolfram and Schilling-Estes (1998:82–3) note that working-class African-American parents may be more direct than European-American parents in issuing directives or corrections to their children. Similarly, Native-Americans employ many strategies of indirectness, but Lakota English-speaking children may phrase requests in a way that seems too direct or abrupt to other groups, e.g., *Teacher, you must give me a pencil!* (Leap 1993:86).

A final area in which indirectness is relevant is humor and joking. While humor in almost all cultures will sometimes take an indirect form, the specifics of how this is accomplished can vary considerably. This topic will be discussed separately below.

8.2   TURN-TAKING, SILENCE, AND BACKCHANNELING

When we act as speakers or listeners in a conversation, we bring to bear a large and complex system of norms for the exchange of conversational turns. Part of what we acquire as we are learning our language and culture is a sense of when it is OK to speak, when we should be quiet, how much we should say, how we know if there is a problem in the conversation, and so forth. In one of the earliest studies of how a conversation works, Sacks et al. (1974) describe several features that they identify as crucial elements of turn-taking systems in conversation. These principles include observations such as "Overwhelmingly, one party talks at a time," or "Transitions (from one turn to the next) with no gap and no overlap are common," or "A current speaker may select a next speaker" (1974:700–1). While such assertions may seem obvious to speakers from certain dominant, English-speaking groups, in fact each of the three I have cited has been shown experimentally to be not at all characteristic of certain cultures or certain groups within a culture. For example, Coates (1996) discusses a group of white British women for whom a great deal of simultaneous speech was the norm, rather than an exception. Philips (1990), in her study of Warm Springs Indians, notes that "Indian speakers do not typically exercise influence over who will speak next through identification of addressed recipients" (1990:339). In looking at the role of inter-actional patterns in the construction of ethnicity, then, we should not expect turn-taking norms from one group to necessarily apply to another.

Again, the relatively large body of research on the discourse practices of various Native-American groups in the USA and Canada is highly relevant. In almost any area related to the structuring of conversation – openings, closings, pauses, paired utterances, speaker selection, body language cues, and so forth – Native-Americans exhibit different patterns from speakers in European-American and other groups. Philips (1990) looks in detail at many aspects of the discourse system of Warm Springs Indians. To begin with, the speakers in this community speak more slowly overall, there are much longer pauses between turns, and the length of turns is very even. Unlike some groups of white speakers, such as the British women in Coates (1996), individuals in the Warm Springs community almost never interrupt each other or speak at the same time. As was mentioned, speakers in this community do not normally select the next speaker directly, or even identify a particular person in a group as the **addressee** (through eye gaze, or some other strategy). In addition, there is very little backchanneling (nods, or verbal agreements like "uh-huh" used to indicate explicitly that the hearer is listening).

With respect to silence, specifically, Stubbe (1998) found that interactions between Maori-ethnicity speakers in New Zealand included relatively frequent silences, which did not disrupt the conversation in any way. She concludes that "Maori speakers are more tolerant of silence than Pakehas" (1998:275). Similarly, a much larger amount of silence is generally considered appropriate in Native-American groups than in comparable European-American or African-American groups. Basso (1970) provides an intriguing discussion of the many strategic ways this silence can be used. In comparison with their own communicative norms, Apaches see European-Americans as not knowing when to be quiet. Their "Whiteman" performances (Basso 1979), discussed in Chapter 6, include comments like *Look who's here!*, which have a quality of communicative emptiness. Such formulas are commonplace among European-Americans. In giving a tour of one's new home to a visiting friend, for example, it is normal to hear comments such as *And this is the bathroom* . . . (as if the listener were standing there puzzled over what a toilet might be doing in the kitchen, and needed this clarification). Clearly, the use of formulas without real communicative content is related to the need to fill "uncomfortable" silences, which affects some groups but not others.

In addition, the norms for linking turns in a conversational sequence can differ greatly between groups. In most of the European-American groups that have been studied, for example, a question requires a response, even if that response is a delaying strategy of some sort or an indication that the speaker cannot answer for some reason. In the Warm Springs Native-American community, though, there is no obligation at all that this response follow immediately after the question. Philips even gives an example of a question that was answered an entire week later (1990:340). An additional implication of this pattern is that a speaker does not automatically give up control of the **floor** by posing a question, as might be expected in other groups.

Though there has been less research on interaction in Asian-American communities than in Native-American groups, the studies that have been done suggest that many of the same patterns can be found. Gudykunst et al. (1988:106–7) report on a number of these studies and some parallels among quite different Asian groups. For example, Japanese-Americans in Hawaii were found to use more indirect forms and more silence in interactions than Caucasian-Americans there. In another community, Chinese-Americans were found to be less likely to perceive talk as "important" or "enjoyable" than Caucasian-Americans. Kang (1994) ties some of these patterns in speakers of East Asian ethnic origins to Confucianism. She discusses how Asian-Americans come from a culture where silence is a virtue, while in European-American cultures there is "[an emphasis] on verbalizing everything" (1994:A20).

Interestingly, many of these same patterns from US communities are found in the English interactions of South African speakers whose first language is Xhosa. Gough (1996) discusses research that shows these speakers use more self-selection and silence, and fewer overlaps and interruptions than native English speakers. Even though this is a group of non-native speakers, and therefore the differences are attributable to language background, rather than simply ethnicity, Gough notes that English is spreading in use among Black South Africans, so it is quite possible that Black native English speakers will continue to show these kinds of discourse patterns.

A related interactional factor is the use of backchanneling. As mentioned above, some Native-American groups tend to use much less of this kind of response in the course of a conversation than speakers from other backgrounds. Stubbe (1998) found similarly that Maori ethnicity listeners produced about a third less verbal feedback overall than Pakeha listeners, in conversation. Stubbe uncovered an interaction with gender in this study as well. Female speakers within each ethnic group were more likely to use what Stubbe called "overtly supportive" responses. As with the structural features that have been discussed in previous chapters, use of discourse features can also be affected by other social factors such as gender, age, and so forth.

In contrast to the more limited amount of feedback given by these groups, African-American communities have an extended system of resources for providing feedback to speakers. The most salient of these is "call and response," a genre associated particularly with church services.[2] In this setting, listeners provide both physical and verbal feedback to the minister in a structured way that encompasses patterns of tempo, a set of typical expressions (such as *Tell it!* or *That's right!*), and norms for the interaction of the minister and the congregation. Although call and response is associated with religious services, it can also take place in other settings. In symposia or lectures that I have attended where a substantial percentage of the audience is African-American, there is often some backchanneling to the speaker, either in response to a question or challenge, or simply as affirmation at appropriate intervals.[3] There is also some carryover of this pattern to conversations among individuals outside of any formal setting (see Green 2002:155).

Besides the overall frequency of backchanneling, the timing of the response is also crucial. Green (2002:148–9) notes that in call and response the congregation uses the minister's intonational patterns as a cue about when to respond, and that responses outside this "rhythm" are more frequent at the beginning than at the end of the sermon. In many cultures, the end of the intonation group or phrase is a key juncture for backchanneling, but not always. I have experienced my own version of the trouble my cousins had with native Japanese speakers. I find that students from Japan often backchannel "too early" when I'm speaking to them, making me want to say, "Wait, I'm not ready for you to agree yet!" Clancy et al. (1996) review the literature showing that Japanese speakers do, in fact, backchannel more frequently than English speakers, and their study confirms that Japanese speakers do not necessarily wait for a "transition relevance place" in the way that English speakers do. I have not encountered this pattern with Japanese-American students, and it may not transfer in this way at all across generations. In general, though, backchanneling has a surprisingly important role in interaction, and differences in its use related to ethnicity may be problematic for interethnic encounters.

8.3 JOKING

Humor, joking, and teasing others can all be important elements in the construction of a cultural identity. As Rickford and Rickford so eloquently put it, "[l]aughter . . . is often nothing more than the fleeting and reflective moment when one lays aside pretension and peers into the shadowy corners of one's own self image" (2000:62). These strategies can be used as an indirect way of enforcing cultural norms, as can be seen in many examples of signifying that Mitchell-Kernan (1972) provides. Humor can also be an important signal of ingroup membership, either because the nature of the joke itself relies on ingroup knowledge to be understood, or because making fun of others is a way of asserting our intimacy with them. In a sense, when we tease someone in a culturally appropriate fashion, we are saying, "I trust you not to be angry with me about this. I'm doing something potentially risky to show that you and I are both members of the same group, and understand that this is not to be taken seriously." In the particular case of minority ethnic groups, humor can be used as a way of fighting, subverting, or at least drawing attention to social injustice. Boskin (2004) discusses the public face of such humor, as part of the tradition of comedic entertainment:

> Protest and resistance have constantly fueled outsider comedy. Concomitantly sustaining morale while resisting encroachment, minorities have woven their way through society's obstacles with raillery. (2004:310)

This public comedy, as discussed in Chapter 6, is also linked to a more private humor among community members, which can form an important part of the construction of ethnic identity.

Research on Native-American communities reveals that many of these have some particular style of humor which is identified as a key element of the cultural identity. Wieder and Pratt (1990) list "razzing" as one of the practices crucial to being recognized as a "real Indian" in the Osage community they studied. Razzing is a type of verbal sparring arising from an ongoing situation or event taking place at the moment of utterance, and, like some other discourse styles that have been discussed, may include metaphors as part of the humor. Basso (1979) describes a very similar pattern among the Western Apache, who have a specific term (banagozdí?) for a type of humor in which "the person at whom the joke is directed is depicted as something he or she is not. In other words, the object of the joke . . . is made the subject of a metaphor" (1979:38). Basso illustrates this type of speech act with an example where an Apache man indirectly compares his tall, thin friend to a hunting rifle. In keeping with the idea discussed above that such humor may serve to highlight ingroup status, Wieder and Pratt report that Indians themselves regard razzing as "distinctively Indian" and "unintelligible to Whites" (1990:55).

Basso's (1979) study of the "Whiteman" performances also reveals how humor is linked to the question of ethnic identity. As discussed in Chapter 6, these performances contribute to our understanding of the construction of "white" as an ethnicity, but they also serve as an important part of the construction of Indian ethnicity in the community. The interactional features that are enacted in the Whiteman performance include, among other things, nosy inquiries about an individual's health, multiple directives (*Come in! Sit down!*), rapid repetition of questions in a series, and a great deal of exaggerated physical contact (back-slapping, hand-shaking, and so forth) (1979:49–53). Each of these contrasts with the appropriate norms for conduct within Apache culture, where it is considered rude to ask a question more than once or inquire about someone's health, and where physical contact in public is usually avoided.

By engaging in joking performances of the Whiteman, the Apaches may accomplish any number of different functions. They can highlight the distinction between Apache ingroup and white outgroup, reinforcing group identity by pointing out boundaries. They can participate in an act that may be highly subversive, a critique of the ethnic group that has historically had power over them and oppressed them, and thereby possibly reinforce group awareness of shared history and social injustices. And they can highlight group norms by enacting their opposites, conveying the message, "We all know how to behave right. We all know how Indians behave, and that is why this performance is funny to us as members of the same group."

Interestingly, a similar imitation of white speakers was found by Heath (1982) among children in a working-class African-American community. Speakers in this community do not normally employ what Heath terms "**known-answer questions**," questions such as "What color is that?," where both speaker and hearer know the answer. However, one 4-year-old boy in Heath's study, after beginning nursery school, produced a series of such questions and then burst into laughter (1982:120–1). It would not be surprising to find that other minority ethnic groups have similar routines, in which the language norms of the dominant group form the basis of joking play.

One of the most well-known joking rituals associated with a particular ethnic group is *playing the dozens* (also known by various other terms including *capping*, *snaps*, *ranking*, *sounding*, and so forth). This practice, found in some African-American communities in the USA, involves an exchange of ritual insults, often directed toward the addressee's mother or other family members (e.g., "Your mother wear high-heeled sneakers to church!" from Labov 1972a:311). This style of verbal dueling has often been associated in the literature with younger males; however, as Green (2002:139) points out, girls can also be adept at the dozens. There are certain similarities between the dozens and razzing, as Wieder and Pratt (1990) note. However, rather than focusing on ongoing events, ritual insults draw on a series of recurring themes, many of them having particular significance within the community. One of the most common "themes" for the dozens is poverty, for example, and in the social context of low-income communities joking about poverty could be viewed as a survival strategy, a way of "sustaining morale" as Boskin (2004:310) puts it. Ethnicity itself can also be an explicit focus of the dozens, and in fact one beginning for a ritual insult is "Your mama so black that . . .". There is also an example in Labov's study of "Your mother so white . . ." (Labov 1972a:312). It is beyond the scope of this text to analyze how these two formulations work together or in contrast to each other. But their use serves as an explicit indicator of how apparently spontaneous and insignificant joking rituals can be crucial windows into the construction of ethnic identity.

8.4 COMPLIMENTING

I once complimented a white, female colleague on her sweater. She plucked at the design on the front and responded, "Thanks! I like it too!" When I have reported this exchange to students from Japan in my classes, they giggle and look shocked, because this type of response would be completely unacceptable in Japan, where a deflection or outright rejection of the compliment is the norm. Both the format and frequency of compliments and the range of acceptable responses are tied to culture, and as such can also serve as markers of ethnic identity. These sorts of differences have been found in very different settings around the world.

A number of studies have focused on compliment responses, because these can be as important as, if not more important than, the compliments themselves. Chick (1996), for example, investigated responses to compliments by South Africans of three different ethnic backgrounds: Black, White, and Indian (meaning people of South Asian origin), and found notable differences among these groups. While White and Indian speakers accepted compliments about 42 percent of the time, for example, Black speakers gave an "accepting" response only 27 percent of the time. Blacks were much more likely than the other groups to produce a "no acknowledgment" response, a fact which Chick traces to possible origins in Zulu interaction patterns. Indian speakers were about three times as likely as those in other groups to respond with overt disagreement, sometimes in a very direct manner, e.g., A: *Your hair looks nice today.* B: *It's a mess.* (1996:277). These patterns are worth investigating, because they could easily be the source of cultural misunderstandings. In addition, as Chick notes, they can be indicators of both the historical social situation of South Africa and current social changes taking place there.

The reticence found among some speakers in South Africa shows up in the norms of a number of other cultures as well. Nhu (1994) discusses how Vietnamese-American parents may be reluctant to compliment their children, and contrasts it with Jewish-American culture, where this norm is not in effect. Similarly, Wieder and Pratt (1990) report that, in the Osage Native-American tribe, putting oneself above others in any way is very negatively valued, even to the point that bragging could lead one to be labeled as not a "real Indian." This view leads to a deflection of compliments. They provide as an illustration that, when a student is complimented on the fact that he or she is getting a college degree, the appropriate response would be, "I've gotten a lot of help" (1990:58).

Holmes (1998) presents the results of a number of studies on complimenting behaviors in different countries and settings. Though her main focus is on gender differences, she also reports ethnic differences for the use of compliments in New Zealand. In particular, she reports that speakers of Samoan ethnicity are more likely to respond to a compliment on a possession by offering it to the person who complimented it. Holmes gives an example of a Pakeha (white) woman who complimented a Samoan woman's necklace, and felt embarrassed when it was offered to her, because in Pakeha culture this response is not expected.

Looking in detail at complimenting behavior, as with the joking rituals discussed earlier, can provide some very specific insights into the construction of ethnic identity. Henderson (1996) focuses on compliments among African-Americans in Illinois, looking both at responses and at the types of compliments given in natural settings. She traces how cultural norms, including those that differ significantly from those in the local European-American communities, affect compliment

and response patterns. A number of the compliments Henderson analyzed stressed ingroup membership specifically, through the use of
ethnically marked terms like *girl* or *Miss Thang*, for instance. Other
compliments involved topics that were by nature related to ethnic
identity, such as the ability to cope in a context of racism and racial
tension, e.g., *Girl, you can really deal with them white folks* (1996a:206).

In terms of the responses Henderson looked at, one of the most
interesting results is that, although rejection of a compliment is a
possibility, "it is clear that the expression of agreement is much
more frequent for African-Americans" (1996a:204). In other words,
the norm of agreeing with the speaker is stronger than the norm
of avoiding self-praise, which differs somewhat from the norms of
comparable European-American communities. Henderson notes that
African-Americans "generally feel they have the right to just praise"
(1996a:204), and the rejection of a compliment may in fact be viewed
negatively by community members. There is a corollary effect of this
pattern in Henderson's data, although she does not discuss it explicitly, which is that a person being complimented can actually intensify
the compliment in his or her response, rather than accepting it neutrally. For example, a woman who is complimented on her appearance
in a beauty salon, including a comment that she is *too fine for this
place*, says in response, *Yeah, but I let y'all look at me anyway* (1996a:202).
A similar example occurs in the citation that opens this chapter, from
the movie *How Stella Got Her Groove Back* (1998), based on a book by the
African-American author Terry McMillan. As can be seen in both of
these examples, humor is an integral part of the intensifying response
category.

There are some parallels between cultural norms for responses
to compliments, and those discussed earlier related to direct-
ness/indirectness. In both cases, there seems to be a scale on which
different ethnic groups occupy different places. When a speaker uses
a form that is more direct or indirect than what speakers from another
group expect, it will be noticed, and the same is true of compliment
responses that are more "accepting" or more "rejecting" than those of
other cultures. The effects of such differences will be discussed more
in Chapter 9.

8.5 ACQUISITION OF LANGUAGE NORMS

We are seldom explicitly instructed about interactional norms. Our
parents don't usually say to us, "You don't leave a long enough pause

before coming in," or "You should rephrase that so it's more indirect" (much less "You should make a joke now"). So how, then, do we learn the norms of our community, including those that will be specifically associated with our ethnic background?

A number of scholars have looked at this question from the perspective of ethnicity. One clear result of their findings is that socialization of this type by the parents begins quite early, even before the child has any verbal abilities at all. Heath (1982), for example, gives the example of a European-American mother addressing her 2-month-old infant; the mother asks the infant a question, pauses, and then continues acting as though the child had given an "answer" in that space. This type of socialization prepares children to receive and respond to certain types of questions, such as "known-answer questions," that are typical of middle-class European-American culture (and that, not coincidentally, will be central to the mainstream educational system).

Acquisition of discourse norms by a child who has become verbal begins quite early as well, and again many of these are related to ethnicity. The European-American middle-class children in Heath's study (1982) had learned to respond to known-answer questions by the time they were 2 years old. The working-class African-American children in the study produced "story-poems," in which an event was described in a series of verse-like utterances, when they were as young as $2^1/_2$ (Heath 1983:170–3). Ritualized insults were also a genre found in this community, and Heath reports that, by the age of 3, children were experimenting with them. A boy who was $3^1/_2$, for example, produced the utterance *Yo' daddy have false teef* (Heath 1983:176). Similarly, Wyatt (1995) gives examples of children in the 3–5 age range practicing ritual insults and also rapping. In practical terms, these data indicate that many of the interactional norms related to ethnic background will be in place by the time the child reaches the school system, the implications of which will be discussed more in Chapter 9.

I began this section by noting that parents would never say to a child, "You should rephrase that so it's more indirect," but somehow children acquire directness and indirectness norms for their culture as well. Research by Clancy (1985) on interactions between Japanese children and their caretakers illustrates how this might, in fact, be accomplished. Clancy found that the caretakers often verbalized explicitly for the child the feelings or other information that were implicit in the indirect utterances of others. Sometimes these feelings were exaggerated beyond what was probably intended by the original speaker as a way of drawing the child's attention to the mismatch between surface words and hidden intentions. Even though this study is not focused specifically on the construction of ethnicity, we can see the implications for research on interethnic differences. Unfortunately, there is a striking paucity of research on Asian-American groups in the US. It is possible, however, that indirectness norms of this type might be transmitted to, e.g., Japanese-American children, who arrive at school speaking completely native English, but use it in ways that differ slightly from European-American children the same age. Even if they do not, in this specific case, the general idea is an important one: children who don't bring to the classroom any differences in language *structure* related to ethnicity could still bring differences in language *use*. These types of issues will be discussed in more detail in Chapter 9.

DISCUSSION QUESTIONS

1. How might stereotypes about groups arise out of differences in language use related to ethnicity? Have you ever been in a situation where there was a cultural misunderstanding due to differences in language use? What happened? How did you find out what was going on?
2. Think about two different ethnic groups that can be found in the area where you live. How do those groups compare in terms of indirectness? Use of silence? Design a research project to explore possible differences in some other pragmatic area, such as complimenting strategies.
3. Joking rituals often play a key role in the language use of particular ethnic groups. Why do you think humor might be so important to the construction of ethnic identity?

SUGGESTIONS FOR FURTHER READING

Goodwin, Marjorie Harness. 1990. *He-Said-She-Said: Talk as Social Organization Among Black children*. Bloomington, IN: Indiana University Press.

One of the first book-length studies of the acquisition of gender norms in language. Particularly interesting because so much research in the area has focused on white, middle-class speakers, while Goodwin's study looks at working-class African-American boys and girls.

Heath, Shirley Brice. 1983 *Ways with Words: Language, Life, and Work in Communities and Classrooms*. Cambridge and New York: Cambridge University Press.

A classic study of different interactional norms related to ethnicity, focusing on middle-class European-American, working-class European-American, and working-class African-American children in the southern USA. Heath shows how these norms affect children in the school setting.

Mitchell-Kernan, Claudia. 1972. Signifying, loud-talking and marking. In T. Kochman (ed.), *Rappin' and Stylin' Out: Communication in Urban America*. Chicago: University of Illinois Press. 315–35.

This article focuses on three different speech events among African-Americans in the USA, analyzing the structure and function of each of them in the social and historical context of African-American culture.

Morgan, Marcyliena H. 2002. *Language, Discourse and Power in African American Culture*. Cambridge and New York: Cambridge University Press.

A recent and comprehensive work on the use of various interactional patterns in African-American communities. Morgan highlights in particular areas that have been neglected in previous research, such as the particular strategies used by women.

Philips, Susan U. 1990. Some sources of cultural variability in the regulation of talk. In D. Carbaugh (ed.), *Cultural Communication and Intercultural Contact*. New Jersey: Lawrence Erlbaum. 329–45.

An article focusing on conversational strategies in a Native-American group and how these contrast with the expectations of other groups, and with analyses in the linguistic literature on discourse that have focused mainly on European-American middle-class speakers.

9 Interethnic communication and language prejudice

I have wrassled with an alligator. I done tussled with a whale. I done handcuffed lightning, throwed thunder in jail. That's bad. Only last week I murdered a rock, injured a stone, hospitalized a brick. I'm so mean, I make medicine sick. (Muhammad Ali, *When We Were Kings*, 1996)

9.1 TENNIS, ANYONE?

In 1996 Richard Williams predicted that his daughters, Venus and Serena, would dominate the world of tennis (Malley 2002). Among his other predictions at various points were that they would be ranked numbers one and two in the world, that they would play each other in the finals at Wimbledon, and that they would become "the next two female Michael Jordans" (CNN.com). The mainstream US media consistently reported on Williams' comments in a very negative fashion, as well as on other comments made by Venus and Serena themselves, such as Serena's "It's our ambition to take over tennis . . . and we're doing a decent job of it" (Baines 2000) or Venus's saying of her $40 million contract with Reebok "If you ask me . . . I'm worth it" (Puma 2005). The adjective most often used to describe them by the media? "Arrogant."

But are they? I was not surprised by the reaction of the media, but still I found it disappointing, mainly because as a researcher on language and ethnicity I saw in the media coverage something that most European-Americans did not see. The mainstream US media, unremarkably, presents everything from the perspective of the dominant white, middle-class culture. In this culture, speaking openly and explicitly of one's own accomplishments, and making sweeping predictions of future success, is generally taboo. Of course, the taboo is lifted in certain situations: job interviews, statements about company performance by CEOs. But otherwise, individuals are not expected (or permitted) to praise themselves openly. Therefore, someone who does so is seen as arrogant.

In African-American communities, however, a different set of norms is in play. Kochman (1981:63ff.) lays out the complex social norms governing acts of self-praise in detail. For African-Americans, too, certain types of bragging are considered unwarranted and objectionable. Speaking at length about one's possessions or financial success, for example, is usually viewed negatively (although in the subculture of rap artists this rule is clearly suspended). On the other hand "boasting," which is distinguished by its exaggerated quality, is generally seen as just for fun, and not objectionable. When Muhammad Ali, in the excerpt given above from the documentary *When We Were Kings* (1996), says, "I'm so mean, I make medicine sick," this clearly falls under the category of boasting, and even the attendees at Ali's press conference who were not African-American seemed to understand the intent and chuckled along with him.

Bragging about one's abilities is in some ways the most complex category. Kochman reports that this type of bragging can be viewed negatively. If the speaker can back up claims about abilities with performance, however, then it is no longer counted as bragging, and unlikely to be criticized. The different evaluations of bragging about possessions and about abilities may be related to a sense that an outstanding performance by a community member – for example, a great athlete – may be unifying and uplifting to the community. In 2002, Venus and Serena became the first siblings to rank numbers one and two in tennis. That same year they played each other in the finals at Wimbledon for the first time, and in 2003 they met in the Wimbledon finals yet again. In the African-American system of discourse, Richard Williams' comments have now crossed from "brag" to "simple fact." Within this complicated system of interactional norms, the comments of the Williams sisters and their father fit perfectly and are quite appropriate to community values.[1]

As with other elements of cultural practice, it is easy to see how norms for language use might be tied to the historical and social context of a particular community. As Gudykunst et al. note in their discussion of verbal communication styles, "there may exist a set of deep-rooted historical-political logics that surround the use of one predominant style over another in different cultures" (1988:104). In a context of pervasive and persistent racism, African-American children have historically been told by teachers, employers, and others that they could never do, or be, certain things. In this context, it seems natural that communities would develop a strategy to counter those negative judgments, summed up loosely as "If others won't give us the praise that is our due, we'll give it to ourselves. If others are going to tell us we can't, we will preempt them by saying openly that we can." Nonetheless, knowledge of the cultural and historical bases for these language patterns is usually not found in other ethnic groups (including the dominant one). In the media reports on Venus and Serena Williams, as in so many other matters, ignorance of cultural differences among ethnic groups has led members of the dominant group to judge others by a standard that comes from outside the group, and is therefore inappropriate. This one case exemplifies many of the issues that come up in looking at interethnic communication.

9.2 INTERETHNIC COMMUNICATION

When two individuals who speak different languages try to communicate, in a service encounter for example, the difficulties are clear. They may use body language and gestures to try to get a concept across, or throw out whatever few words of the other language they know, and smiles or shrugs may play a prominent role in the exchange. At least in the encounters like this that I have witnessed, though, there is not usually a sense of great frustration or hostility. Everyone understands the nature of the problem, and usually there is an agreement to muddle through if possible and, if communication fails, to let it go without too much fuss.

When people of different ethnic backgrounds are using the *same* language, however, very different problems can arise. To begin with, neither person may be aware that there even exists a difference in language use associated with the other group. As was discussed in Chapter 8, interactional differences, like all aspects of culture, are relative to the norms of a particular community. What is perceived as somewhat abrupt in one group may seem unnecessarily polite to another, but our socialization is such that we are blinded to this relativity. Instead we feel confident that certain things are just "obviously" rude, bad manners, arrogant, and so forth, without any sense of how these judgments can vary from community to community. When individuals are native speakers of the same language, each of them is particularly likely to expect familiar interactional norms from the other person, but these norms can vary quite a bit across ethnic groups. Interethnic encounters can reveal many aspects of how ethnicity is indexed through language, some of which have important practical and social ramifications.

Many of the features discussed in Chapter 8 as being representative of the discourse patterns of different ethnic groups, such as the use of indirect speech or the notion of how much silence is appropriate, can lead to interethnic miscommunication. I will present a selection of data from research on interethnic communication from a range of communities, exploring the effects of different discourse styles in personal interactions, particularly in public settings where multiple ethnic groups interact. It is easy, of course, to focus on how differing linguistic styles related to ethnicity can lead to interethnic conflicts. Such conflicts are very salient in our experiences and in the body of linguistic research. Putting a more positive spin on this topic, though, we can focus in addition on the wealth that different interactional styles might bring to settings such as the classroom or the workplace, and explore how such differences might be used as an advantage.

Research on linguistic differences related to ethnicity can also illuminate a more general discussion of language and dialect prejudice. While many of these prejudices, as with the media coverage of Venus and Serena Williams, stem from interethnic differences in communication style, not all of them can be explained in this way. A number of cases are presented here that show how language can stand in for a wide range of biases related to ethnicity, revealing the diverse forms that language prejudice can take.

9.3 DIFFERENCES IN LANGUAGE USE NORMS IN PUBLIC SETTINGS

When multiple ethnic groups interact in public settings, interactional norms tied to ethnicity can become very salient. Let's begin with what seems like a simple question. How do you end a conversation? As with so many areas, native speakers may have no intuitions (or rather no *accurate* intuitions) about this type of discourse pattern, but in fact ending a conversation can be a complex, many-step ritual. In many English-speaking cultures, for example, one of the elements of this winding-down process is the use of formulas such as *See you later* or *Take care*. For Athabaskans in the USA and Canada, however, such formulas violate a norm involving not talking about the future. As Scollon and Scollon (1981) report, in their analysis of this and other interactional patterns among Athabaskans, there are a number of areas in which the norms of Athabaskans and those of the European-American or mainstream Canadian cultures conflict. When individuals from the different groups meet in public settings, many miscommunications can occur, so these contact points are a good place to begin looking at interethnic communication.

The dialect of English that Athabaskans speak, as Scollon and Scollon describe it, has some distinctive features but is not so different from other varieties as to pose inherent problems for communication. It is in the area of interactional patterns that the major differences appear. To begin with, the two groups have different views of the use of silence, an important part of the turn-taking rules. In general, Scollon and Scollon report, Athabaskans talk less than other Canadians and Americans, and also have a longer interval of pausing between speaker turns (a pattern similar to the Japanese–Spanish difference discussed at the beginning of Chapter 8). They also tend to avoid direct questions. As a result, Athabaskans may see people of other ethnic groups as too pushy and talkative, while those same people may view them as taciturn, or talking only with close acquaintances.

Some interactional differences are heightened particularly in the types of settings where the two groups are most likely to encounter each other, such as job interviews or petitioning situations in which the interviewer is from a mainstream group. In a job interview, for instance, the interviewer expects the candidate to talk about past accomplishments and future goals. (If you yourself are from one of these mainstream groups, you are probably thinking, "Well, of course!" – a good illustration of the point made earlier about how interactional norms are naturalized.) But Scollon and Scollon note that, for Athabaskans, talking about accomplishments is a kind of bragging. In other cultures this same taboo is lifted slightly in situations like a job interview, as long as the person doesn't exaggerate beyond a certain point, but Athabaskans do not share this implicit permission to brag. As for discussing future goals, the Athabaskan reluctance to talk about the future has already been covered, and will of course make this difficult to accomplish. If it is the Athabaskan who is conducting the interview, he or she will probably see the speaker from the mainstream group as boasting too much, and talking carelessly about the future – the same problem, but in reverse.

We find a similar situation in Australia – about as far as one can get from northern Canada, where the Athabaskan research was conducted. Here, occasions of interethnic communication between Anglo-Australians and members of First Nations ethnic groups (often called "Aboriginal people") can run into the same sorts of difficulties based on differing interactional patterns, although again the language of communication (English) is shared. Eades (1991) discusses several features of the communicative style associated with speakers of "Aboriginal

English." Speakers from these ethnic groups, for instance, avoid direct questions in certain situations. Instead, they will seek information by offering some statement of their own knowledge about a topic and then pausing to allow the listener to respond if the person so chooses. Like the Warm Springs Indians discussed in Chapter 8, First Nations speakers, according to Eades, may answer questions as much as several days later. Also like the various Native-American groups that have been discussed, they are not at all uncomfortable with silence, in the way that many European-based cultures can be, and don't feel a need to have minimal gaps between turns in a conversation.

In general, requests are formulated by First Nations people in ways that encompass indirectness and ambiguity. Eades gives the example of a person who wanted a car ride to town, asking, *You going to town?* (1991:88). While this type of strategy can also be used in other groups, of course, it usually coexists with other more direct forms, which First Nations people are unlikely to use, such as *Could you possibly give me a ride to town?* The formulation of refusals is similarly indirect, as in the examples Eades gives of possible negative responses to the ride request, such as *Might be later* or *Not sure* (1991:88). Another related strategy involves seeking information about people's motivations. Eades notes that First Nations speakers almost never use the question *Why?*, preferring instead indirect formulations of questions such as *You went to town yesterday?* (1991:88).

Another important characteristic of interactional patterns in this group is a degree of hesitancy in presenting personal opinions. Eades notes that First Nations speakers prefer to discuss topics very generally before presenting any views and, if they feel there might be a conflict between their views and those of others, they tend to downplay their opinions. This pattern is related to the high value placed on harmony among members of these communities. As Liberman (1990) notes, the preservation of consensus among participants in a conversation is a primary constraint among First Nations people. Among the Western Desert people with whom Liberman did his research, this goal is often achieved by a discourse process in which a summary of the conclusions of the group is offered by someone and then repeated by other participants in no particular order until a consensus has been reached. The rapidity and volume of this process sometimes startles Anglo-Australians who observe it. All of these discourse strategies tie in to elements of the culture associated with First Nations people (see Eades [1991] for more discussion of this issue).

The differences between First Nations people and Anglo-Australians have important practical repercussions. In courtrooms, for example, the tendency of Western Desert people to prefer harmony may lead them to agree with whatever the person questioning them suggests (Liberman 1990). In interactions with government officials, speakers from First Nations communities may need a relatively long time to discuss any proposals and reach consensus. In the meantime, the official, presumably a member of the dominant Anglo-Australian culture, often grows impatient and leaves without providing the needed services (Liberman 1990). As in other settings, the lack of understanding about differences in discourse styles can make it difficult for individuals in interethnic conversations even to identify what went wrong.

Another setting of interest to the theme of this section is the city of Los Angeles, where (in 1992) interethnic conflicts culminated in several days of riots throughout that city that led to 53 deaths and millions of dollars of damage. The initial spark for the riots was the brutal beating of an African-American man who had been pulled over for speeding by four white police officers. But many believe that interethnic communication problems that had been simmering for years before this event also played a prominent role in the nature of the rioting that took place. Specifically, many of the people rioting targeted Asian and Asian-American business owners (particularly Koreans). Why?

For years, Asian immigrants had been establishing local businesses such as grocery and liquor stores in predominantly African-American areas of Los Angeles. In service encounters between these groups, a number of cultural norms had emerged as different enough to cause conflict. Bailey (1997) analyzes videotapes of a number of conversations in liquor stores between African-American customers and Korean storekeepers. He contrasts the African-American interaction patterns with those of Korean customers, looking at how each group shows respect. African-Americans use more positive politeness strategies (such as maintaining eye contact or making small talk) to communicate respect. Bailey places this view of what is "polite" in the context of the type of racism and discrimination that African-Americans have experienced, including a history of being treated by storekeepers as if they are not legitimate customers. Koreans, in contrast, appear more "restrained," because they tend to use negative politeness strategies to communicate respect, privileging the idea of not imposing on others. Although both groups appear to have exactly the same goal in the interaction, because their ways of encoding respect into the discourse are so different, there is an overall miscommunication based on expectations related to the patterns typical for each ethnic group. Bailey suggests that these differences in discourse patterns play a crucial role in the social maintenance of ethnic boundaries, and that, no matter how much exposure each group might have to the other's behaviors, they are unlikely to assimilate to each other because the dominant ideology constructs them as being in opposition.

One point that has not yet been covered is the role of interethnic differences in the expression and interpretation of emotion. Many of the basic elements of interactional style associated with a particular ethnic group may map onto elements that convey a particular emotion in the repertoire of some other group. For example, Conklin and Lourie (1983) note that Japanese-Americans may respond to embarrassment with nervous giggling. For European-Americans, however, giggling is generally not appropriate in situations of serious shame or embarrassment (although it may be acceptable if something is both embarrassing and funny). In European-American groups, giggling maps onto feelings of amusement, at least in some tangential way. A European-American friend of mine who had been teaching an English as a Second Language class became very angry when she handed back some exams which most of the class had failed, and several of the Asian students giggled. "Do you think this is funny?" she asked them, in a hostile tone. Of course, they didn't.

A contrasting example comes from the interactional style of Korean-Americans. Bailey (1997) finds that a number of the behaviors among the shopkeepers he observed were rooted in Confucianism, a dominant influence on Korean ideologies. A key principle for Korean adults is restraint in expressing affect. As one of the Korean-American speakers in Bailey's study put it, "If you laugh or smile, you don't have enough in your head. You're supposed to be stoic and expressionless" (2000:93). (As a side note, one of the points clearly illustrated by the previous two examples is the fallibility of categories like "Asian-American," since two groups that would fall within the scope of this term in US-dominant racial ideologies construct the expression of emotion very differently.)

A similar principle is involved when we ask: How do you know if someone is angry? In most cultures, the words "I am so angry at you" occur only occasionally, if at all, in situations where a speaker wishes to express anger. Depending at least partly on the directness or indirectness of the culture, anger is expressed in different ways and, as with other discourse patterns, the interpretation of an interactional style as anger is completely relative. Kochman (1981) analyzes in detail how some discourse strategies used by African-Americans are often interpreted by European-Americans as being "too emotional." He explains how, in African-American verbal tradition, when one is arguing a point, it is normal to show passion and emotions that reflect an engagement with the material, as well as a serious and sincere attitude about what one is arguing. European-Americans, on the other hand, tend to invoke a "cool, rational" mode for debates of this type, in which the appearance of affect is eliminated. This mismatch leads them to misinterpret the affective format of African-American speakers as signifying anger or hostility, rather than seriousness of purpose (1981:18–19). On the other hand, African-Americans may perceive European-Americans who are using a detached argument mode as being "insincere" (1981:22).

Just to show how relative these "emotional mappings" are, we can compare the above scenario with interpretations of European-American interactional style in another setting: interaction with Native-American groups. To the African-Americans, the style of the European-Americans, if anything, conveyed an inappropriate lack of emotion. Native Americans often interpret the style of European-Americans differently. Basso (1979) notes that the Western Apache tend to speak in low modulated tones to each other, so that the relatively louder and higher-pitched intonation used by European-Americans maps onto a critical or indignant emotional function for them. As one Western Apache informant put it, "Whitemen make lots of noise . . . it sounds too much like they mad at you. With some, you just can't be sure about it, so you just got to be careful with them all the time" (1979:55). A similar problem arises in the interactions of Anglo-Australians with First Nations people. Liberman notes that Anglo-Australians value the ability to "think for oneself," even if this means expressing disagreement with others; among First Nations people, though, "[t]he more forceful style of self-presentation of Anglo-Australians is sometimes viewed to be evidence of anger where none exists" (1990:183). I am struck by how similar this description seems to that of interactions between African-Americans and European-Americans, except that in the two cases the role of the European-descent groups is reversed. What is really illustrated here is that, even though emotional mappings of interactional patterns may seem particularly "obvious" to us, in the end they are as relative as anything else.

Up to this point, all the interethnic miscommunications that have been discussed have focused on interactional style. It is clearly possible to have misunderstandings even when the linguistic forms are perfectly clear. There are occasions, though, when specific differences in linguistic structure between dialects can also cause misunderstanding. Structural differences are particularly salient in the case of AAVE, which, as discussed in Chapter 3, has a complex aspectual system that can be difficult for speakers of other English dialects to comprehend fully. Heath (1983:277) gives an example of a European-American teacher who asked a child from Trackton about a girl who was absent. He responded, "She ain't ride de bus." The teacher misinterpreted this as meaning that the girl never took the bus to school, but in fact the boy was using *ain't* as a variant for *didn't*, meaning that she didn't ride the bus on that particular day. Reports of these types of structural misunderstandings are fairly sparse in the literature, though, so it seems reasonable to suggest that interactional differences are a more frequent cause of miscommunication.

It is easy to abstract from these specific cases of interethnic miscommunication to how stereotypes are formed, based on differences in interactional style. Given how common such differences are, we might expect that in any interethnic encounter there will be at least some norms that differ slightly and will probably lead to miscommunication. Furthermore, these issues are not trivial ones. The term "miscommunication" seems inadequate to describe the full range of social situations that can result. The example of the Los Angeles riots shows us that differences in interactional patterns among ethnic groups can have extremely serious consequences. Bringing attention to these issues is a crucial application of research in the field of language and ethnicity.

At the same time, we must be very cautious about encouraging people to change their interactional patterns in order to reduce interethnic friction. As Scollon and Scollon put it,

> If we suggest change we have to be very aware that we are not only suggesting change in discourse patterns. We are suggesting change in a person's identity . . . If someone says an Athabaskan should talk more about plans, should speak out more on his [or her] own opinions, or not be so indirect, he [or she] is saying that he [or she] should stop being so Athabaskan. (1981:37)

We cannot simply tell Korean shop owners to smile more, or African-American customers not to make eye contact. Being aware of patterns in other ethnic groups, though, is always a good thing. As in so many areas, in interethnic communication knowledge is power: by understanding where our conversational partner is coming from, we have a better chance of achieving whatever goals we have for the interaction.

9.4 LANGUAGE VARIETIES AND INTERACTIONAL STYLES IN THE CLASSROOM

In most multiethnic societies, the classroom is one important setting where people of different ethnic backgrounds come into contact. Teachers are often members of the dominant ethnic group, and even if they are not they will probably have assimilated the predominant interactional norms in the course of their professional preparation. The students, on the other hand, at least in most large urban areas, may represent a wide range of linguistic varieties and interactional norms. As with other settings where intercultural communication takes place, ignorance of ethnic differences related to language can cause misunderstandings and lead to unwarranted negative evaluations of students whose interaction patterns do not exactly match the school culture.

One of the most basic questions in language interaction, at school and elsewhere, is: When is it OK to talk? Students of different ethnic backgrounds may answer this question in different ways. In some African-American communities, for example, children are discouraged from providing personal information to outsiders (Heath 1982). Heath reports that in Trackton, the working-class community she studied, when adults associated with the school asked personal questions, the African-American children tended not to respond, and as a result they would be "judged uncooperative, 'stupid', or 'pathetic'" (Heath 1982:116). Conklin and Lourie (1983) discuss how Hawaiian children in the classroom sometimes follow the pattern of traditional Polynesian cultures, where narratives are produced by many voices speaking at once. These children may overlap with and interrupt other students in their responses to the teacher. Heath (1983:280) reports a similar pattern for African-American children in Trackton, who sometimes interrupted the teacher or talked to other children during an activity such as story time, where only the teacher was "allowed" to speak.

In general, students may be hesitant to talk when a classroom speech event is completely unfamiliar to them. Both Heath (1982) and Labov (1972a) look at the reactions of African-American students to known-answer questions, which as discussed in Chapter 8 are not typical of these communities. Heath (1982) notes that one African-American boy, Lem, did not participate in nursery-school activities that involved labeling items and discussing their features. If possible he would try to "escape" to some other activity. On the other hand, when the activity involved learning how to perform a particular task, where known-answer questions were uncommon, Lem participated enthusiastically. Heath reports that older children either would not respond to these questions, or would simply repeat an answer given to a previous question. Since teachers often consider these types of questions to be the "easiest" ones, it is not surprising that they evaluate very negatively the children who cannot answer them. Similarly, Labov (1972a:206) provides the example of an African-American child who, as part of a school evaluation, is brought into a room with a European-American interviewer and asked questions about a toy airplane sitting on the table. These known-answer questions (like "What color is it?") disorient the child, who has no context in the norms of his community for understanding why someone would ask a question to which they can clearly see the answer. This results in pauses of six to twenty seconds before and during his answers. Not surprisingly, this hesitancy is often interpreted by teachers as lack of verbal ability, when in fact it is a sign of interethnic differences.

Strikingly parallel patterns of hesitation or silence are found in children from other ethnic groups, although the basis for the patterns may vary from culture to culture. Since Native-American ethnic groups tend to have a more varied and extensive use of silence, children from these groups often use silence to respond to unfamiliar situations. Leap (1993:87) notes that when Native-American children are given language development tests, the period of silence before they respond is often several times that of other children their age. A similar phenomenon is found among children from First Nations ethnic groups in Australia. In the culture of these children, as discussed earlier, group consensus is emphasized and individuals are not singled out and forced to respond. When the teacher singles out a child from this ethnic group in the classroom, then, the child often does not respond, and in general shows signs of being embarrassed (Liberman 1990). Among Black South African English-speaking students, de Klerk and Gough note that "lack of student participation may indicate respect for the teacher as the repository of knowledge" (2002:366). In each of these cases, the students' use of silence stems from cultural values related to ethnicity. Unfortunately, it is easy for teachers and speech pathologists to interpret these responses as evidence of a learning problem, or even of a negative attitude, rather than simply as cultural differences.

There are other expectations and practices that children bring to the school setting that may conflict with the norms of the educational culture, many of them related to the ethnic differences in interactional style that have already been discussed. In terms of directness and indirectness, for instance, differences between the teacher and student can be problematic. Heath reports that the parents of African-American children in Trackton normally used plain directives such as *Pick up your coat* to instruct children on what to do. In contrast, teachers in the schools often used quite indirect and ambiguous forms such as *Is this where the scissors belong?* or *Someone else is talking now; we'll all have to wait*, which were often difficult for the African-American children to interpret (1983:280). As a result, the teachers might think that the children were being willfully uncooperative, or that their level of comprehension was inexplicably low, when, again, an interactional difference was responsible. A slightly different version of this phenomenon is reported by Leap (1993) for Lakota English-speaking schoolchildren. When the teacher has something the child needs, the child may frame his or her request in a very direct way (e.g., *Teacher, you must give me a pencil!*), which middle-class teachers of other backgrounds find impolite (1993:86). At the other end of the spectrum, First Nations children may phrase requests to the teacher in indirect ways, much like the patterns typical among adults discussed earlier. To the Anglo-Australian teachers, these vague observations or comments are frustrating and difficult to interpret as requests.

Another area of potentially serious difference among ethnic groups in the classroom encompasses turn-taking norms and the non-verbal behavior associated with speakers and listeners. First Nations children, because of the same cultural values mentioned earlier, try not to single others out, and this includes not looking directly into another person's eyes (Liberman 1990). Anglo-Australian teachers may see this as a sign of disrespect, when in fact the opposite is intended. This pattern of averting gaze to show respect can be found in many other groups, including African-Americans (Hecht et al. 1993), Asian-Americans (Conklin and Lourie 1983), and Native Americans (Philips 1990). In terms of turn-taking specifically, teachers report that the First Nations children sometimes talk over one another and don't know how to "take turns" (Liberman 1990). This phenomenon probably seems paradoxical to the teachers who were just moments earlier complaining about the same children's excessive silence. But, like the other patterns, viewed in light of the interactional style typical for this ethnic group, all the children's uses of language are perfectly consistent, and are furthermore tied to the expression of cultural values related to ethnicity.

9.5 TEACHING A STANDARD VARIETY TO SPEAKERS OF VERNACULAR VARIETIES

Issues of language and ethnicity in the classroom involve not only interactional patterns of the type that have been discussed, but also the specific language varieties that children bring to the classroom. Perhaps the biggest concern, and certainly one to which a vast amount of sociolinguistic research has been dedicated, is the teaching of the standard language to speakers of other dialects. I cannot hope to cover this topic adequately here. Instead I will give a brief overview, and then focus mostly on the specific role of ethnic identity in the debates about how (or whether) to teach a standard dialect, looking particularly at cases of teaching Standard English to AAVE speakers in the USA.

Rickford (1999: 329ff.) provides a comprehensive discussion of the difficulties faced by speakers of a vernacular dialect in the classroom. These include not only those directly related to dialect differences themselves, but also some linked to prejudice against non-standard varieties on the part of the teachers, and even towards students of minority ethnic backgrounds who speak a standard variety (see the discussion of Williams [1983] below). Among the startling facts that Rickford uncovers is this: the longer African-American children stay in the US public school system, the more they, as a group, fall behind other groups in scholastic achievement tests. Research of many types from across the country confirms this massive failure on the part of US schools.

It is an awareness of this failure to help African-American students progress in the educational system that sparked one school district in Oakland, California to pass a now famous resolution on Ebonics (AAVE) in 1996. A number of top scholars have written extensively on this controversy, which I will summarize only briefly here.[2] The Oakland School Board's resolution basically called for the recognition of Ebonics as the main language of African-American children in the system, and proposed the use of Ebonics in the classroom to facilitate their acquisition of English-language skills (meaning the standard variety, although the original wording did not necessarily make this clear).

In what is probably the most intense media event ever in the USA revolving around language and ethnicity, this resolution exploded into public awareness, controversy, and, at times, overt racism. To cite just one particularly heinous example, Ward Connerly, an African-American regent of the University of California system, said:

> I think it's tragic . . . These are not kids who came from Africa last year or last generation even . . . These are kids who have had every opportunity to acclimate themselves to American society, and they have gotten themselves into this trap of speaking this language – this slang really – that people can't understand. Now we're going to legitimize it. (*San Francisco Chronicle*, December 21, 1996)

Where to begin discussing a citation like this one? There are the linguistic facts, of course: AAVE is not slang, in fact there is no such thing as a variety that consists only of slang; comprehension between AAVE and other dialects can be quite good except for certain specific forms (like those discussed earlier) that cause misunderstanding. But beyond this, Connerly's statement ignores everything we know about language and ethnicity. People do not speak in a particular way because they fell into a "trap." They use language deliberately to construct their identities, positioning themselves with respect to ethnicity and many other factors. The children Connerly refers to are using the variety that is most appropriate to their circumstances, the one that their friends and family most *fully* understand, not just in terms of structures and content, but in terms of the messages it sends about who they are and how the community fits together. They have, in fact, "acclimated" to "American society," the part of American society that surrounds them every day.

One sad part of the Oakland Resolution is that in the media frenzy two important points were covered over or lost. The first point is that, as mentioned earlier, there was compelling evidence that the public school system was failing African-American students on an almost incomprehensible scale. The second point is that there was also, even at the time, compelling evidence that the use of a vernacular variety (and specifically of AAVE) could help students in their mastery of a standard variety. Rickford (1999:336–42) summarizes a number of studies showing that African-American children learn more and do better on evaluative measures of language when AAVE is incorporated into the instruction process. The studies represent very different methods and tasks: some evaluated reading comprehension and others evaluated composition; some involved "**Contrastive Analysis,**" a focus on specific points of difference between the two varieties, while others focused on building specific skills in the vernacular and then switching over to a standard variety, so that students would be able to transfer their skills. In each case, however, the students acquired more facility with the standard variety than comparable students who were taught with traditional methods where the vernacular was treated as irrelevant if not unmentionable. Although these studies all focused on AAVE, the principles involved should be applicable to ethnic minority groups in other settings, and in fact Rickford (1999:343–4) cites a number of similar studies in other countries. Unfortunately, despite being so successful, the use of these methods in the USA has not yet been embraced by the public. Still, linguists and educators in a number of school systems are working to establish teaching methods based on linguistically (and psychologically) sound approaches.

One of the most important points to keep in mind when thinking about language, ethnicity, and the school system is that teaching a standard dialect is nothing like teaching math. Children do not arrive at school already using a mathematical system that is an integral part

of their identity. They do not employ particular mathematical principles in expressing their relationship to family and friends. It is unlikely
that they will risk charges of "selling out" in their community if someone catches them solving an equation. For these reasons, we cannot
approach the teaching of a standard dialect as we would that of any
other subject. There has been abundant evidence in the research presented so far to show that language is at the very heart of identity. An
educational system that plows ahead while ignoring this information
is doomed to fail.

It is this strong role of language in identity that leads Wolfram and
Schilling-Estes to conclude that the teaching of Standard English must
take into account the "**group reference**" factor, and that speakers of
a vernacular variety will be most likely to learn Standard English if
"their social orientation is geared toward a standard English speaking group" (1998:288). In the context of the perspectives on the role
of language in ethnic identity presented here, such a statement may
seem unsurprising, yet it is hardly ever a primary focus in materi-
als on teaching the standard to vernacular speakers. Possibly, there
is a conflation of this idea with assimilation to the dominant group,
a misinterpretation of it as meaning, for example, that if we wish
to offer African-American children the best chance to learn Standard English, we must convince them to want to be like middle-
class European-American speakers. But of course, this is inaccurate.
As discussed at length in Chapter 3, African-American communities
in the USA encompass a wide range of varieties. We only need to find
a group of people within the community, or in some larger group
beyond the community, with whom a child can identify, and who are
using a standard variety at least some of the time. Only in the context of understanding the construction of ethnic identity through language can the teaching of a standard variety have any chance of being
successful.

9.6 ACCENT HALLUCINATION

Much as we might hope for a day when all dialects of a language
are equally valued, we know that is not currently the case in most
modern societies. When someone speaks a non-standard dialect of a
language, they are often subjected to discrimination. The perception
of stigmatized forms in language can lead to prejudice on the part of
hearers. But another intriguing question is: Can prejudice on the part
of the hearers lead to the perception of stigmatized forms (even where

in reality these do not exist)? The answer, unfortunately, appears to be yes.

One place where perceptions may color expectations of language is in the school setting. Williams (1983) presents the results of several studies of the stereotypes that teachers in the USA have about students of different ethnic backgrounds, in language and in other areas. One of the most interesting studies asked a group of European-American student teachers to watch a videotape of a child who could be seen speaking from the side. There were three different versions of the video, one with a European-American child, one with an African-American child, and one with a Mexican-American child. Regardless of which video they saw, the accompanying audio file they heard was of the same standard English-speaking child. The African-American and Mexican-American children were rated as significantly more "non-standard" in their speech than the European-American child, even though the voice was the same in all three cases. So it is possible for expectations about language and ethnicity to override the actual linguistic nature of an individual's speech in the minds of hearers. A final note of interest from this study: Williams mentions that in pilot studies he performed, teachers would gladly fill in ratings scales both for very short samples of speech, and also "when simply told of a particular type of child who was to speak and where no tape was presented as a stimulus" (1983:359). It says something about the strength of our prejudices about language and ethnicity that they can apply even to imaginary individuals about whom hearers have no real information at all.

Lippi-Green (1997:126–9) looks at the issue from the other side, focusing on perceptions of teachers by students. She reports on an alarming study by Rubin (1992), which investigated how attitudes about ethnicity and race shaped perceptions of language. Sixty-two undergraduates, all native speakers of English, listened to a short lecture while viewing a picture which they were told was of the instructor. The person speaking was a native speaker of English with no marked regional accent. Half of the students saw a picture of a European-American woman, and the other half saw a picture of an Asian woman. The students who saw the picture of the Asian woman were more likely to rate the instructor as having "an Asian accent" (even though they were hearing the same, unmarked speech as the students who saw someone who looked white). In essence they "hallucinated" a foreign accent that was not actually there, based on the speaker's alleged ethnicity. What is even more disturbing is that the students who saw the picture of the Asian woman actually scored lower on a comprehension test about the lecture, good evidence that language prejudices can be quite harmful to those who hold them.

There is also research to suggest that the relevant issue here may be perceptions of race, rather than some more generalized concept of foreign origin. Atagi (2003) conducted a follow-up study to Rubin in which she asked US undergraduates to rate the "accents" of three speakers who were identified to them as "international graduate student instructors." In fact, the three individuals were monolingual native speakers of English, and in a control experiment where no information was given they were all judged as having no accent. In the main experiment, Atagi assigned a foreign identity to each voice (French-Canadian, Korean, or Mexican) and asked monolingual English speakers to rank the voices by accent, leaving open the possibility of ranking them all as equally accented or as having no accent. In this version of the task, *only two* out of the twenty test subjects did not hear an accent for any of the speakers. Furthermore, the French-Canadian identity was much more likely to be ranked as the "least accented" than were the other two identities, even though all three were in reality native speakers of American English. The results for the Korean and Mexican guises were quite similar to each other. In the second phase of the experiment, a group of monolingual and multilingual subjects was asked to rank the same three voices and identities numerically. Again, the French-Canadian guise received the most native-like ratings. The Korean guise, though, was ranked slightly higher than the Mexican guise. Atagi attributes this difference partly to the high ratings given to this guise by Korean and other Asian speakers in the subject group. Overall, then, it seems that the more "ethnically different" a speaker is perceived to be by the hearer, the more likely the hearer is to perceive an accent where none is present.

9.7 MATCHED GUISE STUDIES AND LINGUISTIC PROFILING

A related but slightly different area of study involves the assessment of speaker attitudes and prejudices where there *is* some objective linguistic difference in the speech samples being evaluated. In particular, the "**matched guise**" technique involves having listeners evaluate two versions of an utterance representing different dialects or languages to reveal stereotypes they may associate with these varieties. A number of these studies have focused specifically on ethnic differences. Tucker and Lambert (1969), a classic study of this type, found that AAVE speakers were rated lower on a number of qualities (e.g., "intelligence," "education") than standard speakers. Linn and Pichè (1982) looked at the reactions of children and adolescents to Standard English and AAVE and found a complex pattern of attitudes. Middle-class African-American girls, for example, gave the lowest ratings to AAVE, while several of the groups rated AAVE speakers highly on physical prowess. Cross et al. (2001), who incidentally give a comprehensive review of studies on this topic, explored the attitudes of students in a teacher education program. Their study revealed, among other things, a correlation between the race of the rater and the evaluation of the varieties. African-American listeners tended to rate African-American speakers more highly than European-American speakers did, and vice versa.

More recently, there has been increased interest in applying such attitudinal data to specific situations that speakers of different language varieties might encounter. One such application is the study of **linguistic profiling**. This term is associated with the research of John Baugh and his associates (Baugh 1999, Purnell et al. 1999). Baugh was inspired to do this research because of his own experience looking for housing in a predominantly white college town. Baugh is African-American, but as a professor he speaks a very standard variety of English, with no phonological or grammatical forms that might provide clues about ethnic identity. He found that, in several instances, he would be offered an appointment over the phone to see an apartment, but when he arrived he was told that the apartment had been rented or that there had been a mixup of some sort. Baugh suspected that his race might be a factor in these incidents; the managers had been unable to determine his race over the phone, and were reluctant to rent to him when they discovered that he was black. He predicted that individuals whose ethnicity was identifiable from the dialect of English they used might not be given appointments at all in these situations (Baugh 1999:136).

Baugh began a series of matched-guise style studies in which he would call the same prospective landlord using either his Standard English variety, or one of two non-standard varieties: AAVE or Chicano English. The distinguishing features in each case were phonological rather than grammatical. He was then able to test whether the use of one of the non-standard, ethnically identifiable varieties negatively affected his chances of getting an appointment. Purnell et al. (1999), one of the most comprehensive studies of linguistic profiling, provides some results of these experiments. In geographic areas where the population was predominantly white, the Standard English guise yielded a much higher number of appointments. In Woodside, for example, which is 94.7 percent white, the standard guise elicited appointments to see apartments 70 percent of the time, while the AAVE guise yielded appointments only 29 percent of the time, and the Chicano English guise, only 22 percent of the time.

Since its inception, this line of research has proven very fruitful in illuminating the mechanisms of linguistic prejudice. One interesting and perhaps surprising result is that, when a speaker does use a linguistic variety linked with a particular minority ethnicity, most hearers need very little speech in order to make the ethnic identification. Purnell et al. (1999), for example, found that listeners could often identify a dialect using only the word *hello*. While it is a matter of common knowledge that hearers can often identify a speaker's ethnicity from linguistic features, studies of linguistic profiling have connected this abstract fact to an explicit pattern of racial discrimination in specific settings and communities.

Imagining a classroom . . .

In the majority of the literature on cross-ethnic communication that I have read, the focus is on the problems that can occur. The "positive" side consists of "fixing" those problems so that there will be less friction in interethnic encounters, or so that children in school will be more likely to succeed on tests designed by speakers from the dominant ethnic group. I support these laudable goals, and appreciate the efforts of researchers to address these crucial issues. I believe, though, that research on ethnic differences in communication style could also set its goals on a different plane altogether.

We know from research in areas as disparate as biology and organizational studies that diversity is a Good Thing. The more diverse your crew, the more resources they bring to sailing the boat, and to any problems that might arise on the journey. It stands to reason, then, that the diverse interactional styles of people of different ethnic backgrounds could serve as a very positive resource, in settings like the workplace or the classroom. Getting employers and educators to use these resources may be tricky, but it certainly won't be possible until we can describe these resources and say with some confidence exactly what the potential benefits might be.

I should note that there are some researchers who do focus on different styles of communication as a resource. Heath (1982), for example, was very successful in helping the European-American middle-class teachers in the community she studied expand their repertoires so that they included teaching elements based on discourse patterns used by the working-class African-American members of the community. She takes as a basic motivating principle in her research that "knowledge about language use [can] proceed along a two-way path, from the school to the community and from the community to the school" (1982:125). Heath points out the contrast with most previous research, which had emphasized the dichotomy between "school talk" and "at-home talk," and focused on "how 'we' of the school can enrich the background of the 'they' of culturally different communities" (1982:126). The teachers in her study were surprised to find that some of the types of questions brought to the classroom by their working-class African-American pupils corresponded to questions that were valued highly by education textbooks as ways of promoting certain types of knowledge, and could be beneficial to students of all backgrounds.

Similarly, Foster (1995) looks at a middle-class African-American teacher and her use of African-American communication styles in the classroom. In particular, the teacher would shift into a performance style characterized by features such as repetition, use of figurative language, and variations in intonational contours and tempo. Metaphors, which as discussed in Chapter 8 feature prominently in African-American discourse, played a particularly crucial role in her classroom. Foster found that the use of these patterns reinforced ethnic identity and shared group values, and encouraged students to engage in classroom discussion.

Focusing on Native-American students, Yamauchi and Tharp (1995) argue that certain similarities in terms of the learning culture emerge in research on different tribes, and that knowledge of this culture could be used to enhance educational success for Native-American children. They report on a study in Alaska that looked at the practices of Native-American teachers. The children at the elementary school where the study was based were performing at or above national standards on test scores, and there had been no major discipline problems there. They found that Native-American teachers tended to allow more time for events in the classroom to unfold and also spent more time listening to the students and less time specifically directing their activities.

The number of studies like these that show the positive effects of patterns from outside the mainstream educational system are unfortunately very few. The resources that children from differing ethnic backgrounds bring to the classroom are numerous, and it would be a worthy goal for linguists and anthropologists to apply their research to making these more salient to educators. Heath's research shows that the incorporation of new patterns in this way need not be complicated or expensive. Often it is simply a matter of making things visible; even teachers who care deeply about all their students and want to know more about them so they can be more effective may not be able to identify the discourse patterns that differ, for the reasons discussed in Chapter 8.

A teacher in Heath's (1982) study, for example, asked the children about a new mathematical sign they had learned (presumably either < or >), pointing to it and asking what it was "like." The teacher expected the students to give the response that had been rehearsed earlier, that it looked like the mouth of an alligator. However an African-American student pointed to a bulletin board for a different subject that had yarn forming the same shape as the sign. Heath reports that the teacher was somewhat confused by this response, and found it less relevant than the expected one. However, the child who gave it was performing a very specific skill – pattern recognition – which one could even argue is at a more complex level than the skill embodied in the expected response (simple recall). What if the teacher had asked the kids to get up and move around the classroom finding every example of a pattern that looked like a "<" sign? What if she asked them to draw other analogies from memory? We know from Heath's work that this ability to recognize parallels is also connected in African-American communities to a frequent use of metaphor and other analogical skills, skills that presumably would be useful for all the children, regardless of background. If it is less emphasized in, for example, the working-class European-American community, these children would have the opportunity to learn the skills by watching the model of the African-American children for whom it is more familiar.

An example of another learning style altogether comes from Native-American communities. To begin with, as has been discussed in other chapters, a collective rather than individual orientation is evident in many tribes, as is an emphasis on group harmony and avoidance of conflict. In the educational system, this means that Native-American pupils will often disprefer activities that involve being singled out and questioned individually. Conklin and Lourie (1983) report that when a Native-American student was asked to read aloud, his or her classmates would often whisper along in order to help if the student stumbled on a word. They also note that many Native-American children work better in groups, and tend to provide each other with answers, rather than competing with each other for the teacher's praise and attention. This type of behavior is often classified as "a problem" because of the ways in which it does not line up with the ideologies of the mainstream US classroom, where, for example "sharing answers" is defined as "cheating." But are these kids not exhibiting some skills that

194

194

we would very much like our children to have? Concern for others? Humility? An ability to work cooperatively? Instead of classifying this behavior as a problem, wouldn't it make more sense to think about how we might incorporate it as part of a lesson, how we might equip with these same skills those children from other groups who do not already bring them to the classroom?

We might go a step further and explore the entire culture of learning that can be found in Native-American communities. A number of researchers have focused on teaching and learning practices among Native Americans, finding that they differ in essential ways from the practices of the mainstream US classroom (see, e.g., Philips 1972, Conklin and Lourie 1983, McCarty et al. 1991, Yamauchi and Tharp 1995). In the Native-American communities that have been studied, learning is experiential; rather than explain in detail how a task should be done, the "teacher," possibly a parent or older sibling, demonstrates the task, allowing the student to observe and ask questions. When the student feels comfortable, he or she may attempt the task alone. If the student fails, nobody in the community will call attention to this fact. There is a very high degree of emphasis on the individual's ownership of knowledge and responsibility for his or her own part in the learning process. Native Americans do not generally view knowledge as something that can be passively received. As a result, Native-American children participate most enthusiastically in lessons that are structured with a demonstration at the beginning, rather than a lengthy verbal explanation. In addition, they seem to feel comfortable interacting in small peer groups, and cooperate easily with other students in the group to complete a task, especially in comparison with students of other ethnic backgrounds. These practices could enhance learning for students of all ethnic backgrounds. Even students who do not come from a Native-American culture could benefit from teaching practices that emphasize powers of observation, and provide an opportunity to test out one's skills without criticism.

I have selected a classroom as the setting for this exploration of how interactional patterns from different ethnic groups might enhance learning and ultimately provide all participants with a wider range of skills. The basic idea, however, is also applicable to corporations, the media, and any number of other settings. For example, the "consensus-building" style of Western Desert speakers in Australia could have interesting applications in business settings. So could the "learn by watching" style of Native-American groups. I try to stress to my students, when we discuss these topics in class, that this is not about being "politically correct." While we may feel it is laudable ethically to add the practices of different groups to, e.g., a business setting, a major corporation is unlikely to do so simply so that everyone feels represented. However, there is good evidence that diversity is a positive thing practically speaking, even a lucrative thing, and it is not necessary to appeal to good intentions or political correctness in promoting a greater appreciation for it.

DISCUSSION QUESTIONS

1. What types of exercises would you design to increase awareness of cross-cultural language differences among teachers? What about for executives in large, diverse companies?
2. In the discussion, it was mentioned that you cannot ask someone to change the way they use language without asking them to change something essential about their identity. Try to generate some ideas about how to teach children from different backgrounds the interactional patterns needed to succeed in school, while minimizing the threat to their sense of identity.
3. Can you think of settings besides renting an apartment where linguistic profiling might take place? Try to identify a setting of this type, or one in which you think "accent hallucination" might take place, and design a research project to test your theory.

SUGGESTIONS FOR FURTHER READING

Baugh, John. 1999. *Out of the Mouths of Slaves: African American Language and Educational Malpractice*. Austin: University of Texas Press.

A recent work by a prominent AAVE researcher, focusing on how linguistic varieties and patterns found among African-Americans affect their experiences in the educational system and other settings. Baugh highlights numerous aspects of the political and social policies that foster linguistic discrimination against African-Americans.

Carbaugh, Donal, ed. 1990. *Cultural Communication and Intercultural Contact*. New Jersey: Lawrence Erlbaum.

A collection of articles about cross-cultural communication and misunderstanding across a number of different types of ethnic communities around the world.

Kochman, Thomas. 1981. *Black and White Styles in Conflict*. Chicago: University of Chicago Press.

This book presents an in-depth look at the interactional patterns of African-American and European-American students in the university setting. Drawing on experiences from his own classes, Kochman analyzes the assumptions that underlie various uses of language by each of the groups.

Lippi-Green, Rosina. 1997. *English with an Accent*. New York: Routledge.

An excellent work on language, identity, and discrimination in the USA. Lippi-Green covers a diverse range of topics, from language in the media to legal issues surrounding non-standard varieties.

Scollon, Ron and Suzanne B. K. Scollon. 1981. *Narrative, Literacy, and Face in Interethnic Communication*. Norwood, NJ: Ablex Publishing Corp.

An in-depth look at cross-cultural communication between Athabaskans and other groups in Canada, focusing on assumptions that each group makes about conversation and interaction, and how these can lead each group to develop negative stereotypes of the other.

10 Crossing: may I borrow your ethnicity?

They should stick to their own culture and not try to impersonate no one else.
(15-year-old black adolescent boy in South London, from Hewitt
1986:161)

The term "crossing" (also called "language crossing" or "code-crossing")
comes from the work of Ben Rampton (1995, 1999) in Britain, and can
be defined as "the use of language varieties associated with social or
ethnic groups that the speaker does not normally 'belong' to" (1995:14).
Rampton's work follows in the path of some similar work by Hewitt
(1982, 1986), also in Britain. We know from a large body of sociolinguistic research that people generally speak like the people they want to
be like. Despite a widely held belief that the omnipresent availability
of television is leveling out dialect differences, linguists have shown
that this is not the case. If we live in Alabama, we don't suddenly begin
to talk like a newscaster from Chicago, because for the most part we
want to sound like those around us, our peers, the members of the
communities of practice (see Eckert and McConnell-Ginet 1992) with
which we identify. In a sense, this entire book up to this point has
been an illustration of how that process works.

So why would someone use a speech variety associated with another
group altogether? And how would this individual get access to that
variety in the first place? Research on crossing is of great interest to an
understanding of language and ethnicity, because it reveals processes
of ethnic identity construction that are otherwise often hidden. When
a working-class African-American kid says *aks* we may not even notice
it, but when a middle-class European-American kid says it, it is much
more likely to receive attention. (In fact, Cutler [1999] reports that the
family of Mike, the white teenager from New York City discussed in
Chapter 2, commented openly on his speech, saying that he sounded
like a street kid or a hoodlum.) In this chapter, I will address some
key issues about crossing, in the context of research from Britain and
elsewhere, including the following questions:

- Who is likely to take part in crossing?
- Why might an individual choose to do it? Does crossing indicate a desire to be a member of the other ethnic group?
- How does an individual get access to a linguistic code other than his or her own?
- How "extensive" is crossing, linguistically? What linguistic areas (lexicon? phonology?) are individuals who cross most likely to use?
- What is the attitude toward crossing among members of the ethnic group whose code is being borrowed?
- Does crossing lead to less racism?

Although this area of study is fairly recent within sociolinguistics (which is itself a field with a very short history), the research that has been done so far provides preliminary answers to a number of these questions. At the end of the chapter, I will also discuss the phenomenon of "passing," which might be viewed as a particular type of crossing.

To begin with, we might ask, What counts as crossing? There are linguistic occurrences that might look superficially similar to crossing but don't count, in a sense. So, for example, if we take the case of a speaker of a particular ethnicity brought up completely in a community of speakers of some other ethnicity, we would expect this individual to acquire the code associated with that second group. The use of that code would be the speaker's own "native" way of speaking, then, and unremarkable linguistically, whatever the social implications of its use by a person of another heritage might be (see, for example, Sweetland 2002). It is useful to reserve "crossing" for a situation where an individual deliberately chooses a code that is not the default for him or her within the local context. It entails, as Rampton puts it, "a disjunction between speaker and code that can not be readily accommodated as a normal part of ordinary social reality" (1995:278). For this same reason, code-switching also does not typically count as crossing, even though the two phenomena share some important qualities (and some exceptions will be discussed below). There is still some debate in the literature about exactly how broadly the term "crossing" can be applied; a new term, "styling," has also emerged, which seems to be targeted more broadly to encompass clear instances of crossing as well as a host of related but more ambiguous speech events (Rampton 1999). For the discussion here, crossing will be limited to instances that fit the definition given above: the use of language varieties associated with a group to which the speaker does not belong.

10.1 CLASSIC STUDIES OF CROSSING IN THE UK

Because the works of Roger Hewitt (1986) and Ben Rampton (1995) have been so central to the study of crossing, it is worth giving a brief overview of what they found, before moving on to the wider implications of crossing for language and ethnicity. The first in-depth study of crossing across an entire community was Hewitt (1986). The research was conducted in South London in the 1980s, and examines the use by white (i.e., Anglo-descent) adolescents of Creole or "patois" (an English-based creole brought by immigrants to London from the Caribbean). Hewitt looked at a number of factors relating to Creole use, including whether the speakers were interacting with black or white peers at the time, how extensive their use of Creole was, and what the attitude of black adolescents was towards this appropriation of their code. He found that Creole served a number of different functions among white adolescents: especially 1) a competitive function in verbal teasing rituals; and 2) a cultural function, where white adolescents create a fictive social identity momentarily as a way of aligning themselves with certain elements of black culture (see Hewitt [1986:135ff.] for a full discussion of these two modes). He also described in detail how white kids negotiated the right to use the creole, with their black friends. In particular, the existence of a multiracial local vernacular, not tied specifically to speakers of any one ethnicity, provides a sort of "cover" for the appropriation of Creole features, some of which may then pass into general usage (similar to what has happened with numerous slang terms and phrases from AAVE passing into American-English usage). Hewitt connects all of these linguistic patterns with the larger social and political context of race relations in which they are embedded.

Rampton (1995) also focuses on adolescents and crossing, working in a slightly different location, a multiethnic town in the South Midlands of England, with a population of about 100,000. His study expands on Hewitt's in both the number of linguistic varieties included and the types of participants whose language was studied. The varieties that were available for crossing in the community were 1) Creole, as in Hewitt's study, 2) stylized Asian English, and 3) Panjabi, and Rampton looks at crossing into each of them. In addition, he looks at the use of crossing by speakers of Anglo ethnicity, but also at speakers of Asian and Afro-Caribbean origin and their use of the various codes. In addition, Rampton stresses the importance of the interactional context, particularly whether the young speakers who are crossing are interacting with their peers, with an adult, or in a more specialized setting such as a musical performance. In general, Rampton found that crossing in this community served a variety of functions, including resistance to adult dominance, challenging of expectations about ethnicity, and the signaling of identities *other than* ethnic ones. Both Hewitt's and Rampton's studies clearly highlight both the complexities, social and linguistic, involved in an analysis of crossing, and the many potential contributions to sociolinguistic theory that this phenomenon provides.

10.2 WHO CROSSES?

It seems clear from the literature that the highest concentrations of true crossing occur among adolescents. The borrowing of slang terms from other ethnic groups, or the use of "faux" registers like Mock Spanish (Hill 1999) may be widespread in a society, but the appropriation of an entire code, across the linguistic levels of phonology, syntax, and lexicon, seems to be linked most clearly with adolescence, at least in the Western societies that have been studied so far, from the US (e.g., Bucholtz 1999b) to the Netherlands (e.g., Vermeij 2004). Hewitt notes that most of the youngsters in his study who were Creole users stopped speaking it at about the age of 16, and, though it is possible for an individual to continue using it beyond this point, it is quite rare (1986:160). This pattern makes sense in light of what we know about adolescence and language generally. Adolescents lead other groups in the use of vernacular forms, for example, a factor which Eckert attributes to "that age group's positive motivations for the use of innovative and non-standard forms" (2000:4). And what could be more innovative, or more provocative to one's parents, than using a (stigmatized) code to which, in some sense, one is not entitled?

There also seems to be a gender difference in some cases, although I hesitate to emphasize it unduly, since there has been a tradition in sociolinguistics of focusing on the language of young men and treating that of young women as somehow less interesting. In a number of the studies discussed here, however, crossing seems to be more prevalent among boys than girls. Vermeij (2004), for example, found that gender had a highly significant effect on crossing among adolescents in the Netherlands, with girls crossing less often. Hewitt found that in general white girls used less Creole overall, and used it in a more "low-key" way, than white boys, which he ties to factors such as girls' general lack of participation in verbal sparring, as well as a lower use of Creole by black girls as compared with black boys, limiting its availability to their white (female) friends (1986:155–9). Rampton reports very similar findings for the low use of Panjabi on the playground by girls of Caribbean or Anglo descent, which he attributes to a lack of contacts with Panjabi girls in school, and the girls' non-participation in competitive games of the type that triggered Panjabi use among the boys (1995:189). On the other hand, Rampton found a high use of Panjabi crossing by girls in the context of listening to bhangra music (a style associated with Panjabis). Bucholtz (1999b) presents a study of one European-American boy's use of AAVE in constructing white masculinity, but she reports that girls also use AAVE elements (although there is no data presented here on the frequency of use). As with other issues of language and ethnicity, we cannot expect crossing to be about ethnicity only, without taking into account the role of other factors such as gender.

At still another level, a key factor in who crosses is the structure of personal networks and contacts. Both Hewitt (1986) and Rampton (1995) discuss this issue in detail, so I will not try to cover it comprehensively here. As we might expect, those adolescents with social networks that involve many peers of other ethnic backgrounds have more opportunities to acquire the forms needed for crossing. Hewitt observes that for whites within a predominantly black friendship group, particularly, a kind of "conspiracy" often develops in which permission to use Creole is extended, sometimes involving a kind of suspension of ethnic boundaries (1986:165–6). It would be a mistake, though, to assume that such a network is a prerequisite for crossing. Mike, for example, the boy whose self-correction began this chapter, has mostly white friends, according to Cutler (1999). Some of the Asian boys in Rampton's study also had relatively little contact with Afro-Caribbean peers. The problem of how such speakers get access to the other code will be discussed further below.

Finally, many of the examples of crossing that have been studied involve crossing by members of a dominant ethnic group into a minority ethnic group's code (e.g., Hewitt 1986, Bucholtz 1999b, Cutler 1999, Hill 1999). This does not mean that members of other groups never cross. Rampton's study, for example, looks in detail at crossing into Creole by members of a minority ethnic group, Asian adolescents, and also mentions the use of Panjabi by black adolescents. There does seem to be a high frequency of crossing by members of the dominant group, however, which makes sense in the context of the ideologies about whiteness discussed in Chapter 6. As Bucholtz notes,

"European-Americans are often viewed as lacking an ethnicity. Laying claim to another ethnic group may allow whites to 'become ethnic'" (1995:367).

10.3   WHY DOES A SPEAKER CROSS?

If the question of who crosses is somewhat complex, the question of why is even more so. To some extent, of course, the answer to why an individual crosses will be deeply embedded in the social and political context of a particular community and cannot be generalized to other settings, yet some common themes do emerge across studies. To begin with, we can return to the association of crossing with adolescents, where crossing may serve as a type of rebellion. This is eminently clear in the subversive way that adolescents in Rampton's study, for example, used stylized Asian English to adults. Among other things, the informants themselves perceived it as something done by students who like to "mess around" and joke, and Rampton describes it as more common among adolescents who had "uneasy" relationships with authority figures, although he notes that it is not always used in a hostile way (1995:71). Similarly, Hewitt remarks on the use of Creole by white boys to teachers as a kind of "secret language" used to undermine their authority, a context, incidentally, which unlike some others did not draw any objections from Afro-Caribbean peers (1986:154–5).

Other studies reveal more nuances of this rebellious aspect of crossing. Vermeij seems surprised to discover that a large proportion of the crossing among Netherlands adolescents involved taboo language and offensive expressions, commenting on the "discrepancy between the seemingly offensive content of language crossing and the friendly social context in which it is used" (2004:165). However, from another perspective, taboo language and crossing serve some of the same functions: both signal rebellion against authority and expectations, and both can play a role in humorous rituals such as verbal insults. Their co-occurrence, then, can be viewed as a natural pooling of resources. In addition, switching to a language that adults may not understand provides "cover" for the use of taboo forms, as well as a form of exclusion. Also important in understanding these particular types of crossing is the role of humor in constructing identity, as discussed in Chapter 8.

Not all crossing is humorous, of course. In other contexts, crossing mainly signals a desire to affiliate with the values represented by the borrowed code. Since the codes in question tend to be non-standard or vernacular ones, there is a certain consistency in their associations. Rampton found, for example, that Asian and Anglo kids viewed Creole as "tough, cool and good to use," and they associated it "with argument, abuse, assertiveness, verbal resourcefulness and opposition to authority" (1995:37). This list sounds quite similar to the types of connotations that go with AAVE in the US, as discussed in Chapter 3. Clearly these connotations dovetail with the idea of "rebellion" expressed above.

The values associated with the code may or may not be directly tied to ethnicity. Crossing can be used to signal allegiances beyond ethnicity, as well. Among the connotations that a vernacular code can carry are associations with class and age. Rampton found that both Creole and Panjabi were construed as being associated with lower-class life, in opposition to the language of "posh" outsiders (1995:46). Given the fact that crossing mostly takes place among adolescents, it is also logical that it would be associated with youth. Hewitt talks about the "specific association that creole has with a vigorous youth culture . . . often equated with opposition to hierarchical authority" (1986:155). In time, these associations can become fixed in the linguistic system itself, where terms or expressions that previously had strong ethnic connotations lose them and become simply "youth slang." Both Hewitt and Rampton discuss the ways in which some elements that begin in a context of crossing can eventually pass into a local multiracial vernacular, so that they become a kind of community property.

A parallel case occurs in the US, where the hip-hop culture has provided a kind of access to "urban cool" (based originally in African-American culture) that teenagers of various ethnicities can adopt with less risk of being accused of appropriation. Hip-hop also provides a vehicle by which elements of AAVE – with its connotations of toughness, coolness, and so forth – can pass into general usage, a process that may generate resentment and frustration from the originating AAVE speakers. Williams refers to this as "the mainstream's assimilation of black speech patterns that, once incorporated, are promptly forgotten as such" (1997:8). This type of appropriation of the values of the code, combined with a general desire to project an "urban youth" identity, seems to be the main motivation for crossing both by Mike (Cutler 1999) and by Brand One, the middle-class European-American boy analyzed by Bucholtz (1999b).

Crossing may also be used for more complex purposes, such as indexing multiple identities at a time. Chun (2001) looks at the use of AAVE by Korean-Americans. As Chun notes, there has been much less sociolinguistic study of Asian-Americans than of other ethnic minority groups in the USA. She discusses the status in the predominant US ideology of Asians as in some sense "honorary whites" but also as ethnic minorities. The Korean-American speaker who is the focus of Chun's study uses AAVE to "index both whiteness and blackness" (2001:53), since his crossing is modeled on mainstream white traditions of appropriation, but also on ideologies about African-Americans. In particular, this speaker is using AAVE to access the ideology that associates African-American men with extreme masculinity, a way of challenging the dominant stereotype of Asian men as passive and less masculine. Therefore, we see in this speaker's use of crossing the indexing of three different ethnic identities (European-American, African-American, and Korean-American) and additionally an indexing of gender, a clear example of crossing that serves multiple functions at once.

One thing that crossing does not generally indicate is a desire to be an actual member of the other ethnic group. Mike, for example, despite his prolific use of AAVE features, did not have many black friends, and in fact made a number of disparaging remarks about African-Americans (Cutler 1999). Many uses of Creole in the British studies, as mentioned above, were joking uses, clearly not intended as a bid for group membership. However, there are a few individual exceptions, adolescents who pass through a phase in which they actually wish to affiliate with another ethnicity completely. Hewitt gives one such example, of an Anglo boy who described himself as having gone through a period where he had a sense of "being black in a white person's body" (1986:164), and had even gone so far as to make up a fictitious Jamaican grandmother. The same boy stopped using Creole entirely, though, as he got older, and seemed to look back on that period fairly judgmentally. Much more prevalent is the *perception* that crossers see themselves as potential members of another group. Numerous disparaging comments were made in the various studies about people "acting as if they're black." In fact, both the motivations of the crossers and the frequency of crossing tended to be overestimated. As Hewitt puts it, "the notoriety of white creole use is far greater than the actual activity itself" (1986:161).

10.4   HOW DOES AN INDIVIDUAL GET ACCESS TO A LINGUISTIC CODE OTHER THAN HIS OR HER OWN?

For crossing to take place, at least one serious logistical problem must be addressed: the crosser needs to get access to the other code. In some cases, transmission may take place fairly naturally, through participation in mixed peer groups. Many of the adolescents in Hewitt's (1986) study seemed to have acquired other codes in this fashion, and in fact subtler differences in how much crossing took place, based on gender or geographic location, could sometimes be traced to the strength of interracial peer networks. One Anglo boy even described asking his best friend, who was Afro-Caribbean, explicit questions about the meanings of words and phrases in Creole (1986:165). Others, however, may carry out this acquisition more subtly, almost covertly, due to the possibility of negative judgments from the ethnic group that "owns" the variety. As Rampton notes, it is not uncommon for speakers in the community he studied to "camouflage their learning, obscuring it in the refracted Creole forms . . . [of] the local multiracial vernacular" (1995:221).

Direct transmission from interethnic peer groups, however, is not the only possible source of crossing. First of all, individual crossers who participate in such groups may serve as a secondary source for outgroup adolescents who have little direct contact with speakers of other ethnicities. In doing so, they become what Hewitt calls a "Janus-like cultural sign" (1986:144), providing access to cultural norms and transmitting specific words, which then become dispersed generally among the adolescent population. This role may be particularly important in cases where the crosser is middle class, and therefore less likely to have peers who regularly use non-standard varieties. In the case of Mike, for example, a white friend who lived in a socioeconomically depressed area and had more access to "black culture" played a key role in his acquisition of AAVE (Cutler 1999).

Even more indirect sources of transmission may also play a role. For Mike, Cutler cites a number of other possible sources of access to AAVE, emphasizing particularly the increasing role of the media. Mike and his friends, for example, had seen many 1990s African-American films (e.g., *Boyz 'N the Hood, House Party*) numerous times. The role of the media in crossing should not be underestimated. On the Internet, there are websites that provide definitions of hip-hop terms, and chat-rooms where participants can practice crossing (often while "hiding" their ethnicity if they so desire). Perhaps most importantly, popular music, with its lyric sheets and music videos, is a key source of access to AAVE for millions of European-American adolescents. Similarly, the bhangra music style facilitated access to Panjabi in Rampton's (1995) study, particularly for Anglo girls, and for some of the boys in Hewitt's study reggae music played the same sort of role. Music has many advantages as a source of transmission: it removes the dependence on direct interaction with speakers of the other ethnic group, it provides "deniability" in the sense that quoting lyrics is a less direct voicing of an identity than simply using another variety casually, and music itself plays such a key role in youth culture that it is a natural conduit for expressions of identity.

10.5 HOW EXTENSIVE IS CROSSING, LINGUISTICALLY? WHAT LINGUISTIC AREAS ARE INDIVIDUALS WHO CROSS MOST LIKELY TO USE?

As with so many sociolinguistic phenomena, there are ambiguities in defining what counts as crossing. If a particular European-American boy uses an AAVE term once, is that enough? If a Creole term becomes part of the local multiethnic vernacular, will its use by a Panjabi girl still count as crossing? Even more intriguing, can it count as crossing if the speaker uses a variety associated with a group to which he or she *does* belong – for instance, a Cajun speaker performing an exaggerated Cajun dialect unlike his or her usual speech (Walton 2004) or a European-American speaker who normally uses AAVE performing a stereotyped "white" identity (Sweetland 2002)? Rather than focus on these borderline cases, however, it is probably more instructive to get a sense of the usual patterns of crossing, among speakers who do it on a regular basis. How extensive is their use of the other code? For how many turns might it continue in a single interaction? What are the restrictions on when it can and cannot be done? Are different linguistic areas more or less conducive to crossing? The answers to these questions can give us a clearer picture of what crossing actually looks like in action.

To begin with, there is a great deal of variation in the overall amount and frequency of crossing in particular situations. Rampton, for example, identifies three types of Creole users: minimal, more extensive but jocular, and extensive and serious (1995:207). The Anglo speakers he interviewed almost always fell into the first category. The Asian speakers were distributed across all three groups, but the last category was the least frequent. In the middle category, crossing events themselves could occur frequently, but each event lasted for only a few turns. Hewitt reports that a large number of Anglo kids might use an occasional Creole **expletive** from time to time, for example, but far fewer used Creole for extended interactions (1986:161). It was possible, though, to find sections of dialogue where individuals exhibited an extensive knowledge of the outgroup variety in their crossing, and the speech of these individuals will be discussed more below.

Somewhat different is the case of Mike, where AAVE seems to have become his "everyday" way of speaking for a certain period of his life; Cutler (1999) describes a transition away from this pattern later, when he was more likely to use standard forms with authority figures, but even at this point Mike used AAVE phonology and lexical items across all his speech styles. The implications of Mike's case are interesting, because in general the word "crossing" calls up an image of a speech event of limited duration, a switch *in* from some other variety, accompanied by a later switch *out*. In Mike's case, these switches may have been separated from each other by a period of several years, and been too gradual to identify distinctly.

It may be that a lack of sustained contacts with African-American peers paradoxically facilitated Mike's sustained adoption of an AAVE speech style. Hewitt's and Rampton's studies contain numerous examples of Afro-Caribbean speakers, for example, "policing" the use of Creole. On occasion, this sort of conflict over who was entitled to use the variety actually led to physical fights. In general, Creole use was often avoided when Afro-Caribbean peers were present. For Anglo speakers, it was more common in interaction among Anglo peers. Asian boys used Creole to Afro-Caribbean girls, but rarely in the presence of Afro-Caribbean boys. On the other hand, Mike did not have the presence of African-American peers to inhibit him, and this, along with some association of the code with hip-hop culture, may have led to his prolonged use of the outgroup code.

In terms of the levels at which crossing takes place, again there is some variation. Hewitt provides the example of "Papa Danger," an Anglo boy who was the only white member of a group that ran a "sound" – boys who collected sound equipment and used it to mix music at parties (1986:146–7). In interaction with another Anglo boy, Papa Danger makes extensive use of Creole, over several turns. One of the utterances in this dialogue is *Papa danger com fe nice op dis area!*, which alone contains features of Creole at all levels: lexical items (such as *nice up*), grammatical constructions (such as the infinitive marked with *fe* instead of *to*), and phonological elements (*up* as [ɔp], *this* as [dɪs]). Hewitt notes that this is Creole use at an unusually high level. Nonetheless, the fact that it covers variation across so many linguistic areas is of interest.

Particularly noteworthy in this example is the use of Creole phonology, because Hewitt discovered that phonology was the area most likely to trigger a negative reaction among Afro-Caribbean peers. Rampton gives a parallel example of extended switching into Creole by an Asian boy, where segmental phonetic features were nonetheless *not* switched (1995:214). While crossing of lexical items and grammatical structures is sometimes interpreted as a marker of peer group affiliation, and thus "allowed," phonology is strongly tied to ethnic group membership, and is often avoided by Asian and Anglo kids where Afro-Caribbean peers are present (Hewitt 1986:152). Interestingly, no such restriction was associated with Stylized Asian English, where phonology was usually a crucial element of the switch (see Rampton [1995:68] for more discussion). Much more common in both Hewitt's and Rampton's studies were briefer, less extensive switches to Creole, particularly use of a small core of lexical items and phrases (again, with the accompanying segmental phonology appearing only in ingroup interactions).

In comparison, Mike, in his use of AAVE, shows a completely different pattern. His speech features a high concentration of phonological and lexical items, but almost no marked grammatical elements (Cutler 1999:431–3). In terms of phonology, for example, Mike had intervocalic r-lessness (in a context like *four o'clock*), which is not typical of the European-American New York dialect. In terms of the substitution of [d] for [ð], which is found in the regional European-American dialects, the rate at which Mike used it was more consistent with its use by working-class African-Americans. He also had a large repertoire of lexical items that could be classified as either AAVE specifically or hip-hop, such as *phat*, *mad* (as an adverb), *chill*, *bomb*, and so forth. Conspicuous by their absence were the features of AAVE grammar: habitual *be*, third singular –*s* absence, copula deletion, and the other features discussed in Chapter 3.

There are a number of possible reasons for this pattern, and for the ways in which it differs from the British data on Creole. To begin with, as mentioned earlier, Mike had no regular interactions with an African-American peer group. As was discussed in Chapter 2, a number of linguistic studies suggest that the syntactic component of a variety may be harder to acquire than the phonology or lexicon. It may be that listening to rap music is an insufficient learning environment, and that face-to-face interaction is crucial for grammatical acquisition. It may also be the case that the purportedly "multiethnic" hip-hop culture has claimed for itself certain lexical items, through the process of dispersion from AAVE mentioned earlier, and with them their accompanying pronunciations, which then introduce new phonological patterns to the system. The corresponding grammatical patterns may not have been claimed or transferred in this way yet. If that were the explanation, then interestingly Mike's pattern turns out to be identical to that of the British crossers into Creole. In each case, the features associated with general youth culture are used extensively, and the features that are seen as marking ethnic membership more specifically (phonology in the UK, grammar in the USA) are avoided.

Finally, the examples discussed so far have all focused on crossing as the use of another variety or dialect of one's primary language. Crossing into another language, however, is also possible. It can be distinguished from ordinary code-switching by the fact that the language to which the speaker switches, as in all these cases, is associated with a community to which the speaker does not belong. Rampton's (1995) study discusses this type of crossing in some detail, looking at the use of Panjabi by children of Anglo or Afro-Caribbean descent. As might be expected, their actual knowledge of Panjabi was very limited, and so the crossing was not as extended as with the use of Creole. Interestingly, though, Rampton reports that this type of crossing was generally viewed positively by Indian and Pakistani informants, and was not as socially risky as crossing into Creole. Similarly, Vermeij (2004) looked at crossing among Dutch teenagers of different ethnic origins, who often used words borrowed from Sranan Tongo (a language spoken in Suriname) and Arabic, particularly taboo words (which Hewitt also found in the use of Panjabi). In the Dutch context, crossing was not found to be a "sensitive issue" at all.

It would be tempting to generalize and say that crossing to another language is tolerated more easily by the group whose code is being used than crossing to another dialect or variety. However, there is a study by Lo (1999), one of the few studies addressing the linguistic construction of Asian-American identities, which seems to contradict this hypothesis. Lo analyzes a conversation in which code-switching is used as a way of crossing by a young Chinese-American man, interacting with a Korean-American friend. The Chinese-American speaker knew some Korean because he had a number of Korean-American peers and had studied Korean in college. In the exchange Lo observed, the Korean-American speaker sometimes ratifies the Chinese-American speaker's use of Korean, but in other cases he specifically rejects the speaker's appropriation of Korean-American ethnicity, by insisting on continuing in English. As with so many other cases, context is crucial to the interpretation of crossing.

10.6   DOES CROSSING LEAD TO LESS RACISM?

It is often suggested that crossing as a practice could restructure language ideologies in a way that leads to less racism. Rampton, for example, describes the young people in his study as engaging in "a set of

stylised and often playful interactions that up to a point at least . . .
constitute a form of antiracism" (1995:21). In principle, the view that
crossing decreases racism seems reasonable, but in actuality the relationship between crossing and racism is quite complicated, and it is
not possible to conclude globally that the result is positive.

To begin with, there are some cases of crossing that clearly do indicate racism. For example, Hewitt (1986) mentions two examples of this
type in South London. The first is the exaggerated use of Creole by
whites as a parody of black speech, used in a clearly derisive way. The
second is the use of occasional Creole forms, especially obscenities,
by white policemen, in their interaction with black South London-
ers. In addition, where racism can be assessed to some degree apart
from the issue of crossing itself, the results are mixed. Hewitt found
that white adolescents who crossed and had black friends sometimes
developed "a keen awareness of . . . white racism" (1986:144), although
he adds that the potential for eroding racist ideologies in this way is
"only occasionally realized" (1986:148). The case of Mike, the speaker
from Cutler's (1999) study, is much less ambiguous. Despite crossing
into AAVE features all the time, much more intensely and regularly
than Hewitt's adolescents used Creole, Mike gives evidence of many
racist attitudes, such as making fun of overt demonstrations of "black
pride" on African-American television programs. The reverse is also
true: rejecting crossing as a linguistic strategy is not necessarily associated with racism. Bucholtz (2001) found that at the California high
school where she did her research, protests against the dismantling of
affirmative action were organized in part by the European-American
"nerd" students who rejected any use of AAVE features. In contrast,
many of the white students at the school who frequently drew on
AAVE features in their own language use did not participate.

One very important factor in addressing the relationship of crossing
and racism is the attitude towards crossing of the ethnic group whose
code is being borrowed. In general, crossing tends to draw negative
reactions from the "insider" group. For example, the use of AAVE by
European-Americans is often viewed negatively by African-Americans
because it is seen as a co-opting of cultural elements to which
this group is not entitled. Smitherman notes that, in these cases,
"whites pay no dues, but reap the psychological, social, and economic benefits of a language and culture born out of a struggle and
hard times" (2000a:21). Similarly, the young black British speakers in
Hewitt's study often had very negative views of the use of Creole by
white adolescents, suspecting it of being derisive, a reasonable assumption given the cases mentioned above where it is used in this way, or

else seeing it as an unwarranted use of "culturally significant markers" by outsiders (1986:151).

As discussed earlier, however, Hewitt's study also shows that limited acceptance of crossing can be negotiated by white adolescents within black peer groups. Bucholtz's (1999b) study of Brand One suggests that some of the same negotiated tolerance may be found among mixed peer groups in the USA as well. In addition, borrowing by members of another minority ethnic group may be viewed differently from borrowing by members of the dominant ethnic group. Rampton, for example, describes a range of types of Creole users: minimal, extensive but jocular, and extensive and serious (1995:207). He notes that the white speakers he interviewed tended to fall into the first category, while Asian speakers were more likely to be distributed across all three types. Although this is not necessarily a direct reflection of language attitudes, it is likely to be tied in to ideologies about who is and is not permitted to use a particular code. These studies reveal complexities in the attitudes of members of the group whose code is borrowed, and show that crossing, like most of the language phenomena that have been discussed, is highly context-dependent. In some situations it may be seen as racist, and in others it may be seen as an appropriate process characteristic of individuals on the borders of groups.

10.7 CROSSING VERSUS PASSING

In the cases of crossing discussed above, it is clear that the individuals involved were not trying to pass as members of the other ethnic group. The one exception is the Anglo boy described by Hewitt (1986) who during a brief period of adolescence had invented a fictitious Jamaican grandmother for himself. In general, though, crossing can be clearly distinguished from "passing," which has its own history and ideological contexts.

To begin with, crossing can be done by anyone, as long as he or she has access to the other code. It does not require validation from other community members, and may in fact be openly criticized by them, while still clearly counting as crossing. On the other hand, passing does require validation from the outside. As Bucholtz notes, passing generally refers to "the ability to be taken for a member of a social category other than one's own" (1995:351), and, by this definition, passing can involve categories other than ethnicity, such as gender. Because of the ascription factor, the ability to pass (ethnically) is often affected by factors such as skin tone that do not play the same role in cross-ing. Hall's study of women in the "fantasy line" industry highlights a particularly interesting mode of passing. Since customers who call in cannot see the women, skin tone is no longer a factor and linguistic ability becomes dominant. One of the things Hall discovered is that European-American women were often more successful at performing "black" women for callers than women who were actually African-American, because the European-American men who called were usually looking for a stereotype of black ethnicity, rather than a real African-American woman. Conversely, a manager told Hall that "the best white woman we ever had here was black" (1995:202).

Bucholtz's (1995) study of mixed-race women in the US is one of the more detailed studies available on the role of language in passing; it focuses on how the women construct their ethnic identities in different contexts. Bucholtz replaces the definition of passing given earlier with a slightly different and more action-oriented one: "*passing is the active construction of how the self is perceived when one's ethnicity is ambiguous to others*" (1995:352; italics in original). Bucholtz argues that the social motivations for and meanings of passing are more complex than has been assumed. In the lives of these women, passing served a number of functions; it could be temporary and even unintentional, and did not necessarily signal a rejection of their "real" identity. The ability to use a particular language or variety played a key role for them in their projection of an ethnic identity. Interestingly, some multiracial women may choose to affiliate with ethnicities that are not a part of their biographical origins at all, such as a woman mentioned by Bucholtz who was Japanese-American and European-American, but went through a period of identifying herself as a Latina. Bucholtz's research highlights the "constructed" aspects of ethnic identity, and the complex nature of passing.

Passing as a member of the dominant "white" ethnic group is often viewed differently from any other type of passing. McCormick, for example, discusses how people classified as "Coloured" in South African during apartheid would sometimes be able to pass for white if they spoke English, because "white Afrikaners who were vigilant about infringements of race laws were less able to detect coloured origin by accent in English than in Afrikaans" (2002a:103). The attempt to be reclassified as white was, unsurprisingly, viewed very negatively by members of the "Coloured" community. Interestingly, though, the legacy that this has left in post-apartheid times is that English is seen by this group as a kind of "weapon" that can be used against discrimination by white Afrikaners, since those who supported the apartheid system were unable to distinguish racial identity reliably when English was used. The Puerto-Rican Americans in Urciuoli (1996) also discussed "pretending to be white" as something that was negatively viewed in the community. One speaker discussed how a Puerto-Rican American born with light skin and "nice hair" might be able to pass as white if he changed his name. Another speaker argued that white people never try to pass as any other ethnicity. When Urciuoli asked him if white people ever "hide" their race, he responded, "They don't have to. They were born white. They hit the lottery when they were born" (1996:147). Of course, the Anglo boy who tried to pass as black in Hewitt's study shows that this ideology about white speakers is not necessarily accurate, and they, too, may engage in passing.

Passing seems to have a particularly crucial role in places where there are people of many different ethnic backgrounds, or large populations of mostly mixed-race people (as in the example from South Africa). Particularly interesting is an example from Bailey's (2000b) study set in a highly multiethnic high school in Rhode Island. A couple of Dominican-American boys engage in two separate events of "passing" as a joke, within a very short stretch of discourse. In the first event, one boy tries to convince a Southeast-Asian classmate that the other boy is African-American, and the second boy supports the ruse. Interestingly, it is language that the girl appeals to in denying the claim; as soon as it is established that the boy speaks Spanish, she rejects his claim of being "black." In the second instance, another boy tries to convince the interviewer and a Guatemalan-American classmate that one of the Dominican-American boys is actually Haitian (an insult in this cultural context). Although the Dominican-American boy initially plays along, he later attempts to reclaim his Dominican ethnicity by speaking Spanish. However in this case, he has difficulty convincing the Guatemalan-American woman, a fact which Bailey attributes to the boy's African-descent phenotype, which makes a "black" category like Haitian seem more realistic to the woman than a "Latino" category like Dominican.

The latter example leads to what might be categorized as a third category different from both crossing and passing: *re-racing*. I first encountered this term in Sweetland (2002), the study discussed in Chapter 2 of a young European-American woman who grew up in a predominantly African-American area and speaks AAVE as her primary linguistic variety. In this study, an African-American peer responded to questions about the young woman's language use by saying she was "basically black" (2002:525). Similarly, the European-American boy in Bucholtz's (1999b) study describes an incident (which may or may not be completely true) in which an African-American peer refers to him as *my nigger*, thereby, as Bucholtz notes, "temporarily reassigning Brand

One's racial and cultural identity from white to black" (1999b:454). These cases are slightly different from that of the Dominican-American man. In the previous case, the racial classification was based on phenotype, and corresponds closely to what has generally been termed "ascription." But in the latter cases a community member who has full biographical knowledge of an individual's background nonetheless chooses to reclassify the person ethnically, often as a result of linguistic factors.

In many ways, crossing, passing, and re-racing bring us full circle to the issues raised at the beginning of the book. I began with an exploration of what "race" and "ethnicity" mean, how they are constructed by the individual, by others in his or her community, and by those outside the community. I have explored the role of language in that process from numerous angles, seeking to explain how language indexes, constitutes, and reproduces, ethnicity. Now, at the end, it seems inevitable that the key components in answering these questions are complexity and flexibility. So many things are going on at once when an individual speaks that to try to fix a direct line between some utterance and ethnic identity is too simplistic. In addition, if individuals can borrow the ethnicity of others, pass as members of another group, and even be re-raced by their friends, then whatever definition of ethnicity we might use must carry within it fluidity, the possibility of changing, flowing in a new direction, as the complex social context of an individual's life unfolds around their linguistic acts of identity.

DISCUSSION QUESTIONS

1. Crossing often seems to provoke annoyance or anger among members of the group whose variety is being borrowed. Why might this happen? Is there a "better" or "worse" way to cross? Are some sorts of individuals or groups more likely than others to be granted "permission" to cross?

2. In the past, sociolinguistic differences have often been seen as providing evidence for deep social divisions between groups. Do the phenomena of crossing and passing have any implications for this viewpoint? How do they support or contradict it?

3. Is there such a thing as "crossing" into the dominant ethnic group, as distinct from the process that is usually called "assimilation"? Is the analysis of the comedy routines presented in Chapter 6 relevant to this question? How?

SUGGESTIONS FOR FURTHER READING

Bucholtz, Mary. 1995. From Mulatta to Mestiza: language and the reshaping of ethnic identity. In Kira Hall and Mary Bucholtz (eds.), *Gender Articulated: Language and the Socially Constructed Self*. Routledge. 351–74.

One of the few sociolinguistic studies looking specifically at mixed-race individuals and their use of language in the construction of ethnic identity. An excellent exploration of many crucial questions in the study of ethnicity and identity.

Bucholtz, Mary. 1999b. You da man: narrating the racial other in the production of white masculinity. *Journal of Sociolinguistics* 3:443–60.

This article focuses on one European-American teenager and his use of AAVE features in constructing his ethnicity. It explores the construction of masculinity simultaneously with ethnic identity.

Hewitt, Roger. 1986. *White Talk Black Talk: Inter-Racial Friendship and Communication Amongst Adolescents*. Cambridge and New York: Cambridge University Press.

The classic study that launched a research tradition in the area of "crossing." Hewitt's book looks in great depth at the use of Creole features by Anglo teens in the UK.

Rampton, Ben. 1995. *Crossing: Language and Ethnicity Among Adolescents*. New York: Longman.

Rampton's follow-up to Hewitt's work, which extends the study of crossing in a number of directions. Rampton includes three different ethnic communities, and an expanded range of varieties in his study, also set in the UK, providing the most comprehensive study to date of the phenomenon of crossing.

Notes

Chapter 1

1. Many Native Americans in the USA use "Indian" as their preferred term of ethnic identification. This leads to ambiguity with South Asian immigrants from the Indian subcontinent in the same areas. In trying to respect speakers' right to select their own ethnic labels, I have used "Indian" when referring to tribes where that has been explicitly identified as their preferred term, and "Native American" elsewhere.
2. In reality, this category also included individuals of unmixed ancestry, such as Malay slaves and their descendants or people from Khoe-San groups (Raj Mesthrie, personal communication). For lack of a better term, I will continue to use "Coloured" in quotes to refer to this group.

Chapter 2

1. In this excerpt, "Spanish" is the local term used to refer to Puerto-Rican Americans (and sometimes other Latino groups).
2. "Mexican" is an unmarked label for Mexican-Americans in the community.
3. The speaker in question turned out to be Puerto-Rican American in reality.
4. "Spanish" is an unmarked label for ethnic/racial identity among Dominican-Americans.
5. Two of these people, "Foxy" and "Mike," are given pseudonyms by the researchers who interviewed them. Muzel Bryant was not given a pseudonym in order to "honor the strength and dignity of the Bryants and to recognize the uniqueness of their family tradition on Ocracoke" (Wolfram et al. 1999:171, n.), and because it would not have assured anonymity in any case.
6. See Rose (1994) for a discussion of hip-hop culture.

Chapter 3

1. For those interested particularly in lexical items, see Mufwene et al. (1998), Smitherman (2000b), or Green (2002).
2. See also Mufwene (2001) for a discussion of this question.
3. See Weldon (1994) for more discussion of AAVE negation patterns.
4. For more on several of these features, see Labov (1972a); for more on *steady* and *come*, see Baugh (1999).
5. This alternation has a long history, dating back to Old English forms *āscian* and *ācsian*.
6. Bailey and Thomas list this feature as being unique to AAVE; however, Fought (2003) reports that it is an extremely common feature of Chicano English also, so I have included it under this section instead.
7. For an analysis of syllable timing in AAVE, see Thomas and Carter (forthcoming).

8. See also Lanehart (2002).
9. See Rickford (1999:276) for a discussion of habitual *be* as a particularly salient "distinctively black form."
10. See particularly the discussion of Rickford's Sea Island study in Chapter 7.
11. A slang term for a person who is "black on the outside and white on the inside."

Chapter 4

1. As with African-American groups, there is a wide range of terms for self-reference in communities of people whose ancestry traces back to Spanish-speaking countries in North, Central, or South America. In my own research, and sometimes in the literature, I have found that *Latino* generally carries more positive connotations for ingroup members than other terms, such as *Hispanic*. In addition, its denotation is generally taken to extend to many different countries of origin, so this is the term I will use in this section.
2. See Chapter 3 for a description of AAVE.

Chapter 6

1. Although I have chosen not to look at this particular issue here, a systematic study of differences between settings where there are perceived racial differences and those in which there are not would be fascinating, especially from the perspective of language and ethnicity.
2. This idea seems to have some basis in truth, since self-help manuals for business types often suggest repetition as a way of remembering someone's name at a business gathering.

Chapter 7

1. Perhaps this pattern may account for the use of the reclaimed pejorative term *nigger* as a symbol of ingroup solidarity among some African-Americans (see Smitherman 2000b:362–3), since it represents one of the few words that mainstream speakers cannot easily appropriate.
2. The Portuguese islanders, of course, would technically be European-American also, but they were clearly considered to be a separate group ethnically from the dominant white group in the culture of the island.

Chapter 8

1. The continuing relevance of this cultural reference is revealed in the 1990 movie *House Party*, where the character of the African-American father makes several references to the signifying monkey.
2. See Smitherman (1977:Chapter 5) and Green (2002:Chapter 5) for more on this topic.
3. We might want to label the response-to-a-question comments as "call and response," and the ones that take place without any prompting from the speaker as "backchanneling."

Chapter 9

1. When I made this explicit connection in a class on "language and ethnicity," an African-American student raised his hands in the air and said, "Yes! Thank you! Finally! I'm so tired of hearing everyone criticize Venus and Serena!"
2. For more on the Oakland Resolution, see Rickford (1999:320ff.), Baugh (2000), and Smitherman (2000b:150ff.).

Glossary of terms

AAVE *see* **African American Vernacular English**

accent (1) A popular label for dialect, especially in terms of pronunciation. (2) Speech influenced by another language (e.g., "Bob speaks with a French accent").

acrolect, acrolectal A range of varieties within a dialect that represent the forms that are closest to the standard.

addressee A person to whom speech is directed.

African American Vernacular English The non-standard variety of American English spoken by some people of African descent in the US. Often abbreviated AAVE.

agreement A co-occurrence relationship between grammatical forms, such as that between the subject and verb of a sentence.

alveolar A sound produced by touching the blade of the tongue to the alveolar ridge in back of the upper teeth.

ascription The process by which other members of a community assign an identity (ethnic or otherwise) to an individual.

aspect A grammatical category applying to verbs which indicates type or duration of an activity; for example *has eaten* (perfect aspect) vs. *was eating* (imperfect aspect).

aspiration A puff of air after the production of a stop, as in the pronunciation of *t* in *tie* [t^{h}aj]; usually indicated by a raised [^{h}] after the sound.

assimilation *see* **linguistic assimilation**

auxiliary A form occurring with a main verb, often referred to as a "helping verb"; for example, *has* in *has left*.

back vowel A vowel produced with the tongue toward the back of the mouth; for example, the [u] of *boot*.

backchanneling The linguistic and extralinguistic strategies used by a listener for indicating that he or she is listening to the person speaking; for example, *mm-hm* and *ok* may serve as backchanneling devices.

basilect, basilectal A range of varieties within a dialect that represent its most vernacular form. Used particularly in pidgin and creole situations.

bidialectalism (1) The ability to use two different dialects. (2) The position in teaching Standard English that maintains that the standard should be taught in addition to a vernacular variety rather than replacing it.

borrowed variety A variety used by a social group that originates with another, outside group.

borrowing A language item that originates in another language; for example, *piche* "peach," borrowed from English into Puerto-Rican Spanish.

centralizing Pronouncing a vowel closer to the center of the oral cavity.

code A speech variety, either a dialect, a language, or a mixed form like **code-switching**.

code-switching Switching between two different languages, either within a sentence or between sentences.

community of practice A group of people who come together through some shared social enterprise – for example, a sewing circle, a church membership, etc.

completive A form emphasizing completion of an action at a previous time; for example, "completive" *done* in *She **done** told him to look out.*

consonant cluster A sequence of two or more consonants without an intervening vowel; for example, [st] in *star* or [ld] in *cold*.

consonant cluster reduction The elimination of one consonant in a cluster; for example, the [st] in *list* [lɪst] may become [s], as in *lis"* [lɪs].

constraint *see* **linguistic constraint**

contrast When two sounds can form the phonetic basis for a distinction in meaning between forms; for example, the initial sounds of *pat* and *bat*.

Contrastive Analysis A language-learning technique in which structures from two different languages or dialects are placed side by side to focus on the contrast between forms.

convergence The adjustment of a language variety over time to become more like another dialect or other dialects.

copula The form used to connect a subject with a predicate; in English, a form of *be* when used as a linking verb, as in *The book **is** long, Walt **is** the king.*

copula deletion *see* **zero copula**

count noun A noun that can be enumerated (*one potato, two potatoes*). *see* **mass noun**

covert prestige The positive value associated with language forms that is based on their local social value rather than their value in larger society. *see* **overt prestige**

creole language A contact-based language that begins as a **pidgin**, but becomes the first language of a generation of speakers, and thus becomes more grammatically complex. *see* **pidgin language**

critical age The age period, usually somewhere before adolescence, during which it is hypothesized that a completely native acquisition of a language must begin.

crossing The use of a code associated with a group to which the speaker does not belong.

devoicing The changing of voiced sounds to their voiceless counterparts; for example, [z] to [s] (*fuzz* to *fuss*).

dialect A variety of the language associated with a particular regional or social group.

diminutive Affixes or other morphemes that add a component of "small size" to the meaning of a word; for example, the suffix –*y* in *the piggy*.

diphthong A two-part vowel consisting of a **nucleus** followed by a **glide**; for example, the [aj] of *bite*.

directive A speech act in which the speaker directs the listener to do something; for example, *Get out of my room!*

discourse The structuring of language above the level of a sentence.

discourse features Features that have to do with the organization of talk at the level of discourse.

divergence The development of a language variety or language structure so that it becomes more dissimilar from other varieties or structures.

double negation *see* **multiple negation**

Ebonics *see* **African American Vernacular English**

embedded question A question contained within another sentence, such as I *asked him* **where did he sleep last night** or *You should tell him* **what John said**.

ethnic group A group whose members are perceived by themselves and/or others to share a unique set of cultural and historical commonalities, particularly in contrast with other groups that adjoin them in physical or social space.

ethnic identity *see* **ethnicity**

ethnicity The quality of belonging to an **ethnic group**.

ethnographic study A study in which the researcher spends time in the community, observing people in natural environments and collecting data about all aspects of how the community functions.

existential A form used to indicate existence but having no referential meaning of its own; for example, the form *there* in **There** *are ten chapters in this book*.

expletive (1) An interjection, often used with reference to profane words (e.g., *Damn!*). (2) *see* **existential**

extralocal orientation The perspective in terms of identity of a community member who is oriented toward contacts and future opportunities outside the local community.

floor The right to speak, as in *holding the floor*.

fricative A sound produced with a continuous flow of air through a narrow opening in the mouth so that there is friction at the point of articulation, e.g., [s], [f].

fronting Pronouncing a vowel closer to the front of the oral cavity.

gender The complex of social, cultural, and psychological factors that surround sex; contrasted with sex as biological attribute.

glide A sound considered to be somewhat intermediate between a vowel and a consonant. It can form the secondary vowel of a **diphthong** (e.g., [j] in *bite* [bajt]).

glide reduction The loss or reduction of the glide or second half of a diphthong; for example, in many Southern varieties, the /ay/ vowel in words such as *time* [tajm] is unglided to [a], as in [ta:m].

glottal stop A stop articulated by the rapid opening and closing of the vocal cords.

glottalized A consonant that is articulated simultaneously with a glottal stop.

grammar The system of rules for the formation of words and sentences out of their constituent parts.

grammatical (1) Sentences and forms that conform to the (unconscious) grammar rules of a language or dialect. (2) In popular usage, language forms and constructions that conform to norms of social acceptability; in this usage, "grammatical" constructions may or may not be linguistically well formed; conversely, linguistically well-formed constructions may or may not be socially acceptable.

group reference Identification with a particular group in terms of sociopsychological self-definition.

habitual An aspectual distinction on a verb, indicating that an activity is ongoing or takes place at regular intervals over time.

habitual *be* The use in AAVE of the form *be*, without inflection, to make habitual aspect in the verb.

hedge A modifier used to diminish the force of an utterance, such as *kind of* or *maybe*.

heritage language A language associated with an ethnic group from which an individual is descended, whether or not that individual speaks the language.

high vowel A vowel made with the tongue in high position in the mouth, as in the [u] of *boot*.

intensifier A modifier used to give more emphasis to an utterance, such as *really*, *very*, or *so*.

interdental A sound produced by placing the tongue tip between the upper and lower teeth, for example the [θ] of *thug*.

interethnic communication Communication or interaction that takes place between members of different ethnic groups.

interethnic variation Variation among members of different ethnic groups.

intervocalic Occurring between vowels; for example, *r* in *scary*.

intonation The pitch contours that accompany phrases and sentences; for example, rising intonation on the question *Are you crazy?* vs. falling intonation on the statement *You are crazy*.

intraethnic variation Variation among members of a single ethnic group.

inversion A reversal of the order of words; for example, *Are we there?* vs. *We are there*. One pattern that occurs in some dialects is **negative inversion**, as in *Can't nobody do it* vs. *Nobody can't do it*.

known-answer question A question to which the person asking it already knows the answer; often asked to test the addressee's knowledge.

labiodental A sound produced with the lower lip and upper teeth, e.g., the [f] in *four*.

language acquisition The unconscious learning of language rules which results in implicit knowledge of language.

language attitudes Subjective beliefs about language and its use (at the level of the individual or community).

language ideology Ingrained, unquestioned beliefs about the way the world is, the way it should be, and the way it has to be with respect to language, shared by a community.

language shift The widespread loss of a language (often a **heritage language**) in a community over subsequent generations.

lax vowel A vowel produced with comparatively little muscular tension; the [ɪ] of *bit* is a lax vowel compared with the [i] of *beet*, which is a "tense" vowel.

leveling The reduction of distinct forms within a grammatical paradigm, as in the use of *was* with all subject persons and numbers for past tense *be* (e.g., *I/you/[s]he/we/you/they was*).

lexical item A word or morpheme found in a particular language or dialect.

lexicon The vocabulary of a language, including words and morphemes.

linguistic assimilation A change in language features by an individual or group so that their dialect becomes more like that of some other group.

linguistic constraint A linguistic factor, such as a type of linguistic environment or structural composition, which systematically affects the variability of fluctuating forms.

linguistic environment The linguistic context that surrounds a form, such as the sounds that occur next to a given sound.

linguistic inferiority principle The principle which holds that the language of a socially subordinate group is linguistically deficient compared to the more standard variety spoken by the superordinate social group.

linguistic profiling Discrimination based on the identification (whether correct or incorrect) of a person's ethnic or other social identity based on their voice.

linguistic variable A varying linguistic structure which may correlate with social factors such as region or status, or with other linguistic factors, such as linguistic environment.

local orientation The perspective in terms of identity of a community member who mainly has strong ties within the local community.

long vowel In English, a tense vowel, such as the [i] in *seat*.

marking A speech act in which the speaker imitates and exaggerates the tone and mannerisms of another person, in order to comment indirectly on something about that person, such as his or her personality or perceived motives.

mass noun A noun that cannot usually be enumerated, e.g., *milk, sand*. *see* **count noun**

matched guise Study in which listeners hear the same utterance in different languages or dialects (often secretly by the same speaker), and are asked to provide evaluative judgments.

merger The elimination of contrast between sounds; for example, the formerly distinct vowels in *caught* and *cot* now sound the same in many American English dialects. Also called neutralization.

mesolect, mesolectal The range of varieties intermediate between acrolectal and basilectal forms.

metaphor Use of a non-literal expression that implicitly presents one concept in terms of another.

metathesis The inversion of two sounds in a sequence, as in [æks] for *ask*.

mixed-race individual *see* **multiracial individual**

modal An auxiliary verb which expresses certain "moods" related to permission, obligation, suggestion, or the speakers' attitude toward the truth of her or his assertions; for example, *can, may, will, shall, must*.

monophthongization The reduction of a two-part vowel, or diphthong, to a one-part vowel, or monophthong, through the elimination of the glide, as in [ta:m] for *time*.

mood A grammatical category which pertains to speakers' attitudes toward the truth of their assertions (e.g., possibility, probability) or to speakers' expressions of obligation, permission, and suggestion.

morpheme The smallest meaningful components of words; for example, in *dogs*, *dog* and *–s* are morphemes.

morphology The level of language which concerns words and their meaningful components, or **morphemes**.

morphosyntactic Pertaining to the marking of a syntactic relationship through a particular morpheme; for example, third person *–s* in *She looks bedraggled* indicates a relationship between the subject and verb.

multiracial individual A person who claims descent from more than one racial or ethnic group.

nasal A segment produced by allowing air to pass through the nasal cavity, as in the *m* of *mom* or the *n* of *no*.

nasalization The production of a vowel or other segment with a nasal quality.

negative concord The marking of negation at more than one point in a sentence (e.g., *They didn't say **nothing** to **nobody***). Also called **double negation, multiple negation**.

negative inversion *see* **inversion**

non-standard With reference to language forms, stigmatized socially (usually because of an association with socially disfavored groups).

non-standard dialect A dialect that differs from the standard dialects spoken by mainstream or socially favored population groups; usually it is socially disfavored. It is commonly used synonymously with **vernacular**.

Northern Cities Shift A vowel shift or rotation in which the low back vowels are moving forward and upward and the short front vowels are moving downward and backward; found predominantly in Northern metropolitan areas of the USA.

nucleus The core or base of a vowel sound; in a word like *bike* [bajk], the [a] is considered the vowel nucleus.

overt prestige The positive value associated with language forms that is based on their value in the dominant ideology of mainstream society. *see* **covert prestige**

passing Acting so as to be taken for a member of a social category other than one's own.

phenotype A grouping of physical features, often with significance to a community in the ascription of race.

phoneme A basic unit of contrast, or meaning difference, in phonology. Usually established on the basis of "minimal word pairs." For example, /p/ and /b/ are considered to be different phonemes in English because they can be used to make meaning differences, as in *pit* and *bit*.

phonetic Related to the sounds of language.

phonology The sound system of a language.

pidgin A simplified but rule-governed language developed for communication among speakers who do not share a common language; it has no native speakers. The vocabulary of a pidgin language is taken primarily from a superordinate language, and the grammar is drastically reduced.

pitch The degree to which a sound is perceived as high or low by the listener; with voice pitch, this property is based on the rate at which the vocal cords vibrate.

possessive An item indicating possession, such as the suffix *-s* in *John's hat* or the pronoun *his* in *his hat*.

postvocalic /r/ The sound *r* when it follows a vowel, as in the *r* of *star*.

pragmatics The level of language organization pertaining to language use; takes into account such matters as speakers' and hearers' beliefs, attitudes, and intentions.

prescriptive Based on ideologies about how language "should" be used, rather than on describing how it is actually used.

preterite *had* The use of *had* + past participle to represent the simple past tense; for example *Yesterday, he **had** talked to me on the phone.*

prosody, prosodic The aspects of pitch, intensity, and timing that accompany the segments of spoken language. *see* **suprasegmental features**

race A concept which signifies and symbolizes social conflicts and interests by referring to different types of human bodies.

raising Pronouncing a vowel with a higher tongue position; for example, the **Northern Cities Shift** is characterized by the raising of /æ/ to near [ɛ] position.

reflexive pronoun A pronoun ending with *-self* that refers to a noun phrase within the same clause.

regional norm A language norm that is linked to a particular geographic region.

register A language variety associated with a particular situation of use; for example, the register of the type of talk used to infants, often called "babytalk."

remote past *been* The use in AAVE of the stressed aspectual marker *been* to mark that the action of the verb takes place a (relatively) long time in the past.

re-racing The reassignment of an individual from one racial category to another by someone else. It differs from ascription in that the category is changed from one group to another, rather than simply assigned. *see* **ascription**

resumptive pronoun The use of a co-referential pronoun in addition to a noun in subject position; for example, *friend* and *she* in My **friend**, *she has four kids.*

retroflex A sound produced with the tip of the tongue curled upward; for example the consonant sound *r* in *run*.

r-**lessness** The absence or reduction of the *r* sound in words such as *bar* and *weird*.

schwa A mid-central vowel symbolized as [ə], as in the first and last sounds of *America*.

segmental features Properties of the individual speech sounds (i.e., consonants and vowels). *see* **suprasegmental features**

semantic extension Meaning shift in which a word can be used to refer to a more general class of items than previously. For example, the word *mouse*, which used to be only an animal, can now mean a device for controlling the pointer on a computer.

semantics The level of language organization which pertains to word meaning.

short vowel In English, a "lax" vowel, such as the [ɪ] in bit.

signifying A type of speech act found in African-American communities, used to convey meanings indirectly, often in a humorous and culturally specific way.

slang Words with special connotations of informality and ingroup solidarity that replace words with more neutral connotations (e.g., *phat* for "great"; *cheese* for "money").

socially constructed Refers to a property that is not based on elements of physical, objective reality, but rather on social interpretations of reality.

sociolinguistics The study of language in relation to society; the study of language in its social context.

sound change A change in the phonology of a dialect (or several dialects) that takes place over time.

Southern Vowel Shift A vowel shift or rotation in which the short front vowels are moving upward and taking on the gliding character of long vowels, the long front vowels are moving backward and downward, and the back vowels are moving forward.

speech act An utterance which accomplishes a social action. For example, *Put that down!* is a **directive** speech act in which the speaker directs the hearer to perform an activity.

speech community A group of people with shared norms, or common evaluations of linguistic variables. Members of a speech community may use language forms in different ways, but all members orient toward common norms, such as agreeing on which forms have **overt prestige**.

speech event An event within a culture that consists of one or more speech acts.

Standard African American English (SAAE) The variety of American English spoken by some people of African descent in the USA, which consists of standard grammatical forms, but also includes phonological or stylistic patterns that identify the speaker as African-American.

standard dialect The dialect associated with those socially favored in society; the dialect considered acceptable for mainstream, institutional purposes. *see* **Standard English**

Standard English The variety of English considered socially acceptable in mainstream contexts; typically characterized by the absence of socially stigmatized linguistic structures.

stopping The process of producing fricatives as stop consonants, as in *these* [ðiz] being pronounced as *dese* [diz].

stress timing Timing of utterances in which stressed syllables have greater duration. *see also* **syllable timing**

style One of the speech varieties used by an individual on different occasions; different speech styles tend to correlate with such factors as audience, occasion, degree of formality, etc.

subjunctive a verbal mood that expresses a non-factual modality (e.g., *If I were king . . .*).

superstandard English Forms or styles of speech which are more standard than called for in everyday conversation, such as *To whom did you give the book?*

suprasegmental features Features of language such as stress and intonation that accompany the sound segments (e.g., consonants and vowels) of language.

supraregional norm A language norm that transcends regional boundaries and is shared by groups in different locations, who may perceive themselves as having something in common.

syllable timing Timing of utterances in which each syllable in a phrase has approximately equal duration. *see also* **stress timing**

syntax, syntactic The formation of words into phrases and sentences.

taboo word A word having a social prohibition against its use in many situations because of association with topics the society views as sensitive, such as the "four-letter" words of English (e.g., *shit, dick*).

tag question A question formed by items attached to, or "tagged," onto the end of the sentence (e.g., *aren't you* in *You're going to finish this, aren't you?*).

tense (1) Produced with more muscular tension; for example, the sound [i] in *beet* is a "tense" vowel, whereas the [ɪ] of *bit* is a "lax" vowel. (2) The time reference of an activity or event (e.g., "past tense" in *The professor went crazy last week*).

topicalization The shift of an item to the beginning of a sentence; for example, *The bananas* in *The bananas, I don't think will be very popular*, versus *I don't think the bananas will be very popular*.

transfer The adoption of a form from another language, usually a form from a first language carried over into a second language in the process of acquiring the second language.

turn-taking Shifting from one speaker to another in a conversational exchange.

unaspirated *see* **aspiration**

variants Different ways of saying the same thing, whether different ways of pronouncing the same sound, different ways of forming the same construction, or different words for the same item or concept. For example, *brang* and *brought* are two variants of the past participle of *bring*: *He brought a picnic/He brang a picnic.*

variationist An approach to sociolinguistics that focuses on the quantitative analysis of linguistic variables.

vernacular The indigenous language or dialect of a speech community, acquired naturally in the home. The term "vernacular dialect" is often used to refer to **non-standard** or non-mainstream varieties as opposed to the standard variety.

vocalization The change of a consonant to a vowel or vowel-like form, e.g., changing *feel* to [fiju], like *fee-ooh*.

voiceless sound A sound produced with the vocal cords open and not vibrating, as in the [s] of *suit.*

vowel A sound produced without significant constriction of the air flowing through the oral cavity.

vowel reduction The change or neutralization of a vowel to the quality of a **schwa** [ə]; usually takes place in unstressed syllables.

"Women's Language" A concept associated with studies by Robin Lakoff, in which it is proposed that women as a whole have a distinct way of speaking that encompasses certain specific forms, such as **tag questions**. Mostly discredited by later studies.

zero copula The absence of the copula (a form of *be*), as in *You ugly* for *You're ugly* or *She looking good* for *She's looking good.*

References

Anderson, Bridget L. 1997. Adaptive sociophonetic strategies and dialect accomodation: /ay/ monophthongization in Cherokee English. *University of Pennsylvania Working Papers in Linguistics* 4:185–202.

Anderson, Bridget L. 1999. Source-language transfer and vowel accommodation in the patterning of Cherokee English /ai/ and /oi/. *American Speech* 74:339–68.

Anderson, Bridget L. and Becky Childs. 2003. Rounding, coarticulation, and fronting for /u/ and /U/ among Texana, NC and Detroit African American speakers: problematizing the internal/external dichotomy. Paper delivered at NWAVE 32, Philadelphia, PA.

Anthias, F. and N. Yuval-Davis. 1992. *Racialized Boundaries*. New York: Routledge.

Ash, Sharon and John Myhill. 1986. Linguistic correlates of inter-ethnic contact. In D. Sankoff (ed.), *Diversity and Diachrony*. Amsterdam: John Benjamins. 33–44.

Atagi, Eriko. 2003. Are you a native speaker? The role of ethnic background in the hallucination of foreign accents on native speakers. Paper delivered at NWAVE 32, Philadelphia, PA.

Auer, Peter, ed. 1998. *Code-Switching in Conversation: Language, Interaction and Identity*. London and New York: Routledge.

Azoulay, Katya. 1997. *Black, Jewish, and Interracial: It's not the Color of Your Skin, but the Race of Your Kin, and Other Myths of Identity*. Durham: Duke University Press.

Bailey, Benjamin. 1997. Communication of respect in interethnic service encounters. *Language in Society* 26:327–56.

Bailey, Benjamin. 2000a. Communicative behavior and conflict between African-American customers and Korean immigrant retailers in Los Angeles. *Discourse and Society* 11(1):86–108.

Bailey, Benjamin. 2000b. Language and negotiation of ethnic/racial identity among Dominican Americans. *Language in Society* 29:555–82.

Bailey, Guy. 1993. A perspective on African-American English. In Dennis R. Preston (ed.), *American Dialect Research*. Amsterdam: John Benjamins. 287–318.

Bailey, Guy and Natalie Maynor. 1987. Decreolization? *Language in Society* 16:449–73.

Bailey, Guy and Natalie Maynor. 1989. The divergence controversy. *American Speech* 64:12–39.

Bailey, Guy and Erik Thomas. 1998. Some aspects of African-American Vernacular English phonology. In Mufwene et al. 1998, pp. 85–109.

Bailey, Guy and Jan Tillery. 2004. Some sources of divergent data in sociolinguistics. In Fought 2004, pp. 11–30.

Baines, 2000. http://sportsillustrated.cnn.com/thenetwork/news/2000/08/30/ page_one_william s_sisters/

Bakhtin, M. 1981. *The Dialogic Imagination*. Austin: University of Texas Press.

Baldwin, James. 1997. If Black English isn't a language, then tell me, what is? *Black Scholar: Journal of Black Studies and Research* 27:5–6.

Barrett, Rusty. 1999. Indexing polyphonous identity in the speech of African American drag queens. In Bucholtz et al. 1999, pp. 313–31.

Barth, Fredrik, ed. 1969. *Ethnic Groups and Boundaries: The Social Organization of Culture Difference*. Boston: Little, Brown.

Basso, Keith. 1970. "To give up on words," silence in Apache culture. *Southwest Journal of Anthropology* 26:213–38.

Basso, Keith H. 1979. *Portraits of "The Whiteman": Linguistic Play and Cultural Symbols Among the Western Apache*. Cambridge and New York: Cambridge University Press.

Baugh, John. 1983. *Black Street Speech: Its History, Structure, and Survival*. Austin: University of Texas Press.

Baugh, John. 1991. The politicization of changing terms of self-reference among American slave descendants. *American Speech* 66(2):133–46.

Baugh, John. 1999. *Out of the Mouths of Slaves: African American Language and Educational Malpractice*. Austin: University of Texas Press.

Baugh, John. 2000. *Beyond Ebonics: Linguistic Pride and Racial Prejudice*. New York: Oxford University Press.

Bayley, Robert and Lucinda Pease-Alvarez. 1997. Null pronoun variation in Mexican-descent children's narrative discourse. *Language Variation and Change* 9:349–71.

Bell, Allan. 1997. The phonetics of fish and chips in New Zealand: marking national and ethnic identities. *English World-Wide* 18(2):243–70.

Bell, Allan. 1999. Styling the other to define the self: a study in New Zealand identity making. *Journal of Sociolinguistics* 3(4):523–41.

Bell, Allan and Janet Holmes. 1991. New Zealand. In Cheshire 1991, pp. 153–68.

Benton, Richard A. 1991. Maori English: a New Zealand myth? In Cheshire 1991, pp. 187–99.

Bex, Tony and Richard J. Watts, eds. 1999. *Standard English: The Widening Debate*. London and New York: Routledge.

Bharuthram, Sharita. 2003. Politeness phenomena in the Hindu sector of the South African Indian English speaking community. *Journal of Pragmatics* 35:1523–44.

Blondeau, Helene, Naomi Nagy, Gillian Sankoff, and Pierrette Thibault. 2002. La Couleur locale du français L2 des anglo-montréalais. (The local coloring of French as a second language of anglophone Montreal residents.) *Aile: Acquisition et Interaction en Langue Etrangère* 17:73–100.

Bobo, Lawrence. 2001. Racial attitudes and relations at the close of the twentieth century. In Smelser et al. 2001, pp. 264–301.

Boskin, Joseph. 2004. Outsiders/insiders. In G. Goshgarian (ed.), *Exploring Language*, 10th edition. New York: Pearson Longman.

Brander Rasmussen, Birgit, Irene J. Nexica, Eric Klinenberg, and Matt Wray, eds. 2001. *The Making and Unmaking of Whiteness*. Durham, NC: Duke University Press.

Bucholtz, Mary. 1995. From Mulatta to Mestiza: language and the reshaping of ethnic identity. In Hall and Bucholtz 1995, pp. 351–74.

Bucholtz, Mary. 1999a. "Why be normal?": language and identity practices in a community of nerd girls. *Language in Society* 28:203–23.

Bucholtz, Mary. 1999b. You da man: narrating the racial other in the production of white masculinity. *Journal of Sociolinguistics* 3:443–60.

Bucholtz, Mary. 2001. The whiteness of nerds: superstandard English and racial markedness. *Journal of Linguistic Anthropology* 11:84–100.

Bucholtz, Mary, A. C. Liang, and Laurel A. Sutton. 1999. *Reinventing Identities: The Gendered Self in Discourse*. New York: Oxford University Press.

Butters, Ronald. 1986. Linguistic convergence in a North Carolina community. In K. Denning et al. (eds.), *Variation in Language: NWAV-XV at Stanford*. Stanford, CA: Department of Linguistics, Stanford University. 52–60.

Carbaugh, Donal, ed. 1990. *Cultural Communication and Intercultural Contact*. New Jersey: Lawrence Erlbaum.

Chambers, J. K., Peter Trudgill, and Natalie, Schilling-Estes, eds. 2002. *The Handbook of Language Variation and Change*. Malden, MA: Blackwell.

Cheshire, Jenny, ed. 1991. *English Around the World: Sociolinguistic Perspectives*. Cambridge and New York: Cambridge University Press.

Chick, J. Keith. 1996. English in interpersonal interaction in South Africa. In De Klerk 1996, pp. 269–83.

Childs, Becky and Christine Mallinson. 2004. African American English in Appalachia: dialect accommodation and substrate influence. *English World-Wide* 25:27–50.

Christopher Edley, Jr. 2001. Foreword to Smelser et al. 2001, pp. vii–ix.

Chun, Elaine. 2001. The construction of White, Black, and Korean American identities through African American Vernacular English. *Journal of Linguistic Anthropology* 11:52–64.

Clancy, Patricia. 1985. The acquisition of Japanese. In D. Slobin (ed.), *Crosslinguistic Studies of Language Acquisition*. New Jersey: Lawrence Erlbaum. 373–524.

Clancy, Patricia M., Sandra A. Thompson, Ryoko Suzuki, and Hongyin Tao. 1996. The conversational use of reactive tokens in English, Japanese, and Mandarin. *Journal of Pragmatics* 26:355–87.

Clark, John Taggart. 2003. Abstract inquiry and the patrolling of black/white borders through linguistic stylization. In Harris and Rampton 2003, pp. 303–13.

Coates, Jennifer. 1996. *Women Talk*. Cambridge: Blackwell.

Coates, Jennifer, ed. 1998. *Language and Gender: A Reader*. Oxford and Malden, MA: Blackwell.

Cohen, Ronald. 1978. Ethnicity: problem and focus in anthropology. *Annual Review of Anthropology* 7:379–403.

Conklin, Nancy F. and Margaret Lourie. 1983. *A Host of Tongues*. New York: Free Press.

Cross, John B., Thomas DeVaney, and Gerald Jones. 2001. Pre-service teacher attitudes toward differing dialects. *Linguistics and Education* 12:211–27.

Cukor-Avila, Patricia. 1997. An ethnolinguistic approach to the study of rural Southern AAVE. In C. Bernstein et al. (eds.), *Language Variety in the South Revisited*. Tuscaloosa: University of Alabama Press. 447–62.

Cukor-Avila, Patricia and Guy Bailey. 1996. The spread of urban AAVE: a case study. In J. Arnold et al. (eds.), *Sociolinguistic Variation: Data, Theory, and Analysis*. Stanford: CSLI. 469–85.

Cutler, Cecilia. 1999. Yorkville crossing: white teens, hip hop, and African American English. *Journal of Sociolinguistics* 3:428–42.

Davis, F. J. 1991. *Who is Black? One Nation's Definition*. University Park: Pennsylvania State University Press.

De Klerk, Vivian, ed. 1996. *Focus on South Africa*. Amsterdam: John Benjamins.

De Klerk, Vivian and David Gough. 2002. Black South African English. In Mesthrie 2002a, pp. 356–78.

Denning, Keith. 1989. Convergence with divergence: a sound change in Vernacular Black English. *Language Variation and Change*. 1:145–67.

Dow, James R., ed. 1991. *Language and Ethnicity*. Amsterdam and Philadelphia: John Benjamins.

Dubois, Sylvie and Barbara M. Horvath. 1998. Let's think about dat: interdental fricatives in Cajun English. *Language Variation and Change* 10:245–61.

Dubois, Sylvie and Barbara M. Horvath. 1999. When the music changes, you change too: gender and language change in Cajun English. *Language Variation and Change* 11:287–313.

Dubois, Sylvie and Barbara M. Horvath. 2003a. Creoles and Cajuns: a portrait in Black and White. *American Speech* 78:192–207.

Dubois, Sylvie and Barbara M., Horvath. 2003b. The English vernacular of the creoles of Louisiana. *Language Variation and Change* 15:255–88.

Dubois, Sylvie and Barbara M. Horvath. 2003c. Verbal morphology in Cajun Vernacular English: a comparison with other varieties of Southern English. *Journal of English Linguistics* 31:34–59.

Dubois, Sylvie and Megan Melançon. 2000. Creole is, Creole ain't: diachronic and synchronic attitudes toward Creole identity in Southern Louisiana. *Language in Society* 29:237–58.

DuBois, W. E. B. [1897] 2000. The conservation of races. In Robert Bernasconi and Tommy L. Lott (eds.), *The Idea of Race*. Indianapolis: Hackett. 108–17.

Eades, Diana. 1991. Communicative strategies in Aboriginal English. In Romaine 1991, pp. 84–93.

Eckert, Penelope. 2000. *Linguistic Variation as Social Practice: The Linguistic Construction of Identity in Belten High*. Malden, MA: Blackwell.

Eckert, Penelope and Sally McConnell-Ginet. 1992. Think practically and look locally: language and gender as community-based practice. *Annual Review of Anthropology* 21:461–90.

Eckert, Penelope and Sally McConnell-Ginet. 2003. *Language and Gender*. Cambridge and New York: Cambridge University Press.

Edwards, Walter. 1990. Phonetic differentiation between Black and White speech in east-side Detroit. *Word: Journal of the International Linguistic Association* 41:203–18.

Edwards, Walter. 1992. Sociolinguistic behavior in a Detroit inner-city black neighborhood. *Language in Society* 21:93–115.

Edwards, Walter. 1996. Sex-based differences in language choice in an African-American neighborhood in Detroit. In E. Schneider (ed.), *Focus on the USA*. Amsterdam: Benjamins. 183–94.

Edwards, Walter. 1997. The variable persistence of Southern Vernacular sounds in the speech of inner-city black Detroiters. In C. Bernstein et al. (eds.), *Language Variety in the South Revisited*. Tuscaloosa: University of Alabama Press. 76–86.

Escure, Geneviève. 1997. *Creole and Dialect Continua: Standard acquisition processes in Belize and China (PRC)*. Amsterdam and Philadelphia: John Benjamins.

Fasold, Ralph. 1972. *Tense Marking in Black English: A Linguistic and Social Analysis*. Arlington, VA: Center for Applied Linguistics.

Fasold, Ralph W., William Labov, Fay Vaughn-Cooke, Guy Bailey, Walt Wolfram, Arthur Spears, and John Rickford. 1987. Are black and white vernacular diverging? Papers from the NWAVE XIV Panel Discussion. *American Speech* 62:3–80.

Feagin, Crawford. 1997. The African contribution to Southern states English. In C. Bernstein et al. (eds.), *Language Variety in the South Revisited*. Tuscaloosa: University of Alabama Press. 123–39.

Fine, Marlene G. and Carolyn Anderson. 1980. Dialectical features of black characters in situation comedies on television. *Phylon* 41:396–409.

Fishman, Joshua, ed. 2001. *Handbook of Language and Ethnic Identity*. New York and Oxford: Oxford University Press.

Fordham, S. and J. Ogbu. 1986. Black students' school success: coping with the burden of acting white. *Urban Review* 18:176–206.

Foster, Michele, 1995. "Are you with me?" Power and solidarity in the discourse of African American women. In Hall and Bucholtz 1995, pp. 329–50.

Fought, Carmen. 1997. A majority sound change in a minority community: /u/-fronting in Chicano English. *Journal of Sociolinguistics* 3:5–23.

Fought, Carmen. 1999a. The English and Spanish of young adult Chicanos. IRCS report. 97–109.

Fought, Carmen. 1999b. I'm not from nowhere: negative concord in Chicano English. Paper presented at NWAVE 28, University of Toronto.

Fought, Carmen. 2002. Ethnicity. In Chambers et al. 2002, pp. 444–72.

Fought, Carmen. 2003. *Chicano English in Context*. New York: Palgrave/Macmillan Press.

Fought, Carmen, ed. 2004. *Sociolinguistic Variation: Critical Reflections*. New York: Oxford University Press.

Fought, Carmen and John Fought. 2002. Prosodic patterns in Chicano English. Paper delivered at NWAVE 31, Stanford, CA.

Fought, Carmen and Lea Harper. 2004. African-Americans and language in the media: an overview. Paper delivered at NWAVE 32, Ann Arbor, MI.

Fridland, Valerie. 2003. Network strength and the realization of the Southern Vowel Shift among African Americans in Memphis, Tennessee. *American Speech* 78:3–30.

Fridland, Valerie and Kathy Bartlett. 2003. The social and linguistic conditioning of back vowel fronting across ethnic groups in Memphis, TN. Paper delivered at NWAVE 32, Philadelphia, PA.

Gandy, O. 1998. The social construction of race. In O. Gandy, *Communication and Race: A Structural Perspective*. New York: Oxford University Press. 35–92.

Godinez, Manuel, Jr. 1984. Chicano English phonology: norms vs. interference phenomena. In Ornstein-Galicia 1984, pp. 42–8.

González, Gustavo. 1984. The range of Chicano English. In Ornstein-Galicia 1984, pp. 32–41.

Goodwin, Marjorie Harness. 1990. *He-Said-She-Said: Talk as Social Organization Among Black Children*. Bloomington: Indiana University Press.

Goodwin, Marjorie Harness. 1998. Cooperation and competition across girls' play activities. In Jennifer Coates (ed.), *Language and Gender: A Reader*. Oxford and Malden, MA: Blackwell.

Gordon, Matthew J. 2000. Phonological correlates of ethnic identity: evidence of divergence? *American Speech* 75:115–36.

Gough, David. 1996. Black English in South Africa. In De Klerk 1996, pp. 53–77.

Green, Lisa. 2002. *African-American English: A Linguistic Introduction*. Cambridge: Cambridge University Press.

Gudykunst, William B., Stella Ting-Toomey, and Elizabeth Chua. 1988. *Culture and Interpersonal Communication*. Newbury Park, CA: Sage Publications.

Hall, Kira. 1995. Lip service on the fantasy lines. In Hall and Bucholtz 1995, pp. 183–216.

Hall, Kira and Mary Bucholtz, eds. 1995. *Gender Articulated: Language and the Socially Constructed Self*. New York: Routledge.

Harris, Roxy and Ben Rampton, eds. 2003. *The Language, Ethnicity and Race Reader*. London: Routledge.

Hazen, Kirk. 2000. *Identity and Ethnicity in the Rural South: a Sociolinguistic View through Past and Present Be*. Publications of the American Dialect Society 83. Durham, NC: Duke University Press.

Heath, Shirley Brice. 1982. Questioning at home and school: a comparative study. In Spindler 1982, pp. 105–27.

Heath, Shirley Brice. 1983. *Ways with Words: Language, Life, and Work in Communities and Classrooms*. Cambridge and New York: Cambridge University Press.

Hecht, Michael L, Mary Jane Collier, and Sidney A. Ribeau. 1993. *African American Communication: Ethnic Identity and Cultural Interpretation*. Newbury Park: Sage Publications.

Heller, Monica. 1992. The politics of codeswitching and language choice. *Journal of Multilingual and Multicultural Development* 13:123–42.

Henderson, Anita. 1996a. Compliments, compliment responses, and politeness in an African-American community. In Jennifer Arnold et al. (eds.), *Sociolinguistic Variation: Data, Theory, and Analysis*. Stanford, CA: Center for the Study of Language and Information. 195–208.

Henderson, A. 1996b. The short *a* pattern of Philadelphia among African American speakers. *University of Pennsylvania Working Papers in Linguistics* 3:127–40.

Hewitt, Roger. 1982. White adolescent creole users and the politics of friendship. *Journal of Multilingual and Multicultural Development* 3:217–32.

Hewitt, Roger. 1986. *White Talk Black Talk: Inter-Racial Friendship and Communication Amongst Adolescents*. Cambridge and New York: Cambridge University Press.

Hill, Jane H. 1998. Language, race, and White public space. *American Anthropologist* 100:680–9.

Hill, Jane H. 1999. Styling locally, styling globally: what does it mean? *Journal of Sociolinguistics* 1999:542–56.

Hinton, Leanne, Birch Moonwomon, Sue Bremner, Herb Luthin, Mary Van Clay, Jean Lerner, and Hazel Corcoran. 1986. It's not just the Valley Girls: a study of California English. In Jon Aske, Natasha Beery, Laura Michaels, and Hana Filip (eds.), *Proceedings of the Thirteenth Annual Meeting of the Berkeley Linguistics Society*. Berkeley, CA. 117–27.

Holmes, Janet. 1997a. Maori and Pakeha English: some New Zealand social dialect data. *Language in Society* 26:65–101.

Holmes, Janet. 1998. Narrative structure: some contrasts between Maori and Pakeha story-telling. *Multilingua: Journal of Cross-Cultural and Interlanguage Communication* 17(1):25–57.

Holmes, Janet. 1997b. Setting new standards: sound changes and gender in New Zealand English. *English World-Wide* 18:107–42.

Hoover, Mary Rhodes. 1978. Community attitudes toward Black English. *Language in Society* 7:65–87.

Ignatiev, Noel. 1995. *How the Irish Became White.* New York: Routledge.

Jacobs-Huey, Lanita. 1997. Is there an authentic African-American speech community: Carla revisited. *University of Pennsylvania Working Papers in Linguistics* 4:331–70.

Jones, Rachel. [1982] 1998. "What's wrong with Black English?" In Gary Goshgarian (ed.), *Exploring Language*, 8th edition. New York: Longman. 305–8.

Kamwangamalu, Nkonko M. 2001. Ethnicity and language crossing in post-apartheid South Africa. *International Journal of the Sociology of Language* 152:75–95.

Kang, Connie. 1994. When East meets West within the same person. *Los Angeles Times*, October 22, 1994. A20–1.

Kochman, Thomas. 1981. *Black and White Styles in Conflict.* Chicago: University of Chicago Press.

Labov, William. 1963. The social motivation of a sound change. Reprinted in Labov 1972a, pp. 1–42.

Labov, William. 1966. *The Social Stratification of English in New York City.* Washington, DC: Center for Applied Linguistics.

Labov, William. 1972a. *Language in the Inner City: Studies in the Black English Vernacular.* Philadelphia: University of Pennsylvania Press.

Labov, William. 1972b. *Sociolinguistic Patterns.* Philadelphia: University of Pennsylvania Press.

Labov, William. 1994. *Principles of Linguistic Change,* vol. 1, *Internal Factors.* Cambridge, MA: Blackwell.

Labov, William. 2001. *Principles of Linguistic Change,* vol. 2, *Social Factors.* Oxford and Cambridge, MA: Blackwell.

Labov, William and Wendell Harris. 1986. De facto segregation of black and white vernaculars. In David Sankoff (ed.), *Diversity and Diachrony.* Amsterdam: John Benjamins. 1–24.

Lanehart, Sonja L., ed. 2001. *Sociocultural and Historical Contexts of African American English.* Amsterdam: John Benjamins.

Lanehart, Sonja L. 2002. *Sista, Speak! Black Women Kinfolk Talk About Language and Literacy.* Austin: University of Texas Press.

Leap, William. 1993. *American Indian English.* Salt Lake City: University of Utah Press.

Le Page, Robert and Andrée Tabouret-Keller. 1985. *Acts of Identity: Creole-Based Approaches to Language and Ethnicity.* Cambridge: Cambridge University Press.

Liang, A. C. 1997. The creation of coherence in coming out stories. In Anna Livia and Kira Hall (eds.), *Queerly Phrased: Language, Gender, and Sexuality*. New York: Oxford University Press. 287–309.

Liberman, K. 1990. Intercultural communication in Central Australia. In Carbaugh 1990, pp. 177–85.

Linn, Michael D. and Gene Pichè. 1982. Black and White adolescent and preadolescent attitudes toward Black English. *Research in the Teaching of English* 16:53–69.

Lippi-Green, Rosina. 1997. *English with an Accent*. New York: Routledge.

Lipski, John M. 1996. Patterns of pronominal evolution in Cuban-American bilinguals. In Roca and Jensen 1996, pp. 159–86.

Lo, Adrienne. 1999. Codeswitching, speech community membership, and the construction of ethnic identity. *Journal of Sociolinguistics* 3:461–79.

Luthin, H. W. 1987. The story of California /ow/: The coming-of-age of English in California. In Keith M. Denning et al. (eds.), *Variation in Language: NWAV-XV at Stanford: Proceedings of the Fifteenth Annual Conference on New Ways of Analyzing Variation*. Stanford, CA: Department of Linguistics, Stanford University. 312–24.

McCarty, T. L., Stephen Wallace, Regina Hadley Lynch, and AnCita Benally. 1991. Classroom inquiry and Navajo learning styles: a call for reassessment. *Anthropology and Education Quarterly* 22:42–59.

McCormick, Kay. 2002a. *Language in Cape Town's District Six*. Oxford and New York: Oxford University Press.

McCormick, Kay. 2002b. Code-switching, mixing and convergence in Cape Town. In Mesthrie 2002a, pp. 216–34.

MacDonald, Marguerite. 1996. Bilinguals in Little Havana: the phonology of a new generation. In Roca and Jensen 1996, pp. 143–50.

Makhudu, K. D. P. 2002. An introduction to Flaaitaal (or Tsotsitaal). In Mesthrie 2002a, pp. 398–406.

Malan, Karen, 1996. Cape Flats English. In De Klerk 1996, pp. 125–48.

Malley, 2002. http://www.sportinglife.com/tennis/wimbledon2002/news/story_get.cgi?STORY_NAME = wimbledon/02/07/05/WIMBLEDON_Women_Williams. html

Mendoza-Denton, Norma. 1997. Chicana/Mexicana identity and linguistic variation: an ethnographic and sociolinguistic study of gang affiliation in an urban high school. Ph.D dissertation, Stanford University.

Mesthrie, Rajend. 1996. Language contact, transmission, shift: South African Indian English. In De Klerk 1996, pp. 79–98.

Mesthrie, Rajend, ed. 2002a. *Language in South Africa*. Cambridge: Cambridge University Press.

Mesthrie; Rajend. 2002b. From second language to first language: Indian South African English. In Mesthrie 2002a, pp. 339–55.

Mesthrie, Rajend, Joan Swann, Andrea Deumert, and William L. Leap. 2000. *Introducing Sociolinguistics*. Philadelphia: John Benjamins.

Meyerhoff, Miriam. 1994. Sounds pretty ethnic, eh?: A pragmatic particle in New Zealand English. *Language in Society* 23:367–388.

Milroy, Lesley. 1980. *Language and Social Networks*. Oxford: Blackwell.

Milroy, Lesley and Li Wei. 1995. A social network approach to code-switching: the example of a bilingual community in Britain. In Lesley Milroy and Pieter Muysken (eds.), *One Speaker, Two Languages: Cross-Disciplinary Perspectives on Code-Switching*. 136–57.

Mitchell-Kernan, Claudia. 1972. Signifying, loud-talking and marking. In T. Kochman (ed.), *Rappin' and Stylin' Out: Communication in Urban America*. Chicago: University of Illinois Press. 315–35.

Morgan, Marcyliena. 1994. Theories and politics in African American English. *Annual Review of Anthropology* 23:325–45.

Morgan, Marcyliena. 1998. More than a mood or an attitude: discourse and verbal genres in African-American culture. In Mufwene et al. 1998, pp. 251–81.

Morgan, Marcyliena H. 2002. *Language, Discourse and Power in African American Culture*. Cambridge and New York: Cambridge University Press.

Mori, Kyoko. 1997. *Polite Lies: On Being a Woman Caught Between Cultures*. New York: Henry Holt and Co.

Mufwene, Salikoko S. 2001. What is African American English? In Lanehart 2001, pp. 21–51.

Mufwene, Salikoko, J. Rickford, G. Bailey, and J. Baugh, eds. 1998. *African-American English: Structure, History and Use*. London and New York: Routledge.

Myers-Scotton, Carol. 1993. *Social Motivations for Codeswitching: Evidence from Africa*. Oxford: Clarendon Press.

Myers-Scotton, Carol. 2000. Code-switching as indexical of social negotiations. In Wei, Li (ed.), *The Bilingualism Reader*. London and New York: Routledge. 137–65.

Ngom, F, 2004. Ethnic identity and linguistic hybridization in Senegal. *International Journal of the Sociology of Language* 170:95–112.

Nhu, T. T. 1994. Parents' love didn't need to be spoken. *Santa Barbara News Press*. March 20. 4.

Nichols, Patricia. 1983. Linguistic options and choices for black women in the rural south. In B. Thorne et al. (eds.), *Language, Gender and Society*. Rowley, MA: Newbury House.

Ogbu, John U. 1999. Beyond language: Ebonics, proper English, and identity in a Black-American speech community. *American Educational Research Journal* 36:147–84.

Omi, M. and H. Winant. 1994. *Racial Formation in the United States: From the 1960s to the 1990s*. New York and London: Routledge.

Ornstein-Galicia, Jacob, ed. 1984. *Form and Function in Chicano English*. Rowley, MA: Newbury House.

Philips, Susan. 1972. Participant structures and communicative competence: Warm Springs children in community and classroom. In

C. Cazden, V. John, and D. Hymes (eds.), *Functions of Language in the Classroom*. New York: Teachers College Press. 370–94.

Philips, Susan U. 1990. Some sources of cultural variability in the regulation of talk. In Carbaugh 1990, pp. 329–45.

Poplack, Shana. 1978. Dialect acquisition among Puerto Rican bilinguals. *Language in Society* 7:89–103.

Poplack, Shana. 1980. "Sometimes I start a sentence in Spanish y termino en español": toward a typology of code-switching. *Linguistics* 18:581–618.

Poplack, Shana. 1989. Language status and linguistic accommodation along a linguistic border/Statut de langue et accommodation langagière le long d'une frontière linguistique. *Travaux neuchâtelois de linguistique* 14:59–91.

Poplack, Shana and Sali Tagliamonte. 2001 *African American English in the Diaspora*. Malden, MA: Blackwell.

Puma, 2005. http://www.espn.go.com/classic/biography/s/Williams_Venus_and_Serena.html

Purnell, Thomas, William Idsardi, and John Baugh. 1999. Perceptual and phonetic experiments on American English dialect identification. *Journal of Language and Social Psychology* 18:10–30.

Rahman, Jacquelyn. 2002. The role of Black Standard English in the lives of African American students and staff on a university campus. Paper delivered at NWAVE 31, Stanford, CA.

Rahman, Jacquelyn. 2003. Golly gee! The construction of middle-class characters in the monologues of African-American comedians. Paper delivered at NWAVE 32, Philadelphia, PA.

Rampton, Ben. 1995. *Crossing: Language and Ethnicity Among Adolescents*. New York: Longman.

Rampton, Ben. 1999. Styling the other: introduction. *Journal of Sociolinguistics* 1999:421–27.

Reynolds, Katsue Akiba. 1998. Female speakers of Japanese in transition. In Coates 1998, pp. 299–308.

Rickford, John. 1985. Ethnicity as a sociolinguistic boundary. Reprinted in Rickford 1999, pp. 90–111.

Rickford, John. 1987. Are black and white vernaculars diverging? In Fasold et al. 1987, pp. 55–62.

Rickford, John. 1999. *African American Vernacular English: Features, Evolution, Educational Implications*. Malden, MA: Blackwell.

Rickford, John. 2004. Spoken soul: The beloved, belittled language of Black America. In Fought 2004, pp. 198–208.

Rickford, John and Faye McNair-Knox. 1994. Addressee- and topic-influenced style shift: a quantitative sociolinguistic study. Reprinted in Rickford 1999, pp. 112–54.

Rickford, John Russell and Russell John Rickford. 2000. *Spoken Soul: The Story of Black English*. New York: Wiley.

Rickford, John R. and Christine Théberge-Rafal. 1996. Preterite had + V-ed in the narratives of African-American preadolescents. *American Speech* 71:227–54.

Roca, Ana and John B. Jensen. 1996. *Spanish in Contact: Issues in Bilingualism.* Somerville, MA: Cascadilla.

Romaine, Suzanne, ed. 1991. *Language in Australia.* New York: Cambridge University Press.

Rose, Tricia. 1994. *Black Noise: Rap Music and Black Culture in Contemporary America.* Middletown, CT: Wesleyan University Press and Hanover, NH: University Press of New England.

Rubin, D. 1992. Nonlanguage factors affecting undergraduates' judgments of nonnative English-speaking teaching assistants. *Research in Higher Education* 33(4)(August):511–31.

Sacks, Harvey, Emanuel A. Schegloff, and Gail Jefferson. 1974. A simplest systematics for the organization of turn-taking for conversation. *Language* 50:696–735.

Santa Ana, Otto. 1991. Phonetic simplification processes in the English of the barrio: a cross-generational sociolinguistic study of the Chicanos of Los Angeles. Dissertation, University of Pennsylvania.

Santa Ana, Otto. 1996. Sonority and syllable structure in Chicano English. *Language Variation and Change* 8:1–11.

Schecter, Sandra R. and Robert Bayley. 2002. *Language as Cultural Practice: Mexicanos en el Norte.* Mahwah, NJ: Lawrence Erlbaum.

Scollon, Ron and Suzanne B. K. Scollon. 1981. *Narrative, Literacy, and Face in Interethnic Communication.* Norwood, NJ: Ablex Publishing Corp.

Silva-Corvalán, Carmen. 1994. *Language Contact and Change: Spanish in Los Angeles.* Oxford: Clarendon Press and New York: Oxford University Press.

Smelser, Neil J., William Julius Wilson, and Faith Mitchell, eds. 2001. *America Becoming: Racial Trends and Their Consequences,* vol. 1. Washington, DC: National Academy Press.

Smitherman, Geneva. 1977. *Talkin and Testifyin: The Language of Black America.* Detroit: Wayne State University Press.

Smitherman, Geneva. 1986. *Talkin and Testifyin: The Language of Black America.* Detroit: Wayne State University Press.

Smitherman, Geneva. 1998. Word from the hood: the lexicon of African-American vernacular English. In Mufwene *et al.* 1998, pp. 203–25.

Smitherman, Geneva. 2000a. *Black Talk: Words and Phrases from the Hood to the Amen Corner.* Boston: Houghton Mifflin.

Smitherman, Geneva. 2000b. *Talkin that Talk: Language, Culture, and Education in African America.* London and New York: Routledge.

Spears, Arthur K. 2001. Directness in the use of African American English. In Lanehart 2001, pp. 239–59.

Spears, Arthur. 1998. African-American language use: ideology and so-called obscenity. In Mufwene, et al. 1998, pp. 226–50.

Spindler, George, ed. 1982. *Doing the Ethnography of Schooling: Educational Anthropology in Action*. New York: Holt, Rinehart, and Winston.

Stubbe, Maria. 1998. Are you listening? Cultural influences on the use of supportive verbal feedback in conversation. *Journal of Pragmatics* 29:257–89.

Sweetland, Julie. 2002. Unexpected but authentic: use of an ethnically-marked dialect. *Journal of Sociolinguistics* 6:514–36.

Talbot, Mary M. 1998. *Language and Gender: An Introduction*. Cambridge: Polity Press and Malden, MA: Blackwell Publishers.

Thibault, Pierrette and Gillian Sankoff. 1993. Varying facets of linguistic insecurity: toward a comparative analysis of attitudes and the French spoken by Franco- and Anglo-Montréalais/Diverses facettes de l'insécurité linguistique: vers une analyse comparative des attitudes et du français parlé par des Franco- et des Anglo-montréalais. *Cahiers de l'Institut de Linguistique de Louvain* 19:209–18.

Thomas, Anulkah. 2000. The connection between racial-ethnic identity and language among youths of Afro-Caribbean Panamanian descent. Unpublished ms.

Thomas, Erik. 1999. A first look at AAVE intonation. Paper presented at NWAVE 28, University of Toronto.

Thomas, Erik and P. Carter. Forthcoming. Prosodic rhythm in African American English. *English World Wide*.

Trechter, Sara and Mary Bucholtz. 2001. White noise: bringing language into whiteness studies. *Journal of Linguistic Anthropology* 11(1): 3–21.

Troutman, Denise. 2001. African American women: talking that talk. In Lanehart 2001, pp. 211–37.

Tucker, G. R. and W. E. Lambert. 1969. White and Negro listeners' reactions to various American English dialects. *Social Forces* 47:463–68.

Urciuoli, Bonnie. 1996. *Exposing Prejudice: Puerto Rican Experiences of Language, Race, and Class*. Boulder, CO: Westview Press.

Veltman, Calvin. 1990. The status of the Spanish language in the United States at the beginning of the 21st century. *International Migration Review* 24:108–23.

Vermeij, L. 2004. "Ya know what I'm sayin'?" The double meaning of language crossing among teenagers in the Netherlands. *International Journal of the Sociology of Language* 170:141–68.

Wald, Benji. 1984. The status of Chicano English as a dialect of American English. In Ornstein-Galicia. Rowley, MA: Newbury House. 14–31.

Wald, Benji. 1996. Substratal effects on the evolution of modals in East LA English. In Jennifer Arnold et al. (eds.), *Sociolinguistic Variation: Data, theory, and analysis. Selected papers from NWAV 23 at Stanford*. Stanford, CA: Center for the Study of Language and Information. 515–30.

Walton, Shana. 2004. Not with a Southern accent: Cajun English and ethnic identity. In Margaret Bender (ed.), *Linguistic Diversity in the South: Changing*

Codes, Practices, and Ideology, Southern Anthropological Society Proceedings. 104–19.

Waters, Mary. 1990. *Ethnic Options: Choosing Identities in America*. Berkeley: University of California Press.

Wei, Li, Lesley Milroy, and Pong Sin Ching. 1992. A two-step sociolinguistic analysis of code-switching and language choice: the example of a bilingual Chinese community in Britain. *International Journal of American Linguistics* 2:63–86.

Weldon, Tracy. 1994. Variability in negation in African-American Vernacular English. *Language Variation and Change* 6:359–97.

Weldon, Tracey. 2004. African-American English in the middle-classes: exploring the other end of the continuum. Paper delivered at NWAVE 33, Ann Arbor, MI.

Wieder, D. Lawrence and S. Pratt. 1990. On being a recognizable Indian among Indians. In Carbaugh 1990, pp. 45–64.

Williams, Frederick. 1983. Some research notes on dialect attitudes and stereotypes. In Ralph Fasold (ed.), *Variation in the Form and Use of Language: A Sociolinguistics Reader*. 354–69.

Williams, Patricia J. 1997. The hidden meanings of "Black English." *Black Scholar* 27(1):7–8.

Wolfram, W. 1969. *A Sociolinguistic Description of Detroit Negro Speech*. Washington, DC: Center for Applied Linguistics.

Wolfram, Walt. 1974. *Sociolinguistic Aspects of Assimilation: Puerto Rican English in New York City*. Arlington, VA: Center for Applied Linguistics.

Wolfram, Walt. 1987. Are black and white vernaculars diverging? In Fasold et al. 1987, pp. 40–8.

Wolfram, Walt. 2000. On the construction of vernacular dialect norms. Paper presented at the Chicago Linguistic Society, Chicago, IL.

Wolfram, Walt. 2001. Reconsidering the sociolinguistic agenda for African American English: The next generation of research and application. In Lanehart 2001, pp. 331–62.

Wolfram, Walt and Clare Dannenberg. 1999. Dialect identity in a tri-ethnic context: the case of Lumbee American Indian English. *English World-Wide* 20:179–216.

Wolfram, Walt and Natalie Schilling-Estes. 1998. *American English*. Malden, MA: Blackwell.

Wolfram, Walt and Erik R. Thomas. 2002. *The Development of African American English*. Oxford, UK and Malden, MA: Blackwell.

Wolfram, Walt, Phillip Carter, and Beckie Moriello. 2004. Emerging Hispanic English: new dialect formation in the American South. *Journal of Sociolinguistics* 8:339–58.

Wolfram, Walt, Kirk Hazen, and Natalie Schilling-Estes. 1999. *Dialect Change and Maintenance on the Outer Banks*. Tuscaloosa: University of Alabama Press, for the American Dialect Society.

Wolfram, Walt, Kirk Hazen, and Jennifer Tamburro. 1997. Isolation within isolation: a solitary century of African-American Vernacular English. *Journal of Sociolinguistics* 1:7–38.

Wolfram, Walt, Erik Thomas, and Elaine Green. 1997. Dynamic boundaries in African American Vernacular English: the role of local dialects in the history of AAVE. Paper presented to the American Dialect Society, New York.

Wyatt, Toya A. 1995. Language development in African American English child speech. *Linguistics and Education* 7(1):7–22.

Yamauchi, Lois A. and Roland G. Tharp. 1995. Culturally compatible conversations in Native American classrooms. *Linguistics and Education* 7:349–67.

Zack, N. 1993. *Race and Mixed Race*. Philadelphia: Temple University Press.

Zelinsky, Wilbur. 2001. *The Enigma of Ethnicity: Another American Dilemma.* Iowa City: University of Iowa Press.

Zentella, Ana Celia. 1997. *Growing Up Bilingual*. Malden, MA: Blackwell.

Index